Train Wrecks & Transcendence

A Collision of Hardcore and Hare Krishna

Vic DiCara
(Vraja Kishor)

Copyright © 2016 Victor Damien DiCara
All Rights Reserved

ISBN-13: 978-1533073266 ISBN-10: 1533073260

Preface

This is going to get ugly.

And it'll be beautiful.

Ugliness and beauty will stand shoulder to shoulder, each one unashamed of its nudity. It has to be like that, because that's how I lived it. It was an awful train-wreck and it was a wonderful transcendental revelation, at the same time.

I apologize in advance to those in my story who are uncomfortable being portrayed in the nude. I certainly won't go out of my way to reveal your warts and blemishes, but ugliness is an essential part of the reality I experienced, and my story just *won't make sense* if I blur out and censor the unsavory bits.

I can at least throw you a towel by mentioning the fact that this is a memoir, a tale of my own subjective perception of reality. What else *could* it be; consciousness can never perceive reality from anything but a subjective point of view, unless it loses its individuality.

Why should we be ashamed of what we look like in the nude? Only plastic looks like Barbie.

Some think that the sacred must have no flaw and the profane no virtue, but this is the opinion of inexperienced stereotypist blockheads. According to Śrī Rūpa Goswāmī, even Krishna himself exhibits sixteen out of the eighteen classical flaws! Just as the virtues of the wicked do not absolve their essential ugliness, the flaws of the virtuous do not destroy their beauty. Rather, they increase its depth and richness

THE PREHISTORIC ERA — 1

HIGH SCHOOL SUCKS, BUT... — 3
WHY ME? — 4
THIRD PLANET — 5

SCREAMING SOBER? — 7
FRIENDS — 7
STRAIGHTEDGE — 8
KAHLUA AND SLUTS — 9
COCAINE AND COPS — 10
PAPA STRAIGHTEDGE — 11

INDUCTED TO THE THRASH METAL JUNIOR LEAGUES — 13
BLOODY UTERUS & TOXIC PHLEGM — 13
THRASH METAL — 14
SOCIALLY INCORRECT — 15
INNER STRENGTH — 16
ECTOPLASMIC POPSICLES — 17
MEETING MY BICH — 19

THE BEYOND ERA — 21

BA-DUMP-DUMP: BEYOND! — 23
RASTA ROCK — 23
KRISHNA KILLERS — 24
AGNOSTIC OTHERS — 25
THIRD PLANET ⇒ BEYOND — 25
VEGETARIANISM — 26
YO, WE'RE PLAYIN' AT CBS — 27

DRIVING ON THE RAZOR'S EDGE — 29
BLEEKER BOBS & RAZOR'S EDGE — 29
GUIDO *KARMA* COLLISION — 31
"HARE KRISHNA" — 32

REACH OUT AND SHRED THE GRAVEYARD — 34
SACHEM STRAIGHTEDGE FOR LIFE — 34
SHRED ZINE RECORDS — 36
THE GHASTLY 1000 — 37

YOU'RE INTO THAT KRISHNA SHIT, RIGHT? — 38
CHANT AND BE HIPPY — 38
REAL-LIFE ELVISH! — 39
KRISHNA HAS SEX, WHY CAN'T YOU? — 41
EVERYBODY LEAVES, IF THEY GET THE CHANCE — 43

BYE BYE TO 18 YEARS OF GROWING UP — 45
A CRUCIAL BAR-B-QUE — 45
LINGUISTIC LEGACY OF THE KING TUT CREW — 46
CROSS COUNTRY IN A YUGO — 48
A LOT OF MUSICIANS REALLY LIKE THIS BOOK — 50
LOST IN THE SCHISM CHASM — 52

THE INSIDE OUT ERA — 56

FORBIDDEN ADVENTURES IN THE TEMPLE OF DOOM — 58
CLEAN SLATE — 58
OFF WITH HIS DREADS — 59
TEMPLE OF DOOM — 60

HARDCORE HARDCORE, KRISHNA KRISHNA — 63
MOSHING AT THE TEMPLE — 63
ARGYLE CORE — 66
THE KRISHNA PUNK SHOW — 66
BRAHMAN ON BELLECHASE — 68
A CHAIN FROM DYS TO INSIDE OUT — 69

SPIRITUAL EQUALITY FOR MEN — 71
TRY TO MAKE ME BOW DOWN TO YOU... — 71
SPIRITUAL HARDCORE — 73
BUM RUSH THE BIBLE STUDY — 75
MARIANNE IS NOT "LESS INTELLIGENT" — 76
PROUD TO BE BRAINS-FREE — 79

BY A THREAD — 81
CAN'T QUIET THE UNDERTONE — 81
SMOKE SOME *PRASĀDAM*, MOTHERFUCKERS! — 83
GANDHI CORE — 84
SEXISM + NO SEX = FAIL — 85
MY EARLY KRISHNA HEROES — 86
MERRY-GO-ROUND OF MAJORS — 88
ENQUIRER — 89

IMPERFECTIONS IN PERFECTION — 91
GARLIC @ GOVINDA'S — 91
HARE CHRISTIAN — 92
THE GANGSTA PIMP GURU — 93
TELL IT TO THE STRAIGHTEDGE KIDS — 94
FALL OF THE PERFECT LINEUP — 95
THE APEX OF MY MUSICAL CAREER — 96
PUNK DISCOVERS THE DARK SIDE OF KRISHNA — 97

NO SPIRITUAL SURRENDER — 100
KENT OR JORDAN? — 100
RAGE AGAINST ISKCON — 101
DEATHBED & EMPTY DAYS — 102
FASTER, HARDER, MORE INSANE — 103
ZINES FOR THE BIG TOUR — 104

KRISHNA'S TRIAL BY MOSH — 106
INTENTIONAL LEFTOVERS — 106
THE ORIGINAL SINGER OF THE CRO-MAGS IS MY HUMBLE SERVANT — 108
"I LIKE THAT HE FARTED" — 108
YOUR INTELLIGENCE IS THIRD-CLASS — 110
KRISHNA'S TRIAL BY MOSH — 113

GOODBYE FRIENDS — 117
A DISNEYLAND OF KRISHNACORE — 117
DON'T BOTHER US, WE'RE PRAYING — 118
OUT OF INSIDE OUT — 120
WHY DID YOU DO *THAT*? — 121
TEN-THOUSAND DOLLAR LAMPS... FOR KRISHNA — 123
(DON'T NEED) FRIENDS (LIKE ME) — 125
300 BUCKS... SO WHAT? — 126
WE'LL HANDLE THIS — 127

THE END OF INNOCENCE   128

THE SHELTER ERA   129

MOM AND DAD   **131**
600 BUCKS IN THE SEAT POCKET   131
I'M GOING ON TOUR WITH SHELTER   133
PROMISE ME YOU WON'T JOIN A CULT   134
HOW CAN YOU SERVE GOD?   134
HOW CAN YOU LOVE GOD?   135
A BHAGAVAD GITA DIARY   136
EDITORIAL TRICKS & HOMOPHOBIA MAKEOVERS   136

IS THAT OUR SON?   **139**
BARFI BAGS   139
THE PSYCHOPATHIC TRANSCENDENTALIST   140
HAIR FALLING ON PORCELAIN   141
IN OUR OWN LITTLE BUBBLE   143
PARTING GIFTS   144

SHELTER TEMPLE TOUR 1990   **146**
PINK SOCKS   146
ONLY THE BERZERKLY GURUS FALL DOWN?   147
MY FIRST BHĀGAVATAM CLASS   148
STRAIGHTEDGE KĪRTAN FEST   148
DESPERATE (FOR) DRUMMERS   149
BOGUS ANTI-ISKCON DEVOTEES   150
GOLD MINES IN THE GREAT WHITE NORTH   151
GIRLS IN THE BACK, PLEASE   152
A WALL BETWEEN US   153
GET SERIOUS   154
DESTINATION: PHILLY   155

A CRUMBLING MANSION   **156**
BHAKTA UNCLE FESTER   156
PORN-ĀŚRAMA DHRAMA   157
WELCOME TO PHILLY   158
TAPE A CRYSTAL TO YOUR FOREHEAD   159
SINFUL GRAINS   160

THE WISE DON'T LAMENT FOR THEIR MOM	161
WRITING LETTERS > PLAYING POP PUNK	162
EVR2: THE CORE OF EQUALITY	163
EVR3: INDIVIDUALITY	165
EVR4: BLUEPRINT FOR SOCIO SPIRITUAL REVOLUTION	166
THE KRISHNACORE EXPLOSION	**168**
TEMPLE TO THE HARDCORES, HARDCORES TO THE TEMPLE	168
TEXAS KRISHNACORE	169
HI DAD, CAN I HAVE MONEY?	170
FRIENDS IN HIGH PLACES	171
STRAIGHTEDGE GOES BACK TO GODHEAD	172
DEAR STRAIGHTEDGE GURU,	174
TROUBLE IN PARADISE	**177**
BY HOOK OR BY CROOK	177
RUN A MILE IN SANTA'S SHOES	178
RAY VS. VIC	179
I HAVE A DREAM	179

THE 108 ERA — 181

BANNED TO DC	**183**
INSTANT 108	183
VEGANISM - THE NEXT LEVEL OF PURITY	184
ANOTHER SPRAWLING MESS	186
A PRAYER FOR ME?	187
PROUD OWNER OF A SHACK	188
BHAKTA ZAC 108	189
109 INCH NAILS	189
A CHANCE IN ATLANTIC CITY	190
VOCALS	191
VṚNDĀVANA! VṚNDĀVANA!	**193**
OUT OF THE RECORDING STUDIO, INTO THE HOLY LAND	193
RASA-LĪLĀ TONIGHT	195
THE INSIDE OUT OF KĪRTAN	197
NECTAR OF DEVOTION	200
TIME WON'T DYE MY SUBSTANCE PALE	201

BROKEN HOMES, FORGOTTEN FATHERS	**203**
108 HOUSE USURPED	203
FORGOTTEN FATHER'S DAY	204
LET'S TALK ABOUT SEX, BABY	**210**
DISCUSSING CELIBACY WITH HOT HIGH SCHOOL GIRLS	210
THERE IS INDEED A PUNK AMONG US!	212
I ONLY WATCHED...	215
SEXIST THINGS KRISHNA'S SAY	217
WOMEN ARE MORE INTELLIGENT	219
108... SLOW OUTTA THA GATE	**221**
WEIRDER THAN YOU CREW	221
KARMĪ GRAINS	222
YOU KNOW THE CENTER OF A CIRCLE BY ITS CIRCUMFERENCE	224
THIS SONG IS FOR ALL THE LADIES HERE TONIGHT...	225
I GIVE UP (TAKE ONE)	227
ŚRĪLA JESUS	228
BATS IN THE BELFRY	229
A KALI-JOLLY CHRISTMAS	230
YOUR NAME IS... VRAJA KISHOR	**234**
EDITING THE GURU	234
YOUR NAME IS...	235
NĀRĀYAṆA MAHĀRĀJA	237
108 + SHELTER: MUST WORK TOGETHER	239
THE KRISHNA CARNIVAL ROADSHOW	**240**
ROB FISH IS NO TEMPLE THIEF!	240
JEALOUS AGAINST THE MACHINE	242
MULTI-TRACKING WITH A BOOMBOX AND WALKMAN	243
THEY HAVE A GIRL IN THE BAND	244
TAR AND FEATHER EGO	246
NO VISIONS TO IMPRESS ZACK	247
VEGANS IN OUR MIDST	248
SOS ON THE LES	**250**
PEANUTS IN POCKETS	250
SONGS OF SEPARATION @ DON FURY'S	252
WHERE'S TOWACO?	254
GREEN MARBLE AND CANDLELIGHT	256

Franklin, Slayer of Monists	257
Śrīla Thanks List *ki Jaya*	257
Saturday Night Life	259
Irritating Whippersnapper	260

M.A.D. like Insane — 261
Grandma Mindi	261
Makeshift Lineups	262
Red Light Japa Walk	263
Worn Out	264
Blue Busses	265
Deathbed Music Video	265
Ras, Under Arrest	265

Kārtika in Vraja — 268
Once Italian, Now a Brahmin	268
You Should Study Sanskrit with Him One Day	270
Love Krishna, but Not *too* Much	271
Hollow Are the Bones of Lonely	274
Trivikrama Dasa & Baby Gopal	275

Threefold Miseries — 277
This Demo Sucks	277
Killer of Triangles	278
Scandalous Triangles	279
Spin Magazine	280
Who's Triv? Where's Kate?	281
Can't Catch the Roadrunner	283
Fuck Korn, and Fuck You if you Support That Shit	283
Daly is the Reason	284

Misery on Wheels — 285
I Slashed the Fucker's Tires	285
Frustration x Caffination	288
You Are Yamaraja Das	289
The Daughter of my Godsister is my...	289
One, Two, THREE, Four...	290

Misery on Other Continents — 292
108 minus 1	292
Hold the Plane for our Guru	293

A Taste of the Big Leagues	296
These Next Songs… are Covers	296
Swedish Friends, German Dungeons, Italian Nuns, and James Bond's Briefcase	297
Leaving Lenny	298
Past Life Regression	300
A Stupid *Karmī's* CD Walkman	302
Cursed Instincts	**304**
The Incredible Missing Drummer	304
Screams of Death	305
Lost and… Well, Just Lost	306
Baked Potatoes and Portable Ovens	306
The Train Wreck	**308**
Ashes, Ashes, The Soul Falls Down	308
Child Abuse	311
Seven Days Without Oxygen	315
The Train Wreck	317
The Transcendence	**322**
It was Beautiful, for a Moment	322
Seven Days to Live	323
An Evil Presence	325
A Skull at the Edge of Forever	326
Get Me Out of This Filthy Place	328
The End	**330**
Center for Tropical Disease	330
Descent to Berlin	331
The Final Suck	332
Mr. Headmaster President	333
Vṛndāvana? Or Shyama Sakhī?	334
Happily Ever After	335
Liner Notes	**338**

The Prehistoric Era

CHAPTER ONE:

HIGH SCHOOL SUCKS, BUT...

High School sucks, so it's pretty ironic that my amazing train-wreck ride towards transcendence begins in the Sachem High School cafeteria.

It was 1987.

I was 17.

Mr. Lecese, our music teacher, had a coolness mixed with the fragrance of mothballs; confined as it was to the lingo-bingo of freshly bygone eras. We called him "Snaggle Monster" due to the "snaggle" always caked into the corners of his mouth. Today the Snaggle Monster stalked the cafeteria with his curly, thinning hair and bad posture; happy as a button that the highlight of his year was about to begin: The Battle of the Bands.

Actually this was just the *tryouts* for the Battle.

I found myself drifting around like him, moving from band to band as they each set up their drum sets and guitar pedals atop throw rugs on the cafeteria floor. A Rush cover-band here, a Duran-Duran cover-band there, an Iron Maiden cover-band somewhere else. All of them nervous and eager to show their self-worth by demonstrating how well they could imitate rock stars. But there was one spot in the cafeteria that was totally different from all the others. It was an actual stage, complete with a second-tier drum riser, on which a massive black double-bass drum set loomed ominously.

The guys who would play on that stage were the main reason I had come.

Why Me?

It was my new friendship with Kevin Egan that brought me to the Battle of the Bands. He formed a friendship with me because I was a skater, and he was into Anthrax, who were into skating. I formed a friendship with him because he was a hardcore punk, and I was into skating, and skaters were into punk.

The music on the VHS skate tapes I used to watch was at least as interesting as the skating. As a result, I got into Agent Orange, "Everything Turns Gray," and The Sex Pistols, "Never Mind the Bullocks..." Kevin exposed me to a different branch of the punk-rock tree: Thrash Metal and Crossover. The band with the huge stage in the cafeteria today was a Thrash / Crossover band. Kevin was friends with them.

I was a bit more into Dungeons and Dragons and BMX freestyle than I was into music, but always had a deep connection with music. Some of my earliest memories are of my mom playing the Doors and the Beatles really loud in her Opal while she drove to work at the hair salon. We used to sing along at the top of our lungs. "Waiting for the Sun. Waiting for the Sun. Waiting... for the Sun." The best part: "This is the strangest life I've ever known." When Morrison screams right after that, we would usually crank the volume knob all the way up and roll down the windows to scream along with him out into the roadsides. Another favorite was, "Two of Us" by the

Beatles. We would drive home in the rain with this song blasting. "Two of us wearing raincoats... on our way back home."

Dad had a strong thing for the blues and other really weird shit like Frank Zappa and Tom Waits. For the most part, mom and I couldn't really figure that out, but he also had a full collection of Led Zeppelin records, and I loved that. My passion for Lord of the Rings and Dungeons and Dragons worked well there.

Dad had a guitar and tried to play it now and then.

When I was pretty young they bought a six-octave stand-up piano and got me a teacher. I gave up after four or five years, but it gave me a good understanding of how music works.

So even though I was more of a skater than a musician, I could pretty easily get had my feet in both worlds.

Third Planet

The bands playing in the school cafeteria were pretty bad and boring, but here and there they had some interesting equipment, or occasionally sounded surprisingly good. I was just waiting for the dudes with the big stage.

When their turn came, everyone gathered around. The band was nowhere to be seen, but their big PA speakers started playing jungle noises, replete with monkeys and orchestral strings. A few friends of the band clapped with awkwardly unabashed enthusiasm when the drummer climbed up and started checking the tightness of this or that bolt or lever, with his long, straight, Asian-black hair swaying like a rockstar.

Then, everything got tense.

A voice boomed over the PA as the rest of the gloriously longhaired band came onto the stage. It was a loud, deep, and crazy voice. "Greetings Earthlings..." it boomed. "We... are Third Planet."

The rest was more like an explosion than a concert. The drummer laid down a cement-heavy tribal beat while simple, insanely thick chords strode forth from mega-distorted guitars. The singer came out, leaping around in sneakers, jeans, and a sweatshirt (hood up and completely obscuring his face), bounding about like a wild gorilla, even scratching under his armpits. He threw back his hood to revealed a short crop of bleached blonde hair, pale skin, and a big nose, just before the music suddenly changed into some incomprehensibly fast blur of precise noise, while the lunatic "singer" howled and shouted in a mad frenzy and the rest of the band stalked, jumped or brooded around the stage like wild animals.

A fight broke out in front of the stage. At least that's what everyone thought it was. In truth it was John Vitale "dancing"... slam dancing... moshing... scaring the living shit out of everyone.

Snaggle Monster's mouth hung open and disbelief gushed from his eyes. No one in Lake Ronkonkoma had ever even heard of this shit before. Kids would have probably called the police if we had cell phones in those days.

As for me, I was *sold*.

It was the most amazing musical performance I could imagine, and the people who did it were just kids like me, kids from my school, friends of my friends. I was blown away and felt incredibly empowered. I wanted to be *just like them*.

Ironically, Snaggle disqualified Third Planet for inciting a riot - proving the point that High School does indeed suck.

Chapter Two:

Screaming Sober?

Friends

I eagerly made friends with the people in and around Third Planet. Denny Dharmo - the octopus-like drummer. Mike Yanicelli - the virtuoso guitarist. Lance Yeager - the sick bass player with long, straight blond hair who might as well have been on loan from Iron Maiden. Victoria Faella - the beautiful girl from around the block with a songbird voice and love for metal. Danielle Catalano - the artist/poet with a thing for metal and magic - the high-school crush that never went anywhere, but stayed on the brink of it for what seemed like forever. Serena Tupper - a cute and spunky guitarist in spandex, with long, spiked blonde hair and a passion for Metallica, my only girlfriend throughout High School.

The central figure of the whole scene was Third Planet's singer and mastermind, Tom Capone. He was an enigma. My skater friends and I had noticed him a few months ago, walking around like a "burnout" (our slang for *pothead*) with long hair, denim and leather.

Unlike most burnouts, though, his shirts and jackets promoted bands that no one in our school had ever heard of: "Venom" - with a goat's head inside an inverted pentacle; "Slayer" - with demons impaling naked corpses on pitchforks, declaring that hell awaits. These bands were incalculably more ominous than the cheesy "Satanism" PMRC alleged on innocent theatricals like Iron Maiden. And the dude walking around the halls with those bands on his chest and back seemed a whole lot scarier than any burnout or metalhead.

Straightedge

I kept wondering, "What made this kid trade his long hair for a bleach-blonde crew-cut, and his denim and leather for sneakers and Champion hoodies?"

Straightedge did.

And as soon as I made friends with Tom, he let me know all about it.

Straightedge, he explained, was a punk rock movement *against* drugs and alcohol. The sporty hair and attire was consistent with the straightedge idea that abstaining from drugs and alcohol would make you stronger and healthier. I wasn't into looking like a jock, but I liked weird stuff, and this was definitely weird.

I went home one day with his Youth of Today album - "Break Down the Walls." The cover was ugly: a black and white photo that looked like it was taken in the middle of an abandoned subway tunnel. In it, a shirtless guy with ultra-short bleached hair and jock attire grimaced like a bulldog while pointing from a filthy stage into the air, greeted in response by a crowd of raised fists. His other hand was marked with a big "X" and clutched a microphone to his chest. The whole thing felt like a patriotic war photo, because it was framed in red and white over a blue background.

I put it on the turntable.

It sounded like ice getting crushed in a blender while a crazed cat howled outside.

A few days later I went home with Tom's Minor Threat record, called "Out of Step." This seemed more promising. The cover was all white except for the logo and some sheep hand-drawn with a simple black crayon. All the sheep were just outlines, white sheep, except for one totally black one, running the opposite direction. What a cool image! The "black sheep" was "out of step" with everyone else.

I put it on my turntable.

It was fast and loud like Youth of Today, but much more articulate. The lyrics were a lot more discernible, too, and the whole thing just had a lot more *subtlety*. I liked it! Maybe this straightedge thing was something I could get into?

Minor Threat's lyrics seemed to explain the logic of straightedge: Intoxication was just so *ordinary*, so ubiquitous in modern culture. A true revolutionary would shun it all that in favor of facing life alert, awake, and engaged.

Kahlua and Sluts

I was 17 when I got exposed to this idea; still younger than the legal drinking age, but that doesn't mean much to teenagers. All the same, the history of my relationship with alcohol was quite brief.

The first time I drank I was just a toddler, scaring the shit out of my parents when they found me standing at the coffee table in front of my mom's empty cocktail glass. My next swig happened when I was just entering my teens. Dad gave me a beer while we were building a shed and wine cellar in the backyard, digging a six-foot deep hole in the long island sand.

At my first junior high school dance (which was also my last) I was pathetically nervous and decided to surreptitiously raid my parent's liquor cabinet before heading out. Kahlua. I thought, "This one is chocolate, right? It should taste better then the rest of this stuff."

God was I wrong. Anyway, I needed the stuff to liberate me from the fear of following up on any opportunities that "slutty girls" might offer at the dance.

The Kahlua didn't make me heroic, just dizzy and a little out-of-phase.

Cocaine and Cops

My only exposure to big league drugs came a couple of years before encountering Third Planet. In the very first house of our development lived a grown-up who was in metal band called Attila (not Billy Joel's heavy metal duo). A few junior high school friends and I crashed their record release party.

It wasn't a hard party to crash, as it sprawled out of Mr. Attila's plushly finished garage, down his driveway and all over his front lawn. At first we just wandered over to a small group of people standing in the woods on the side of the house. Turns out they were smoking a joint. It somehow came into my hand, and I really didn't know what to do with the tiny thing. The smoke was so hot I coughed it out almost as soon as it came in.

It didn't really seem to do anything special either, except make me feel like I was accepted at the party. My friends and I bravely ventured inside the garage, the *sanctum sanctorum*. An impressive stereo blasted the Attila cassette, and I was pretty impressed by the sound of it. On the cover, the dudes in the band were all done up in their outfits, obviously trying to catch some of the stardust falling from the boot-heels of Long Island's recently ascended metal mega-champions, Twisted Sister.

Nearby, a bunch of guys relaxed in comfy chairs around a coffee table, looking at the Attila album cover atop it. I wanted to get a closer look so I walked over and picked it up. As soon as I did, silence suddenly filled the room and all eyes fixed on me. After a while, I looked up from the album cover. I glanced around wondering why I had just become the most interesting thing in the world. Suddenly, everyone started laughing and things went back to normal. My friends hushed me away and explained that I had just dumped several lines of cocaine into the carpet! They told me it was worth a ton of money and we were lucky those guys laughed it off instead of beating the shit out of us.

Right then the police rolled up, scaring the holy hell out of us. I imagined that I would soon be stuck in jail for years, a POW of Ronald Reagan's "war on drugs." We hightailed it down the bike path and off into the woods and hid there flat on the ground while police flashed their flashlights looking for us. I was terrified and had to pee, but the cops weren't giving up. As I started to fidget, the leaves and branches rustled. I preferred to pee my pants than become Reagan's prisoner.

And that's what I did.

Papa Straightedge

So, drugs and alcohol didn't have any special allure for me and straightedge just seemed smart and easy.

I got into it.

Soon after I did, my dad took it up too and stuck with it for maybe a year or more. He hoped it would influence my mom to drink less. People said she drank too much, but to be totally honest, I didn't notice that while I was growing up.

As you can tell my now, my parents were pretty awesome. A lot of people think that punks, religious converts and other "weirdoes" are the products of bad upbringing, and do what they do as a way to rebel against their parents. That's not my case at all. I wasn't rebelling against *my parents*; I was rebelling against *my peers* and everyone else.

Everyone has disagreements with their parents, and of course so did I, but I don't have a single serious complaint about how they raised me. They were responsible, loving, knowledgeable guides to life. And you know what, maybe that's *why* I became a "weirdo"? I didn't become a punk convert in spite of my excellent childhood. I became a punk convert *because* of my excellent childhood.

Maybe being a weirdo can be a good thing, when "normal" is so lame?

CHAPTER THREE:

INDUCTED TO THE THRASH METAL JUNIOR LEAGUES

Bloody Uterus & Toxic Phlegm

Third Planet's drummer, Denny, was doing a "joke band" named Bloody Uterus. I wanted in. I went to one of their jam sessions and tried to play synthesizer. Either they didn't really want synthesizers in their thrash band, or I just sucked.

They suggested that I could play bass. I didn't have one. Maybe that's why they suggested it? I asked for, and got one from mom and dad that Christmas.

I almost never played it. The way it looked embarrassed me (which really isn't an easy thing to do). It looked like something KISS would play on tour in Japan. More importantly, I just didn't feel like learning the bass after all. Girls like singers and guitarists, not bass and keyboard players. What sense was there in going from keyboards to bass?

I decided to learn guitar. Most of what guitarists played looked really easy; they just moved their hand up and down the neck, practically always in the same position. I took my dad's beautiful Les Paul purple-starburst electric guitar, put Master of Puppets on the turntable at the simplest song ("The Thing That Should Not Be"), turned all the knobs on everything pretty far up, and started figuring out how to make the guitar sound like the song playing over my stereo.

Took a few hours, but I got the hang of it.

I showed Kevin Egan. When he heard me play he invited me to join the band he was in, Toxic Phlegm. I was stoked to be their second guitarist.

Toxic Phlegm was about as good as the name implies, but I was thrilled to be in a band and practice every day in a basement.

Thrash Metal

Most of my new friends were into Thrash-Metal. We loved Exodus, and tried to play all their ridiculous hyper-muted picking patterns. Anthrax was a more serious band than Exodus, but was still more cheese than bread. Learning some of the songs from Spreading the Disease started to prime me for a lot of the musical concepts in crossover hardcore. Metallica was even better than Anthrax. Master of Puppets was fascinating and compelling, musically and lyrically, and sent me digging into their earlier records for more.

My favorite was Slayer. Reign in Blood was simply a perfect record. The rhythms were crooked, the tense and dissonant intervals in the riffs were wicked, and the "satanic" lyrics captivated my attention with their ferocious religious imagery. I was surprised to find that many of them actually made good religious, philosophical and social points.

Still, I think the Crumbsuckers were the most important band for me in those days. Even today, listening to almost anything from their Life of Dreams LP blows my mind. They were pinned as a "crossover" band because they combined elements of hardcore (like short songs, and gruff non-melodic vocals) with elements of metal and thrash (which basically means that, compared to a hardcore band, they had higher quality instruments, better recordings, more skill as musicians... and guitar solos).

Socially Incorrect

After a month or so, I outgrew Toxic Phlegm and decided to put together a new band more like the Crumbsuckers. I had a friend named Vin Novara who was a drummer. He was a prog-rocker, but willing to bang heads with me; a Rush fanatic who could play most of their complicated drum stuff, but was also intrigued by trash metal and crossover. I sang and played guitar. Chuck Vinci - a lanky, older, vocational-schooled, longhaired burnout metalhead Black Sabbath and Pink Floyd fan - played bass. The trio was (aptly) named Socially Incorrect.

We wrote three original songs (I did the lyrics and the main part of the music), covered the Courageous Cat theme and the Italian anthem, Tarantino, and did an original solo-guitar ballad dedicated to my girlfriend, Serena, "The Big S." My dad set up an appointment at a basement recording studio he found in the Yellow Pages. The engineer told him, "I never heard this kind of music before, but these kids have talent and a lot of potential."

Tom Capone came along and sang on the first song, Private Holocaust:

> *Obscured vision — cover your eyes*
> *Reality to bury — under centuries of lies*
> *Fallen from love, more friendship to buy*
> *Even if you see the answer, you say you're too old to try.*

We had a straightedge song, too, Prisoner of Glass:

> *Waste your life hiding from death.*
> *Wanting more, but sick is all you get.*

> *Disown your own personality.*
> *Prisoner of glass, you thought you were free.*
>
> *Shuffling in your drunken haze.*
> *Blinded by your glassy gaze.*
> *What need is there for bars of brass*
> *When the strongest prison is built from glass?*

And an anti-war song, No Burial:

> *A country of madmen*
> *At war with their brother*
> *Seeking destruction*
> *Then running for cover*
>
> *Caught in the foreplay of nations at war*
> *A frenzy of madness, as newsmen tally the score*
> *The lives in each country, just statistics to their rulers*
> *Children taught to worship hate, by government schoolers.*

Socially Incorrect played a small show in the Holbrook VFW hall with a few other local bands. We did everything from the demo but replaced the acoustic guitar ballad with an instrumental cover of Rush's classic, Temples of Syrinx. On another occasion, an opportunity to play a few songs arose during someone's party. That time we also did a cover of "Am I Evil" and both Tom and I sang.

A few dozen copies of our demo tape circulated amongst the musicians at school, like a resume. Soon, a pair of badass metal musicians with long hair, and denim-leather jackets made me an offer. "It's a really cool tape, man!" Scott Oliva and Rob Porta told me in the school hallways. "You wanna play second guitar for Inner Strength?"

Inner Strength

Inner Strength was a serious band, practically an international project by my standards, since half of the members weren't even from my school. They were good, and they played live shows - sometimes even in actual rock clubs on real stages!

The drummer, Alan Cage, was a year or two older than the rest of us, making him practically an adult in my book. He was smart and straightedge; a lean, mean guy with a crew cut, who hit the drums like a blacksmith hitting iron. When I met him I felt like I suddenly got an elder brother.

With them, I played my first show at a real rock club: Long Island's "Sundance." The stage was about four feet high, with a full compliment of professional lighting. The PA was enormous. Huge bands played here: Slayer, Metallica, Anthrax, and Megadeth. To me, it might as well have been Madison Square Garden.

Of course, our show was one of those "buy your own marquee letters" / "sell your own tickets" deals with a whole bunch of other unknown bands on a Wednesday night.

Ectoplasmic Popsicles

Both sides of my family loved bowling. We are New York Italians. My parents would join them every Thursday night to bowl on a league. When I was younger I would tag along and feed quarters to the Donkey Kong, Pac Man, and Tempest games while they did their thing. These days I mostly stayed home and hung out with my friends. On this particular Thursday, Kevin and I were chilling out on my couch, eating orange creamsicles and watching videotapes of The Young Ones while thunder boomed and rain fell outside.

As we laughed at MTV's hysterical show, we gradually noticed that the fern in front of the sliding door was *moving...* erratically.

Even when we stared at it, it didn't stop.

"Maybe it's a poltergoost!" Kevin said, referring to a term featured in The Young Ones. I burst out laughing and threw my creamsicle stick tauntingly at the possessed fern. The stick flew straight but, to our horror, suddenly fell to the floor when it came close to the plant.

Kevin threw his creamsicle stick, and *the same thing* happened!

Our laughter transformed into fear with dizzying speed. "Maybe it's the wind?" We checked the sliding door and found no air coming through. But while we were close to the plant we discovered something else: strange brownish stuff on the leaves.

"Ectoplasm?"

Petrified, we ran out the front door, halfway around the block through the heavy rain, to Victoria Faella's house. There, I called my mom and dad at the bowling alley.

"Dad," I said, breathing heavily, "I'm at Vicky's. There's a ghost in the house... I'm not going back in there."

We did go back, but with Vicky for support, and waited on my front porch for about a half hour discussing the paranormal. I had always believed in magic, devils, spirits, telekinesis and so on - but tonight I actually experienced first hand proof of that whole realm! I was elated to have had a first-hand experience of paranormal phenomenon.

When my parents returned we went inside and explained the whole thing to my dad, who was totally unimpressed. He checked the sliding door thoroughly for air leaks and found none. He examined the telltale ectoplasm. Then, suddenly, he declared, "The ceiling is leaking water from the rain. When the drops fall on the fern, it moves."

I was pissed - devastated, actually - and resisted the rational explanation. "What about the ectoplasm?" I challenged.

He pointed up to the artificial wooden beam directly above the plant, at the apex of the ceiling. It was brown, just like the "ectoplasm." The water was leaking through that stupid thing, taking some of the cheep coloring with it as it fell onto the plant.

My dad seemed like Mr. Spock, dismantling my supernatural experience with cold logic, but I refused to give up. "You think you can explain everything," I challenged, "but you can't explain the Popsicle stick!"

He promptly picked up the stick from where it had fallen to the floor by the paranormal energy field of the apparition, and threw it towards the couch. The stick flew straight and normal for a few meters, and then, suddenly fell straight to the ground - exactly like it had done when we threw it at the paranormal fern. "It's just the aerodynamics of a popsicle stick," he said calmly. "It will always fall like that."

I was so angry with my father, half from the embarrassment of being exposed as irrational and gullible, and half from the feeling that he had robbed me of a life-changing genuine experience of something supernatural. I don't really know how many years it took for that anger to fully subside.

Meeting my Bich

Inner Strength was in a real band, so I needed real equipment. Mom and dad drove me to a guitar store on my seventeenth birthday and I found a guitar that looked wicked, all pointy and curvy and just so *metal*. I picked a white version of that BC Rich "Bich" because the white was a little plain and counterbalanced the otherwise completely over-the-top metal-ness of the thing. As soon as I got it home I put skateboarding stickers all over it, too, making it a perfect symbol of "crossover."

The guitar became as much a part of my identity as my hands or face.

I needed an amp, too; a real one to stand up with Alan's *loud* drumming and the big half-stack the other guitarist played through.

Time to get a job!

My first paying job was as an employee of the IDR division of Reuters (IDR stands for Information Dissemination and Retrieval, but my dad said it stood for "I Don't Remember."). My dad was a first-generation computer programmer from the days before they invented keyboards. He got me the job.

I don't really know what the job actually was. I was supposed to do something on a computer, with a database, but I don't recall doing much of anything at all, and no one seemed to care. Dad would drop me off on Saturday mornings, and I'd go sit at a desk and hit a key every now and then on one of those 1987 IBM PC/AT computers with green-on-black screens. At lunch I'd go next door to the Adventureland amusement park, and eat at Nathan's franks. "I scream, you scream, we all scream for ice cream." After lunch-hour (which steadily became a lot more than an hour) I'd go back to the desk, trying to figure out whether I had no idea what I was doing or if there really was nothing for me to do. Eventually dad would pick me up at the end of the day.

For some reason, they paid me.

As soon as I had the thousand-something dollars I needed, I bought a Carvin X100B half-stack amplifier. Why a Carvin? Don't ask me, I've never been a good shopper. I liked playing with the five EQ sliders on the amp, but after a while it became obvious that the thing's distortion sounded thin and abrasive no matter how I fiddled with the switches.

THE BEYOND ERA

CHAPTER FOUR:

BA-DUMP-DUMP: BEYOND!

Rasta Rock

The more I hung out with Tom, Kevin Egan, and Alan Cage, the more hardcore I heard. Bad Brains was my favorite. Actually everyone loved the Bad Brains. It was Victoria Faella who leant me her copy of I Against I, saying, "This album is *incredible*. You'll *love* it."

I did.

It was a masterpiece, rhythmically a lot like Led Zeppelin 4, sonically a lot like Master of Puppets, with punk's freedom of expression and urgency, metal's accuracy, and reggae's pulse and spiritual overtones. I Against I is probably the #1 record on the list of extremely important rock albums that relatively no one knows about.

They were Rastafarians. That was weird.

And cool.

Rastas were into the bible, so I found one in the house and checked it out. By coincidence, maybe, I opened to one of the most boring sections - a list of Ruth's decedents or something like that - and I closed the book after five or ten minutes, thinking, "How does something this boring inspire such amazing music?"

Krishna Killers

I think it was Tom who gave me a cassette of Age of Quarrel, which immediately skyrocketed to #2 on my list of awesomeness, just a bit behind I Against I. It had great production, without sounding cheesy or metal. The songs were well written and the musicianship was first-rate. After hearing the first three seconds after the opening stick-clicks, I gained a whole new perspective on what the "hard-" part of "hardcore" was supposed to sound like. Age of Quarrel was *hard* as iron. Every note was brutally solid and forceful. They had an incredible tempo too, a really special sweet spot between fast and slow that just felt perfect for skanking and moshing.

The Cro-Mags and Bad Brains had something in common: countercultural spirituality. Bad Brains were Rastas. Cro-Mags were wrapped up in Hare Krishna, the weird cult my mom told me not to get involved with when I was six or seven and we walked by a Krishna temple on a Sunday afternoon while on Vacation in Laguna Beach, California.

I knew Rastas were into the Bible, but I had no idea what Krishna's were about, and had no idea how to find out.

I decided to keep an ear up.

Agnostic Others

I also wore out my cassette dub of Agnostic Front's Victim in Pain LP. It was just catchy and genuine. The last song, "With Time (For Amy)" was my favorite because of its heavy, tom-based drum pattern.

Sick of It All was another New York Hardcore favorite of mine, they had just released a 7" on Revelation records, and I wore it out on my turntable. I also really loved the "joke band" their drummer did, Rest in Pieces.

I was into the metallic New York Hardcore style, but I also really connected with the more sophisticated approach of Minor Threat and a few other bands from Washington D.C., like Dag Nasty and Rites of Spring. The New York bands were very masculine and brutal, and the D.C. bands were more feminine and nuanced.

Third Planet ⇒ Beyond

I was a fan of Third Planet, too, but they self-destructed a few minutes after the battle of the bands. Tom and the bassist took one of the Third Planet songs and formed a new band called Beyond.

When I went from Toxic Phlegm to Socially Incorrect, Kevin Egan went from Toxic Phlegm to Beyond, becoming their singer under Tom's careful and sometimes almost stifling coaching. Kevin's friend, Dominic Biocco became Beyond's drummer. Like the drummer from Socially Incorrect, Dom was a Rush fan who played all sorts of fancy and complex stuff.

Dom got me a job at a bakery where he worked. Frying donuts was a lot more fun than doing nothing at Reuters. I fried enough to make about two hundred and fifty bucks, which I used to buy a red Dodge Dart that was almost as old as me, and had a hole rusted through the floor in the back, on the passenger side.

I quit the job when I drove away in my new ride.

While I was playing with Inner Strength, Beyond put out a demo cassette that was nothing short of *amazing*. It sounded as good as any of my favorite bands, and had a lot in common with the more complex and musically sophisticated D.C. sound. Tom bought hundreds of blank cassettes from Price Club (later known as Costco), and duplicated beyond demos on the tape deck in his room. Adding a Xeroxed cover, he got Some Records, an underground hardcore record shop on the Lower East Side, to sell it.

From there it very soon attracted the attention of the big names in the New York Hardcore scene.

Dom and Lance were amazing musicians, but weren't much into straightedge or hardcore, and it showed. Inner Strength had a similar split: two of our members were into metal, and two others (Alan and I) were straightedge and into hardcore. The fifth member - Rob, the bassist - had a foot in both worlds.

Tom pulled off the high school hardcore equivalent of a corporate merger, splitting both bands and grafting the hardcore halves together into the new Beyond lineup. I did a bit of a hardcore-ization myself, by transforming my long metal hair into dreadlocks.

I played second guitar for a while, until Rob made up his mind that hardcore was for meatheads. That's when I took over on bass.

We played Sundance (another one of those sell-your-own tickets things), and another show opening for Trip 6 at a Long Island dive called The Right Track Inn. We also played the Sachem Battle of the Bands (tryouts), following the footsteps of Third Planet from the year before. They had been disqualified for inciting a riot. Beyond got a similar honor, disqualified for going past our time limit.

Vegetarianism

The most active current straightedge band, Youth of Today, suddenly got into vegetarianism, and within a few months it was more or less a new part of straightedge. Their song, No More, said:

> *Meat eating, flesh eating — think about it.*
> *So callous to this crime we commit.*
> *Always stuffing our faces with no sympathy.*
> *What a selfish, hardened society.*
>
> *No more*
> *just looking out for myself*
> *when the price that's paid is the life of something else,*

Undeniably, it made sense. Why should we kill things if we don't need to? But was vegetarianism really *so important* that I should rearrange my whole life about it? I wondered about it for a few days until mom put chicken on the dinner table one night. Sticking a fork into the "drumstick," I hit a vein.

A big, purple vein.

I have veins. A chicken has veins...

Wait... am I eating a *leg...* from someone's *body*?

I just dropped my fork into the plate and stopped eating meat from then on.

Within a month or two, there was a clan of almost a dozen of us at school: straightedge vegetarians. At first we had no idea what to eat. All we knew was what not to eat. We survived on the likes of pasta, pizza, and french-fries. When a Greek restaurant eventually opened up in town, the falafel pita wraps were like a gift from God.

Yo, We're Playin' at CBs

Thanks to the guitarist of Token Entry, Beyond got a show at one of CBGB's famous Sunday Hardcore Matinees. Token Entry would headline, supported by Swiz from D.C., Wrecking Crew from Boston, and Beyond from... Sachem High School.

Holy crap!

On March 6th, 1988, we piled into Tom's dad's van and drove into the sleazy Bowery on the Lower East Side. A few hours later, just before the show was to start, my mom and dad pulled up in their Lincoln Continental.

Hardcore was supposed to be "from the streets" but I was from the suburbs and my mom and dad had a two-story house and a big, fancy car. Oh well. I was more worried about their car than my image. They parked it in a lot on the corner, next to a god-awful sleaze-rag "hotel."

We opened the show, but there was already a very good-sized crowd, and a lot of them even knew our songs! They were moshing around and even singing along with the catchier lines. Towards the end of the set things really started getting wild. That's when I saw the guitarist from Youth of Today stage diving and moshing. "Holy shit," I said to myself. "The guy from Youth of Today is stage diving to my band!"

Mom and dad were super proud, and they left with all hubcaps intact.

CHAPTER FIVE:

DRIVING ON THE RAZOR'S EDGE

Bleeker Bobs & Razor's Edge

Tom, Kevin and I would drive out to CBGB's or up to The Anthrax in Connecticut for shows. The first time we crossed the border leaving New York, I felt like I was on a journey to the far east. I think it was on that virgin trek to The Anthrax that I first met Gus Peña - the most famous guy in hardcore who wasn't in a band. We hit it off. I guess he liked me because I was in Beyond, and maybe my unusual appearance helped; in a sea of guys with crew cuts and sports gear, I stood out with dreadlocks and Rasta-skatepunk clothes.

My first few CB's shows were terrifying. Shows at CBs made Third Planet's mosh pit look like a preschool. Even shows at The Anthrax seemed like a school field trip in comparison. "Moshing" or "slam-dancing" at CBs back then was no joke. A lot of big, ugly cats prowled the "dance floor," pissed off street kids from the city bearing their fangs and venting their frustrations to very loud, chaotic, angry music. For a suburban middle-class guy like me, it was an act of valor just to stand on the same dance floor.

To my amazement, Alan Cage would get in there and mosh with all those huge, scary characters. He fit right in and seemed as intimidating as they were.

Before or after CB's shows we'd get pizza or falafel and go to record stores like Some Records and Bleeker Bob's. These Lower East Side shops helped the hardcore punk scene by carrying lots of homegrown stuff: Cassettes of local bands, and Xeroxed fanzines.

Tom was scoping out at a rack of zines behind the counter at Bleeker Bob's.

"Hey Vic," he called, "check this out." He pointed to a zine with a drawing of a cow tied around the neck to a post in the ground, struggling to get free from a man in heavy boots and overalls holding an axe above his head. The real mind-blower, though, was that the man holding the axe had a cow's head, and the cow struggling to get free had a human face! A gruesome, horror-movie font identified the zine as issue one of The Razor's Edge.

Tom bought it.

The next day at school Tom showed up at my locker, looking surreptitiously left and right as he handed me the zine, as if it was a bag of weed. "Dude!" he exclaimed in a paranoid hush, looking over his shoulder. "This thing is sick! You gotta read it."

It was nothing I could have expected at all. It had barely anything to do with music, and was all about Hare Krishna. That was fine by me, because ever since I learned in Thrasher magazine that the Cro-Mags were into Krishna, I'd been wanting to figure out what that whole thing was all about.

I was expecting something as weird and incoherent as their brainwashed flower-child cult image, but to my surprise the Krishna stuff seemed rational. In particular, there was an article entitled, "*Karma* and the Origin of Evil." The main illustration for it was the profile of a woman with a snake coming out of her forehead and arching back to bite her neck. My mind was blown by the fact that this article written by mind-melded hippies in a Xeroxed zine picked up from Bleeker Bob's managed to logically answer a question I thought no one was supposed to be able to answer, "Why do bad things happen to good people?"

The answer was *karma*: no one was all good, all of us have done good and bad things in their past lives. It was sure as hell a lot more impressive than any parts of the Bible I had read. Or anything else for that matter.

Guido *Karma* Collision

Tom's dad's van became Beyond's van on weekends when we had shows to play. It soon became dubbed, "The Van of Suffering," since the entire cab had no seats, no windows, and not even a carpet on the bare metal floor. One weekend, we piled in to drive up to our show in Albany, opening up for Warzone and Gorilla Biscuits. We stopped in front of Walter Schreifels' house in Queens to caravan with the "Youth Crew" guys.

Somehow, I was behind the Van of Suffering's steering wheel when we pulled away from the curb, concentrating on the day ahead and the awesomeness of the moment.

Then there was a "crunch."

I looked in the passenger side mirror (for the first time) and saw that one of those little sports cars had its nose crammed into our rear tire. There was no damage to the Van, but the Mazda 280ZX got it's front bent out of shape. An angry Italian guy emerged from the car and started yelling and pointing.

"We were already late," I worried. "Now we're *completely* screwed." I paced around on the sidewalk, waiting eternally for the cops to show up and do whatever it is they would do.

Seeing my fret, Gus sauntered over to offer words of wisdom. "It's like HR says," he told me, about to refer to a line from the solo project of the Bad Brains' singer, "It'll be alright."

I wasn't convinced.

"No really, man," he said. "Don't worry about this. It's all just an illusion."

An *illusion*? I took a closer look at Gus. He looked Hispanic, and positively overflowed with self-confidence. Wooden beads were around his neck tightly - just like the Cro-Mags - and his shirt said *love animals, don't eat them*, around a very un-hardcore painting that seemed to depict the harmony among humans and animals in the Garden of Eden.

"It's illusion, man," Gus continued. "This guy is in complete illusion. His car is an illusion, and he's completely attached to it because he's in the illusion that it makes women think he's attractive. It's all *māyā*. Don't worry about hitting his car, that's just his *karma*."

I laughed uncomfortably, not knowing how to reply to such conversation. It was all so foreign. "That's a really cool necklace," is all I could manage to say.

"Kids call 'em schism beads or Krishna beads, but they are really *kanthi-mālā*," he explained.

"Where'd you get 'em?" I asked.

"From the Krishna temple."

Whoa.

"Hare Krishna"

By the time we finally got to Albany, Warzone was playing. The opening act, Wolfpack, had already played. By the time we all played it was late, and there were only something like 20 people at the show. That was a surprise for me - since I was used to the packed shows at CB's and The Anthrax.

When I got back home I told my parents about the car accident. It was a bummer that my dad's insurance would have to cover the repair of the car, and would get more expensive. Somehow an idea came to me. "Gus and all these Hare Krishna's say there's some power in chanting Hare Krishna? Ok, I'll test it out. I'll chant Hare Krishna, and if this whole problem goes away, I'll become a Hare Krishna, but if nothing happens I'll know they're just daydreaming and are probably a cult like everyone says."

I said aloud, "Hare Krishna," once.

The next day I got a phone call from Alan. He had good news: Shortly after banging into the Van of Suffering, the Italian guy's car got stolen. The whole insurance claim was dropped.

Chapter Six:

Reach Out and Shred The Graveyard

Sachem Straightedge For Life

Meanwhile, back at Sachem High, the straightedge Hardcore Phenomenon just kept growing. A few friends from younger grades, including Larry Gorman, formed a straightedge band called Reach Out. Tom asked me to sing for them, suddenly opting out of his own role in that capacity.

Most of the lyrics were already written when I came down into Eddie Ciappa's basement for my first Reach Out jam session. I finished up some of their unfinished lyrics and wrote one or two new songs. In one of the songs, I put an oblique reference to chanting Hare Krishna:

> *The path laid out is clear.*
> *Just need a tongue to sing, and an ear to hear.*

> Sing it out - the only way,
> To cleanse your heart in these quarrelsome years.

I wrote a D.R.I. style song, extremely fast and short, with an anti-materialism message. "Downward Bound":

> Worshipping money - rejecting God.
> Worshipping flesh - rejecting Love.
> Ignoring the truth, but there's only so much time left.
> And you're still fuckin' going down.

My biggest contribution was a song called Lose to Gain, a sonic sermon on the pervasive evil of treating women like sexual objects, inspired by contrition over my recent breakup with Serena (who had frustrated me by keeping a bible next to her bed and keeping out of sexual relations):

> Sometimes you lose to gain
> But it hurts you all the same
> To find you were caught up in the game
> - of daytime-drama "love."
>
> With your dick glued to the screen
> They've got you cuming in your dreams
> And real-life love seems
> - like a lost naivety
>
> Love is not a kiss
> Or a girlie you can "hit"
> Or a nipple on a tit
> - that's just a sense-trip.
>
> Now I wake to see
> Can't worship love materially
> It must be given and gotten for free
> - this knowledge strengthens me.

Shred Zine Records

Reach Out recorded a demo, and we "released" it on my "record label" - Shred Zine Recordings. The cover was a photo my dad took of me, dramatically looking up at the sky with my hand on my head. You couldn't possibly tell it was me. I drew the logo by tracing a freehand highlighter with a thin black marker - a trademark style of mine for a few years.

Shred was an independent counter-culture magazine I had been doing since I was 16, with help from my dad (a photographer and contributing writer) and Aunt Janet (a graphic artist). It was a collage of dot-matrix printouts glued to poster-boards with exacto-knife graphics, supplemented with stickers and free-hand sketches. The focus was on BMX freestyle, skateboarding, and underground music. We published bits of counter-cultural creative writing, covered major freestyle events, had interviews with famous skateboarders like Neil Blender, reviewed places to ride and skate, and talked about bands and their records and demos. I was the main writer and editor. We even managed to get a few BMX stores and companies to buy advertising spots.

I think it was mainly my dad's idea to do the zine, but it seemed natural to me, since I was almost always writing and had always been infatuated with Xerox machines. My career as a writer started in fifth grade, when, as a homework assignment, I wrote my first short story using a Wordstar word-processor running on the DEC VT180 forerunner to a personal computer. It was a Dungeons & Dragons / Lord of the Rings type of tale, spanning about a dozen pages, which I also hand-illustrated. The main character, "Uraizah the Mystic," was literally the character I used to play at the D&D club I went to every once in a while. My English teacher loved the story, and that gave me to confidence to consider myself a writer. I hardly stopped writing from that moment on, particularly inspired by Tolkien, Jim Morrison, and J.D. Salinger.

Shred survived for about six issues before calling in quits in 1988. The Shred "record label" came late in Shred's life-cycle, but wound up "putting out" a whole bunch of our friend's demos. At one point I think we even put the Shred Zine logo on Beyond demos.

The Ghastly 1000

Reach Out's Shred Zine label-mates were The Ghastly 1000. The original incarnation of this band was a chaotic 2-piece called 1000 MPH. Someone named "Riff" (Inner Strength's singer, Scott Oliva) played guitar and screamed, and someone named "Raff" (Tom Capone) attacked a drum set and screamed in the background. The first demo they did was called "Speed Attack," which was followed up by "On a Run" - an "18-Song Album" that probably lasted less than 10 minutes, and was replete with ridiculously funny clip art of zany characters looking like they were moshing.

By the time I got involved with the band, it morphed from a speed-thrash jamboree to a horror-core hoedown dubbed "The Ghastly 1000." The line-up:

Zombus - Lead Vocals (me)
Gazaboz - Drums / Vocals (Tom, formerly known as "Raff")
Creeper - Guitar / Vocals (Scott, formerly known as "Riff")
Igor Franken poke - Bass (Kevin Egan)

Our songs had titles like Skulls and Bones, Garlic Grin, Foolish Ghoul, 1000 Years of Horror, Cigar Stomper, Ghosts of Our Past, Whitey the Undead Criminal, Sideburn Suicide, Rebels, That Which Sin Created, Satisfaction (a cover of the Stones' classic), Snaggle Monster (a cover of the 1000MPH classic, dedicated to our high school music teacher), and so much more...

The highlight of our career was playing Linda Tosti's backyard Halloween party, in costume. True to the name, Zombus, I used white makeup to make my skin pale and my eyes black, and dressed in an outdated 60s suit and jacket.

Chapter Seven:

You're Into That Krishna Shit, Right?

Chant and be Hippy

Beyond started to play shows with Youth of Today, and thus the time came for me to meet their singer, Ray Cappo who was probably the most famous and important person in the entire international straightedge hardcore scene. He was the guy who was making vegetarianism an official part of straightedge. He wore Krishna neck beads and even had a Krishna ponytail on the back of his shaved head.

The first time I met him, he was wearing a T-Shirt that had a row of vegetables across the chest, and just said "whole foods" in a small font above them. Whole Foods was a grocery store that catered to health food fans. It was probably the last t-shirt anyone would expect the singer of a punk band to wear on stage.

Youth of Today didn't impress me much on record, but live... they were insane. Cappo never stopped jumping and running all over the place, karate kicking every five seconds while snarling half the lyrics and getting the audience to shout the rest. It quickly became obvious to me why he had become the most important guy in straightedge.

I eavesdropped on an interview he was doing. He used these words like *transcendental* and *cosmic*. Unable to contain myself I butted in to ask him about *kali-yuga*, the Age of Quarrel. He said all this fantastic, fatalistic, apocalyptic stuff, which I found fascinating.

It was the end of the night, so he said he would tell me more about Krishna the next time we played together.

The next time we played together was in Connecticut, at a place called "The Brick and Wood." The Vandals headlined, Youth of Today and Beyond opened. Cappo showed up separately from the rest of his band, rolling up with Steve Reddy in their own van, which was full of boxes of Hare Krishna books. We played Frisbee for a while on the lawn outside the club, and then he gave me a book.

It was called "Chant and be Happy" and seemed hokey and culty. The cover had pictures of three people, a smiling Indian Swāmī, John Lennon, and George Harrison. Hello hippies, we have some names to drop. The book turned me off, so I figured I'd put the whole thing on the back burner.

Real-Life Elvish!

After Beyond practice one night, Alan Cage tossed a paperback at me, saying, "You're into that Krishna shit, right? Take this... I hate it."

How strange. Alan Cage, the devoutly atheistic secular moralist, had just tossed me a book with a picture of Krishna on the cover! I had no idea how to read the title: "Śrī Īśopaniṣad."

"Where'd you get it?" I asked.

"The Cro-Mags were selling a bunch of these Krishna books at their show." He said.

"What do you hate about it?" I asked.

"They support the caste system. That's total bullshit."

When I went home that night, I propped myself up against the pillows in my bed and gave the book a chance. Flipping through it, I saw stuff like this:

ॐ पूर्णमदः पूर्णमिदं पूर्णात्पूर्णमुदच्यते ।
पूर्णस्य पूर्णमादाय पूर्णमेवावशिष्यते ॥

Sanskrit! There was even a table at the back of the book explaining how to read the letters. I was raised on Lord of the Rings. When I saw these Sanskrit letters, it was as if the mother of Elvish Feanorian Script suddenly stepped out of the fantasy genre and became a living reality.

To this day I remember the opening words of the introduction almost verbatim, it was the transcript of a public address given by the Hare Krishna leader:

> Ladies and gentlemen, today's subject matter is the teachings of the Vedas. What are the Vedas? The Sanskrit verbal root of Veda can be interpreted variously, but the purport is finally one. Veda means knowledge.

There was a yellow highlighter in the introduction where Alan had marked the part he hated:

> The divisions of society are brāhmaṇa, kṣatriya, vaiśya, śūdra. Brāhmaṇa refers to the very intelligent class of men, those who know what is Brahman. Similarly, the kṣatriyas, the administrator group, are the next intelligent class of men. Then the vaiśyas, the mercantile group. These natural classifications are found everywhere. This is the Vedic principle, and we accept it.

This *did* sound like a reference to the caste system, but a few paragraphs down from this statement the Swāmī said:

> Dvija-bandhu refers to those who are born in a high family but who are not properly qualified. A man who is born in the family of a brāhmaṇa but is not qualified as a brāhmaṇa is called dvija-bandhu.

This meant that the Krishna's were *not* in favor of the caste system, because the key flaw of the caste system is that birth into a particular family is the sole determinant of social position. The Krishna's were saying that someone might be born into a high-class family, but if they don't have high-class qualities they should not be held in a high social position.

I guess Alan had stopped reading before he got to this point.

As for me, I really liked the book because, just like the article I had read a few months ago in that zine, it seemed rational and systematic, especially compared to anything else I had ever heard about religious subjects.

Krishna Has Sex, Why Can't You?

The more I read that book, the more I became the local authority on the subject of Krishna. Not many people asked me much, but Tom was a bit interested in the whole Krishna thing, so at one point, while we were driving slowly through my neighborhood, he asked, "So, Krishna's have four rules, right? And one of them is 'no sex,' right?"

"Yeah," I said. "'No *illicit* sex.'"

"OK, whatever," Tom said. "But why should Krishna be allowed to have sex with all these girls?"

"Gopīs?"

"I guess," he said. "Is that what you call all those girls who are always around Krishna?"

I tried to answer as I made a right turn. "Well, we're not Krishna." I said. "Krishna lifted a mountain with one hand - so obviously he's a bit different than you or me."

"What's so different about him?" Tom asked.

"It's hard to explain," I said, "But the difference is that, by nature, Krishna is male and we are female."

Tom squinted at me, trying to figure out what the hell I had just said.

Hoping to explain how two guys driving a car were actually female, I said, "*Male* means 'predominating' and *female* means 'predominated.'"

His squint turned to incredulous frustration.

"I'm not talking about sexism or social stuff," I said. "I'm talking about psychology, you know, about the basic psychological natures of men and women, which happens because of the way our bodies are. Men have a penis and women have a vagina." I used my fingers for visual aids. "The vagina *receives* the penis, that's what I'm talking about with 'predominated.'"

Tom backed away from me in his seat, looking at me like I was a raving lunatic who might say or do *anything* next. "Dude, what the *fuck* are you talking about?"

"Ok, Ok," I tried to pull it all together, "Krishna is the source of everything, so everything belongs to him, everything is his to enjoy. So for him to enjoy is totally right. But for us to imitate him, that's not right."

"So a Krishna devotee isn't supposed to enjoy anything?" Tom asked.

"Well, being enjoyed is enjoyable!" I said. "Women enjoy sex too, right? So, we enjoy life, but not in the male position, in the female position."

"Yeah," he said, "but Krishna is supposed to be your role model, right? Your leader; the example you try to follow, right? So why should his followers not be allowed to do what he did?"

"Krishna's not our 'leader' or 'role-model'," I said. "Krishna is our object of love. Guru is the role-model and leader, and lives the way you are talking about: never doing anything that we shouldn't follow."

I don't know if I helped or hindered Tom's comprehension of Krishna, but at least it was starting to make some sense to me.

Everybody Leaves, If They Get the Chance

My mom had a thing for Southern California. When she was a girl she visited there with her dad, and since then dreamed of living the California Dream. As I approached high-school graduation, my dad made ready to make that dream come true for her.

I remember visiting California to scout out potential new homes. Escondido was one of the towns mom and dad considered.

I said I would rather die than move there.

They wound up buying a house a little south of Escondido and gave me a choice, "You're eighteen now. You don't have to come with us. It's up to you."

I felt close to my New York family, especially my Aunts. Tom and Kevin were like my brothers; Alan, too, like an older brother. Everyone else was a blast. Yet, I left all that behind and moved to California, just south of Escondido.

Why?

I was really starting to like this Krishna-stuff, and wanted to get more seriously involved, but I felt it would be harder to do that in New York where everyone had known me for years and expected me to keep being basically the same Vic DiCara I had always been. I figured I could reinvent myself much more easily in California.

I went to one of those "college fairs" in the gymnasium of my high school and applied to the first college I found from California: Cal Poly Pomona.

They accepted me.

CHAPTER EIGHT:

BYE BYE TO 18 YEARS OF GROWING UP

A Crucial Bar-B-Que

We decided to throw a going-away bash, the End-of-Shred Party. 45 zillion people showed up, and only 20 zillion were invited — music friends, BMX friends, skateboarding friends, friends from school, friends from the neighborhood, friends of all these friends, with their friends... and almost all of my family, too.

We built skate ramps and set them up on the road in front of my house, blasting music towards them from my bedroom window. In the backyard, my family mostly hung out at the wooden table and the built-in benches of the deck my dad and I had built under the roof's overhang. They drank wine and beer, and laughed themselves silly about how wild and crazy my friends and I were.

Outside the deck, my dad had built a brick patio featuring a huge bar-b-que. Chef Fishfeet (Dad's nickname as the Shred photographer) manned the grill and my hardcore friends circled around it singing the Murphy's Law song, "It's gonna be a crucial bar-bar-ba-bar-bar-bar-b-que!"

It *was* pretty crucial, probably the first major all-vegetarian BBQ ever held on Long Island. My dad roasted veggie kabobs and corn on the cob, and I am pretty sure we had a boatload of veggie dogs and veggie burgers (not at all easy to come by in those days).

Out in the yard was a huge wooden quarter-pipe and trick-ramp half-pipe. It was a plywood playground, and Skaters and BMXers were all over it like ants on an anthill as we blasted music into the backyard from out of the family-room windows.

The main event happened under the covered portion of the wooden deck my dad and I had built around our huge L-shaped in-ground swimming pool. Just about all the "Shred Bands" played, including Reach Out and Beyond. Bloody Uterus reformed to play their hits. Members of Third Planet played as a joke band named Rotting Fetus. The teenage hardcore boys in Bermuda swim-shorts moshed around the deck and did "stage dives" into the pool, while the minority of girls at the party stood at a little distance laughing and pointing along with my mom and aunts, who were practically on the floor in hysterics, especially when Bloody Uterus would announce their songs, which had titles like Spit or Swallow and Vaginal Discharge.

The party achieved "monumentally crucial" status, earning an enduring place in the annals of Long Island history.

Linguistic Legacy of the King Tut Crew

A little bit after the going-away party, a moving truck carted everything away and my parents relocated to the other side of the continent. I stayed behind, spending a week here, and a week there, and a week somewhere else on the spare beds or couches of friends. It was a non-stop straightedge party, constantly lounging around and making up new aspects of our exclusive micro-subculture.

Some cliques have handshakes. Some have fashion statements. Us... we mainly had words.

Funny words.

Funny words no one else on earth would use,

...or understand.

We were the "King Tut Crew." No one knows why. Maybe it's because King Tut was ancient, and we wanted to be known as "Ancient Heads," people who loved ancient stuff?

I was "Rasta the Hut." Maybe it was a reference to how I used to play with Star Wars figures with our chief nicknamer, Anthony D'aiuto, in first and second grade?

Everyone had a nickname. Snaggle Monster. Grimace. Garlic Grin. Almost all of them were insulting and never spoken directly to the named. A lot of them the title "Dahg." This moniker was born when Kevin Egan told Anthony, "Robert Rodriguez wants to play drums in a band with you."

Anthony replied, "Who? Dahgdeedus?"

The original Dahgdeedus had coarse, frizzy hair that frustrated his desire to be a proper metalhead, so we honored anyone with frizzy hair by appending the title Dahg to a condensed and stylized version of their real name. Vin Novara, for example, became known as Dahg Vera.

Besides nicknames, the King Tut Crew had an arsenal of original words. Sap was one of our most beloved and widely known. We could use it as a noun - "don't be a sap." We could use it in the vocative, "Yo, Sap!" We could use it as an adjective, "That's a sappy guitar solo." We could even use it in imperative for giving commands: "Sap slaughter!" (to incite a mosh-like frenzy), or "Sap alert!" (a "heads-up" of impending or approaching sappiness).

Besides words, we also had killer pronunciations to commandeer common phrases as King Tut Crew property. Instead of calling someone a dick, we would say, "ah dheeee" with an abundance of breathiness and just the slightest hint of final consonant. We applied this term ubiquitously for anything slightly clumsy or uncool.

Instead of saying "I know" we'd assume the persona of an old Jewish grandma and draw the phrase out with nasal sarcasm, "mmmnyeaiknyooow" to stop anyone from saying anything a little pretentious or boring.

This kind of stuff was way better than drugs. The King Tut Crew could laugh forever. We didn't need a reason, all we needed was enough ridiculous nicknames for everyone and anyone, sufficiently obscure adjectives and catchphrases, and our plethora of caricatured pronunciations. This word play was like free and unlimited LSD — everything suddenly looked *different*, and *better*, with the right nickname, keyword or pronunciation to describe it.

I was goofing off like the old Vic, but also giving serious consideration to Krishna consciousness and the new me, studying that Hare Krishna book Alan had given me. Thus our King Tut / Reach Out basement goof-off headquarters had "Krishna" and "Rāma" spray-painted on the walls near a pin-up picture of Krishna I had cut from an incense box.

Cross Country in a Yugo

In that ancient pre-Facebook epoch it wasn't so easy to communicate with people in distant places - making it quite difficult for a band to organize a tour. World tours were the exclusive glory of bands backed by major management companies. In the hardcore scene, only the most austere and popular bands like Black Flag could manage to play shows across the ocean - and even they rarely did it. National tours were also pretty much the exclusive domain of relatively huge bands. In Beyond's provincial scope of things, "tour" was a word you could use to describe an extended weekend with three or four shows going to the cities up in New York State and adjoining states, playing in pizzerias, backyards, and an occasional rock club.

We did one such tour with Youth of Today in the summer of 88, playing a handful of shows in a few North Eastern states, starting in New York and winding up in Ohio. Surprisingly, I don't remember having any important conversations about Krishna with Ray. But he and I did solidify our friendship by spending a few days joking around, being weird, and having fun. We played poolside in someone's backyard during the afternoon on the Fourth of July. Then we did a club show — Confront, Beyond, and Youth of Today. The next day, Alan and I got into my car.

In the front seat of my Yugo, Alan reminded me of a yogi I had seen on TV squeezing himself inside a small box; he was really big, and the Yugo was really small. This little four-wheeled scooter had replaced the aged Dodge Dart I had bought at the bakery a year or two ago. It was brand new, but it was also the smallest, cheapest new car on the market. For some reason, my friends *loved* it. I guess it seemed like the perfect compliment to my personal style: Now I was the guy with dreadlocks into elves, Krishna, and hardcore; an ex-skater and freestyler who leapt around a stage like a wild animal playing a bass, yet drove around in a tiny sky-blue tin-can of a car with all the horsepower of several lawnmowers.

The Yugo was such a glorified go-kart that we had to wonder if it would even make the journey across the continent without stranding us in the plains of Kansas or the deserts of Utah. Alan and I bravely set out south on Route 71. At Columbus we turned onto Route 70, heading West - which took us through Indianapolis, to St. Louis. There we crossed the Mississippi and things started looking a whole lot different. Everything became perfectly flat, and pretty empty.

We must have slept once or twice along the way, but I don't remember it. I remember rolling through Denver with the windows wide open. It was early July and *hot*, and the Yugo had nothing fancy like Air Conditioning. Route 70 changed from a highway into a rollercoaster, carrying us higher and higher and higher into the Rocky Mountains as if it was about to drop us into some wild ride. The higher we went, the lower the Yugo's top speed. The pedal was constantly pinned to the metal, but the poor little car went slower and slower, eventually limited to a top speed of about 30mph. We started trying to figure out what we should do if she couldn't make it all the way to the top.

Every few minutes the temperature dropped noticeably and soon we had the windows closed and the heater on!

Eventually the Yugo ascended the peaks and picked up speed through the Rockies, taking us to Route 15, South. The way down the other side of the mountains was like riding a skateboard. Every few minutes the temperature got *hotter* again, a *lot* hotter. We were descending into the Nevada desert.

Sweating like dogs in the hot air that billowed in the open windows, we skirted past Vegas and sooner or later pulled up in front of my new home - a big upper-middle class two-story affair in a new housing development a bit north of San Diego, in a town with a pretty snobby sounding name: Rancho Bernardo.

A Lot of Musicians Really Like This Book

A few weeks later, I flew back.

Beyond had become pretty big by the time I left. What started off as the offshoot of a battle-of-the-bands project now played real shows with real bands to real people paying real money. What started off as a high-school hobby now had national attention in the hardcore punk scene.

We even had a record offer!

Of course we are talking hardcore punk. Our "record offer" was from John Porcel - guitarist of Youth of Today, singer and mastermind of the band who practically invented militant straightedge, Project X, and the Chief Executive Officer and Primary Shareholder of a record label called Schism Records. (Schism's stock traded only slightly higher than Shred Zine Records but was destined for greatness with such an influential figure at the helm).

So I flew back from to record a full-length LP with Beyond.

The flight had one stop, in Texas, where I had to change planes. As I walked through the airport with a guitar, skate-punk clothes, and dreadlocks, a short man walked up to me, middle-aged and with round glasses over his kind eyes.

"You must be a musician," he said. "Are you on your way to play a concert?"

I was thrilled to have the chance to say, "I'm going to New York to record an album."

"Wow, that's great!" he exclaimed, and reached into a large bag. "A lot of musicians really like this book."

I recognized the book the instant he began pulling it from his bag. "That's Bhagavad-Gītā!!!" I exclaimed.

He froze. "You know the Bhagavad-Gītā?" He asked in amazement.

"Yeah!" I said, "Can I have it?"

He was delighted to hand it to me. "How do you know about it?"

"Some bands I like are into Krishna consciousness," I said. "I've read one other book... eye-so-pa-knee..."

"Īśopaniṣad?"

"Yeah! That's it!"

"Great!" he said, eyes as wide as his smile. Then he glanced at the book in my hands and said, "Can you give a donation to cover the cost of printing?"

"Well..." I said, "I sent away for a free copy, you know, you had a card in one of your magazines for a free copy... but it never came. Sooo... can't you just give it to me?"

He thought about it for a moment and then agreed, "Yeah, I suppose so... Sure, why not!"

Finally, I had a copy of Bhagavad-Gītā! Between this and Śrī Īśopaniṣad I felt prepared to learn more about Krishna than any punker had ever dared to learn before.

Lost in the Schism Chasm

Beyond recorded No Longer At Ease in a recording studio called Sanctum. We considered it a big studio because it had a huge 24-track board (even though it did use small recording tape, not the big two-inch wide stuff), and the live room was bigger than a lot of rock clubs, with a full sized stage. Alan set up his drums up there and the engineer setup up Alan's brother's bass amplifier in another room, pointing into a corner. There was a big pane of glass between the control room, where I stood with Alan's brother's bass hanging from my shoulders, and the live room, where Alan poised himself to smash the life out of his drum set.

Then the red bearded old metalhead burnout biker of an engineer, nicknamed for eternity by us as Red Man, took a swig of Jack Daniels and pressed record. The most technical thing we did was probably to tune the bass in between songs. "Wait man, tune up," Tom would remind me before we'd launch into the next song. I don't think we did much more than a second take on any song. So, within an hour or two, fourteen songs had their foundations laid. Alan and I even recorded a fifteenth - a relaxed and dubby drum-and-bass oriented thing that he and I used to break out live whenever Tom broke a guitar string or some other technical mishap presented itself.

Recording the drums and bass did take long enough that I had to pee when we were done. For some reason I remember being in the small studio toilet thinking, "Wow. This is really a good record. I just did something that will affect a lot of people for a long time." It was the first time I ever felt legitimately important to the world at large.

Tom spent the rest of the session recording the rhythm guitar. The next day, he did his guitar solos and some fancy feedback, and then Kevin recorded his vocals. We threw in a few backing vocals shouted as a group, and that was that: the record was done. We mixed it in a few minutes and sent it off to Porcel.

As it turned out, the record would never be released by Schism. It waited for that for a few months, till Schism withdrew from the record-label arena and called it quits, leaving behind only rumors that it ever came close to existing. The recording passed to a friend and die-hard pillar of the hardcore scene, Dave Stein, who released it a few months later on his under-the-radar label: Combined Effort.

I am proud of the record. Even the name of the band "Beyond" seemed to me to indicate a focus on something supernatural, paranormal, or transcendental. Tom wrote the vast majority of Beyond's lyrics, but I really felt them as if they were my own. One of my favorites is Time Stand Still, a song about the need to find relevant meaning in life, or else become consumed by the meaningless void of death:

> *Missing answers to the question*
> *of why I'm even here.*
> *Losing feeling for the things around me*
> *things I once held dear.*
> *Still awake late at night*
> *afraid to let the day slip by.*
> *I'm always feeling empty...*
> *I can't help but wonder why.*

I also really liked Vampire Empire, a song about religious evangelists who use "god" as a tool to control, manipulate, and exploit people:

> *Using a figure like GOD*
>   *to benefit no one except yourself.*
> *The money you make is brought by lies,*
>   *and just increases your wealth.*
> *If you really cared,*
>   *you wouldn't use people like a ruthless vampire,*
> *Feeding off of struggling people and preying on their guilt,*
>   *just to build an empire.*
>
> *Crucify and cast blame*
>   *on anything that threatens you.*

> *Create, and propagate,*
> > *more problems than solutions to work through.*
> *Victims gravely leached,*
> > *gullible to your monopolized divine theft*
> *Manipulated for your gain, and killing for GOD -*
> > *but what does he need with death?*

Self-Interest was an anti-greed and anti-selfishness song:

> *We are on this earth and revolve with it,*
> *but sometimes we think it revolves around ourselves.*
> *There's too much concern about what we can get,*
> *and never any time to consider the world around us.*

The Inside Out Era

Chapter Nine:

Forbidden Adventures in the Temple of Doom

Clean Slate

Back in California and settling in for the long-term, everything seemed a blank canvas. The room was new. The house was new. The street was new. The town was new. The world was new.

The perfect setting to forge a new identity.

The Hare Krishna's had a vegetarian restaurant not too far away, and the food was amazing. I especially loved the coconut "chutney" all over this spicy cake-thing called a *dhokla*. I bought a few things besides lunch: a bumper sticker that said "Friends Don't Let Friends Eat Meat," a magazine with a trippy galactic painting on the front, called "Origins," and a book with a drawing of an old man entering one door, and a boy walking out of another, called "Coming Back."

Through the magazine, I sent away for a free copy of Bhagavad-Gītā (described as the "Bible of India"), and placed an order for a cassette of the Rādhā Krishna Temple Album and a strand of chanting beads.

The free Gītā never arrived, but the beads and cassette wound up in my mailbox pretty soon. Afraid of freaking out mom and dad, I brought them into my walk-in closet and listened to the tape on my Walkman. George Harrison had produced it and played guitar here and there. It had a hippie smell, but also had something very transcendental and appealing about it. I think it was mostly the woman's voice - Yamunā - so compelling, sincere and in another realm of consciousness.

Beads in hand, I chanted along with the tape, very quietly, moving to the next bead after each mantra. The whole Hare Krishna song was over way before I got around the whole strand, so I rewound. About a half hour later I was still only about halfway through the beads and gave up the effort. I had heard or read that devotees chant 16 times around all those beads, and I figured they must spend all day doing that.

Off With His Dreads

Once I got to California I got tired of my dreadlocks. Maybe the fact that I liked the Krishna's so much made me veer away from keeping such long, outrageous hair. All of the Krishna guys either shaved their head or kept their hair clean and short. But at least half of it was just the fact that my dreadlocks were pretty raunchy and my head was getting unbearably itchy.

My mom, a former hairdresser, cut them off. The stench was awful, but we put one in a zip lock and saved it. She cut them about an inch away from my scalp, and then we took pictures and laughed in the mirror. My head looked like a funny drawing of the moon, or a chopped up stalk of broccoli.

After unraveling the moon-crater dread-stubs, I had normal, short hair again!

We threw a little blonde bleach in there for fun.

Temple of Doom

In September, I moved into the dorms. The university was only about an hour and a half from my parent's house, but I was 19 and wanted to live on my own. My roommate turned out to be a Jewish accounting student named Ira. We had practically nothing in common. The guys across the hall, on the other hand, were neo-hippies: Mark, a beat-poet, and Dave Zuckerman, an Israeli with a taste for mysticism and philosophy. I introduced myself as a Hare Krishna and we became three musketeers of Cal Poly Pomona

Now that I was living on my own on the other side of the country, I wanted to get more involved with Hare Krishna; but at the same time, I was hesitant. The philosophy in their books was deep and solid, but a lot of other things about them smelled strange. ISKCON seemed like a garden where beautiful flowers grew amidst festering composts; amazingly precise and clear concepts about the soul and God were mixed with a whole bunch of very cliquey, cultish stuff.

It was like being at the beach very early in the season. The water is freezing, but you want to go in, and as you go in, you want to run out. I wanted more of Krishna, but to get him it seemed I would have to deal with a lot of things I wasn't sure I wanted at all.

There was a Krishna temple about an hour away from campus. Within a week or two I had worked up the courage to go check it out. I convinced myself that I wasn't exactly going to the *temple*, I was going to an exhibit they had, called "F.A.T.E - the First American Transcendental Exhibit," a collection of dioramas illustrating the central messages of the Gītā.

When my Yugo pulled up in front of the saffron buildings at 3764 Watseka Avenue there wasn't a soul around and all the doors were closed. A wave of fear came over me, and, without getting out of the car, I drove away. When I got to the end of the block, however, I stopped, "You drove all the way out here just to turn around? What are you scared of? Go find someone and ask where the FATE exhibit is."

So, I drifted around the front of the temple like an electron without a proton for an awkward while. Finally, someone came by who looked fairly normal, but had neck beads.

"Excuse me," I said. "Do you know where I can see the FATE exhibit?"

They pointed me to double wooden doors at the end of a wide alley on the side of the temple.

The doors were locked.

I hung around in front of them until someone else finally walked by. His head was as bald as a mirror, his face as hairless as a 10 year-old's, his small frame was wrapped in cloth like a citizen of ancient Greece. Round glasses were on his eyes, big leather sandals on his feet, and a small bag hung at his chest from a strap around his neck, big chanting beads slightly hanging out from it.

"Excuse me," I said. "Can I see the FATE exhibit?"

"Well," he replied more softly and slowly than I had ever heard anyone speak before, "normally the exhibit is closed at this hour, but if I can find the key I'll open it for you."

He walked away slowly. Quietly.

A few minutes later he returned with the key. Slowly. Quietly.

I was a bit scared of this gender-neutral little guy who floated around with semi-expressionless peace. I couldn't decide if he was completely brainwashed or completely spiritual.

The exhibit was simultaneously impressive and disappointing; impressive because most of it was absolutely beautiful, disappointing because it was obviously in disrepair. In one diorama, Krishna sat at the front of a horse-drawn chariot speaking to a worried warrior. "Here, Krishna is speaking Bhagavad Gītā to

Arjuna," the little devotee explained, as if I didn't know. In another, Krishna had dozens of heads and dozens of gods and goddesses thronged around him. "This is Krishna's universal form," he said, again not realizing that I already knew. In yet another, a terrified passenger was carried on a wild ride in a chariot drawn by five horses. Each horse, the devotee explained (and I already knew), was one of the five senses. The driver was the mind. The reigns were the intellect. The passenger was the soul.

I already knew what all the stuff was about because the exhibit was essentially a 3D version of all the paintings in the Bhagavad Gītā I had gotten in the Texas airport. What I liked the most was Krishna standing in a moonlit forest playing a flute, with about half a dozen goddesses surrounding him, all singing and playing exotic musical instruments while looking at him with eyes that dripped affection. "This is Krishna and the gopīs in Vṛndāvana," he said, softly and slowly, still not asking if I knew anything about any of this stuff.

I guess he didn't notice that I had Tulasi beads around my neck?

As I walked back out into the daylight, the devotee softly told me, "The temple is open now. Why don't you go..." I couldn't understand the rest of the words but the meaning was clear.

The temple had three big double-doors, and each one seemed ominous with dangerous seductions. I went to right-most doors and quietly pulled one slightly ajar to peek in. On the other side was a huge white circle against a black background, with a black dot in the middle. It was the eye of the figure on the altar, and it seemed to be *right in my face!*

I shut the door, caught my breath, and got in the car.

The inside of a Hare Krishna temple would have to wait for my next brave adventure. But it sure did smell good in there.

CHAPTER TEN:

HARDCORE HARDCORE, KRISHNA KRISHNA

Moshing at the Temple

I had gone to the Hare Krishna temple and made it back with my brain still in one piece, so I felt brave enough to try one of their "Sunday Love Feasts."

The temple was a lot less imposing on Sunday afternoon, because dozens of people were around. There was a lot of "normal looking" people, assuaging my concerns about what might be excessive uniformity in ISKCON. There were also a lot of Indians, assuaging my concern over whether or not ISKCON was authentic.

The temple floor was rich checkered marble. Marble pillars lined the side walls, with beautiful Krishna-paintings in the archways between them. The ceiling was two stories high, and looked like an Indian version of the Sistine Chapel, with a huge painting of beautiful people in robes dancing and chanting in some rural setting. A big, crystal chandelier hung from the middle. Above the pillars, on the second-story level of the walls, were ornate bas-relief statues of Vedic deities dancing, singing, and playing drums and hand cymbals.

At the front of the temple was a stage about a meter high, with three elaborately carved double wooden doors. The doors opened and almost hid behind the pillars and Indian-style arches separating them. Brilliant light streamed out from the altar inside, revealing a huge, incredible wooden structure, carved and shaped more gorgeously than anything I had ever seen before. This wooden masterpiece from another dimension formed a canopy over three sets of "deities," sacred statues. The set on the right consisted of three wooden figures, squarish, with exaggerated and simplified eyes and mouths painted over their black, yellow, and white surfaces. I recognized the big round eye that had jumped out and stared at me when I peaked in the door last time! The middle set of deities was Rādhā and Krishna in marble. They were big, full of flowers, amazingly colorful and, to use some of my favorite words from Prabhupāda's lexicon, "sumptuously opulent." The deities on the left were another two marble figures with arms upraised, Gaura (a recent *avatār* of Krishna who began the whole Hare Krishna movement and granted intimate access to Rādhā and Krishna), and his brother, Nitai (who helped him immensely in that mission).

The sights, sounds and smells were all rich and pleasant, like cake.

Near the altar but out on the temple floor, there was also an ornate seat, more like a sofa, upon which a different sort of sacred statue sat. It seemed to be made of some type of resin, and was disarmingly lifelike. It was Śrīla Prabhupāda, the original guru and founder for ISKCON. I wasn't sure how to feel about it.

Someone sat at the foot of this fancy sofa, on a smaller dais, explaining what the Krishna philosophy is all about. I don't remember much about exactly what he said, but I remember the dancing that came afterward! The Krishna's had these two-headed drums and these hand-cymbals, and could really get something going with them in "kīrtan." Their kīrtan even had mosh-parts! It would speed up and speed up and speed up, and then drop into a huge, slow, moshable stomp. I danced around without much reservation, somehow fitting together a Rasta strut, two-step skank and occasionally even doing the "pick-up-change" mosh. People gave me a little distance as I jumped around, but looked at me with smiles. Some of the Krishna guys would even come over and leap around with me.

By the time it was over, I was sweating and out of breath. It was time for the feast.

I sat there on the floor with paper plate and cup in front of me, in a line with the dozens of other people, plates and cups. Chatter was all around, but I had no one to talk to, and liked it that way. A devotee proceeded down the line, pushing a plastic bucket in front of him, scooping food onto the plates.

Splish... he dumped spinach into my plate.

There was nothing in the world I hated more than cooked spinach. I would gag if my mom put it on my plate. Yet here it was sitting in front of me, its green mass on the white plate, slowly leaking yellow-green juice.

Maybe the next bucket would have something I could stomach?

Splash... carrots.

Besides spinach, there was nothing I hated in the world more than cooked carrots.

I stared at the two dire enemies of my taste buds. "This stuff is *'prasādam,'*" I thought. "Krishna *ate* it. I should at least try it."

I spooned a bit of the spinach into my wary mouth.

It was delicious!

Incredible!

Next, a spoon of the carrots... "What?" I shouted to myself in amazement. "Why do I *love* this?"

65

Argyle Core

I somehow found out about a show in Irvine, and decided to drive out there for my first taste of West Coast Straightedge Hardcore.

I walked into the show with elitism protecting the vulnerability of being alone and knowing no one. I was from the piss-stained, rock-hard streets of New York! The scene I walked into in Irvine was indeed palpably un-terrifying. First of all, it was in a church. Second of all, all the kids were young, clean, and smiley. Third, the music had no "chug."

The bands that played were pretty good, though. Hard Stance jumped around a lot and, most interesting thing by far, the bassist wore Krishna beads and the singer wore a Razor's Edge shirt.

While they played, I got out of my cocoon, dove into the pit, and attempted to demonstrate the New York style. It was a little difficult, since a big part of the New York style revolves around the ongoing effort to clear a space for yourself on the dance floor. People in Irvine stayed out of the way once plowed there the first time.

After the set I went up to the singer and said, "I like your shirt. Are you into Krishna?"

"I think its pretty cool," he said. "But Helmet is more into it than me." Then he introduced me to Helmet - Mark Hayworth, the bass player - who gave me a flier for a show that would be put on by the Razor's Edge Fanzine.

The Krishna Punk Show

I eagerly drove down to San Ysidro on the edge of Mexico for the Razor's Edge show - hoping to meet the person behind the zine that had been my first real exposure to Krishna Consciousness. I got there early and saw a skinny young man a year or two older than me with beads around his neck, a blonde Krishna-ponytail, and blue eyes. He was walking around with a purpose, and seemed to be setting things up.

"Do you need some help?" I asked.

"Sure," he said, "What's your name?"

"I'm Vic."

"I'm Kalki." He said. It sounded familiar, so I asked him, "Are you the guy who does the Razor's Edge?"

"Yeah, that's me."

"Wow! That is a great zine!" I blurted out. He thanked me and I helped him set up some equipment that the Hare Krishna restaurant would be using for giving free vegetarian *prasādam* to everyone at the show tonight.

How cool!

It was a long show with a slew of bands. Two small and new bands opened the night, followed by the local favorites, Amenity. By the time Inside Out played, about 100 kids had come, 98 of whom had never heard Inside Out before. Despite zero audience participation, the singer carried the energy of the whole show with his unbridled emotional outpouring and smart yet emotionally charged rants between songs.

When Hardstance played, I realized that Inside Out's singer was one of their guitar players - Zack de la Rocha. Hardstance was OK, but Inside Out had really caught my attention. They even reminded me a little bit of Beyond in how their music incorporated some of the subtler D.C. style of hardcore.

No For An Answer headlined and sucked. Inside Out and Hardstance had expressed appreciation to the Krishna's for putting on the show and giving out vegetarian food, but No For An Answer brought out the banter: "Religion doesn't belong in hardcore." Hello dude on

67

stage, Bad Brains... Cro-Mags... much of the *best* hardcore was connected with religion.

I hung around late, eating *prasādam* and chilling with Kalki and the Krishna's who had come from the restaurant. One young lady in a sari was standing up, munching on something, when she shyly put her hand to her mouth and said, "I shouldn't eat standing up. I heard that if you eat standing up you'll become a horse in your next life."

That sounded ridiculous.

Brahman on Bellechase

One weekend night, back at my parent's house on Bellechase Circle, I drifted to sleep while reading the Bhagavad Gītā and contemplating the new concepts. In the middle of the night, I woke up uncommonly *calm*.

Everything felt different than usual.

I glanced around the room. Nothing was different. The closet doors were still the closet doors.

Yet they weren't.

The whole room was, like me, calmly *alive*.

The walls were obviously solid, but seemed to breathe. Their solidity was a superficial perception coexisting with the deeper perception I was now immersed it. They slowly drew closer without changing their physical location. They drew closer not in distance but in sameness. Their insentience seemed like a veil that was gradually lifting. The distance between observer and observed was narrowing, gravitating towards one another, revealing that both occupied the same point in reality.

I felt myself becoming the room, and the room becoming me.

And suddenly, it was terrifying - like death. I was losing contact with my separate sense of self.

The fear broke the revelation, and the observer and observed were back in their normal positions. The room was still just a room, and I was still me.

I went back to sleep.

A Chain from DYS to Inside Out

Someone knocked on my dorm-room door to tell me I had a phone call. In the small foyer at the end of the hall, the receiver of a payphone dangled by its metal cord.

I picked it up. "Hello?"

A confident voice asked, "Is this Vic DiCara?"

I thought I might be in trouble for something. "Yeah," I replied. "Who's this?"

"This is Chris Bratton from Chain of Strength. We just got back from an East Coast tour and did some shows with Beyond. Tom Capone gave us your number. We're looking for a guitarist for a project. Are you interested?"

I said, "sure."

He told me where and when to meet them.

A few days later, my trusty Yugo pulled into Riverside, where Frosty's dad had an insurance office that Chain of Strength used as a rehearsal space after-hours. A drum set and amps were set up in a corner, and a bunch of guys with guitars stood amidst office desks piled with files and papers.

After exchanging hellos and I put my guitar case on the floor, opened it, took out my white BC Rich Bich, and strapped it over my shoulder. When I turned around half the guys in the band tried not to laugh.

The other half loved the "metal" guitar.

A few days later, Chris called again. "Ryan and I are doing a D.C. style project with Dave Smalley and we think you'd fit that perfectly."

Dave Smalley from Dag Nasty? I said, "Yes!"

Chris, Ryan and I practiced a few times, ironing out two or three pretty cool and sophisticated songs. Then we rented a pro studio and met Smalley there, only to find out that we were just on a totally different musical page. We wanted to do something like Fugazi or Dag Nasty, but he wanted to do pop-punk.

A few days later, Alex Baretto called (Chain of Strength's bassist and Hardstance's drummer). "Dude," he said, "wanna be in Inside Out?"

Chapter Eleven:

Spiritual Equality for Men

Try to Make Me Bow Down to You...

Inside Out fell apart a little after that Krishna show in San Ysidro, but Alex stepped in with a plan to keep Zack on Vocals and Sterling Wilson on bass, and replace the rest of the members with himself on drums and me on guitar.

I drove Alex's house in Riverside. His large bedroom had a bed shoved into the corner, the rest of it was full of amplifiers, P.A.s, a drum set, and assorted debris. I plugged my guitar into one amp. Sterling plugged his bass into another. Zack turned on a microphone. Alex sat behind his drums.

They showed me the intro to Burning Fight, beatboxing and humming while pointing to the right frets on my guitar. It was easy because it was a whole lot like one of my favorite early Bad Brains songs - Supertouch.

When Alex clicked his sticks, we lost contact with the external world and teleport to an electrified, energetic zone of diversified oneness. We were jumping, head-banging, and moshing around Alex's room. When the music stopped we all started laughing at how ridiculously cool it felt. We must have played that intro ten times in a row.

We learned the rest of the song, and one or two others and then, as we were starting to pack up, Zack told me he wanted to have a song called No Spiritual Surrender. "I wanted to name the band No Spiritual Surrender," he said, "but it's too long. But my idea for No Spiritual Surrender is not to surrender your spirit to the forces in this world that just try to drag you down and make you some meaningless number, some little robot doing whatever you are told."

I told him I'd have a song for them the next time we got together.

That weekend I went home and went through my Dad's Led Zeppelin records, looking for a song I had heard before with a killer drumbeat. After a while, I found it: When the Levee Breaks. After listening to it a few times, I went upstairs with it still playing in my head, took out my guitar and wrote the music to No Spiritual Surrender.

Then I sat down at my desk. An hour or two later, the song had lyrics.

> *Try to make me bow down to you.*
> *Try to take my identity.*
> *Try to make me just another pebble on the beach.*
>
> *A green mind twists the plan.*
> *A cold hand to silence me.*
> *But when you try to grasp me, you'll find I'm out of reach.*
>
> *No Spiritual Surrender.*

The next time we got together, I showed them the song and we were jumping off the walls again, playing it a thousand times, beating it into perfect shape.

The perfect chemistry in the band was undeniable. The approach to music, the concepts behind the lyrics, the qualities of the musicians, and the personalities of the people - everything just *fit*.

Spiritual Hardcore

Ryan from Chain of Strength had convinced a middle-aged Persian restaurant owner in Riverside to open on his doors to hold shows for local bands on Sunday afternoons. I doubt he mentioned that the local bands were hardcore, and the restaurateur surely wouldn't have guessed that Ryan had anything to do with slam dancing.

We had cleared away tables and chairs and set up drums and amps in front of a salad bar. At least a hundred kids had packed in to the place with green carpet and green glass chandeliers.

It was the first show here at Spanky's restaurant, the first show with Inside Out's new lineup, and my first show on the West Coast. I had more than one point to prove. I was the new guy from New York with the weird metal guitar, and I intended to show California what was up with that. Even more importantly Inside Out was a *spiritual* band, and I intended to leave no doubt in anyone's mind that spiritual hardcore crushes and kills.

We were the first band. I stood there with my guitar at the ready, wearing a baseball hat, a white t-shirt with the Lion of Judah carrying a red, gold and green flag, and karate pants cut into shorts with a hand-drawn BBT Logo (BBT stands for Bhaktivedānta Book Trust, the publisher of Śrīla Prabhupāda's books).

I flipped the stand-by switch, and the old Carvin began to hum.

We faced one another, unified of mind and purpose. Back to the audience, I pronounced the opening chords of Burning Fight. When the song dropped into its groove it burst into the room like an elephant knocking over trees. I plowed back-first into the crowd, let everything loose. Everyone came unhinged. The universe shrunk to the size of the room.

When the song slammed shut, the restaurant owner started shouting. "Show's Over! Show's Over! Everyone go home, the show's Over!"

Ryan and Chris tried to calm him down. He was petrified, and furious. "You kids are crazy! You will destroy my restaurant! Everyone, go home! The Show's Over!"

Somehow, the show went on, but with one condition: no slamdancing. Everyone except the band had to sit on the floor.

At least from my point of view, this made the show ten times better. Our music seemed to have more meaning when people were sitting still, paying attention to it. The amount of stomping, moshing and crushing we did more than compensated for the lack of the same from the seated crowd.

At one point a homeless and slightly deranged man wandered in, shirtless and smelly, drinking from a brown paper bag and showing gaps in the teeth behind his bushy, copper beard. He was moved by the music and was shouting his appreciation. A few people started joking or making fun of the guy, and there was some threat of throwing him out, but Zack wouldn't have it. He wouldn't tolerate anything but complete solidarity with and respect for the destitute man.

"This next song goes out to this man," he shouted into the mic. "It's about the plight of the homeless, and it's called Redemption."

> *Children on the street wander so helplessly*
> *Who will pay for their suffering?*
> *We've got the power to set them free*
> *Yet still we do nothing*
>
> *But I believe in redemption.*

Bum Rush the Bible Study

My dorm-mates across the hall, Dave and Mark, thought it was cool that I was into Hare Krishna. They became vegetarian and would often come with me to Sunday feasts at the temple. Every time I went, I'd come back with a new poster, book, incense, or *something*. My half of the dorm room — the top half, since I had the top bunk — became like a makeshift Krishna art gallery.

For a stretch there it seemed like every second day we were getting fliers slid under our dorm-room doors, inviting us to come to the Bible study group just down the hall. Dave and I finally decided to take them up on the offer, and launch a philosophical surprise attack on the sure-to-be unprepared and unsuspecting Asian girls who hosted the thing.

We showed up fashionably late. They were all sitting on the floor, wearing no shoes, reading from bibles - some held in their laps, and some on the floor in front of them. There were no men, only Asian girls.

We sat and patiently waited for the chance to say something. When that chance came, I asked, "Are you vegetarians?"

They weren't, so I asked, "Do you follow the ten commandments?"

It must have become completely obvious that we were intent on harassing them with trick questions. So, they answered evasively, saying something about how the Ten Commandments weren't as important as loving Jesus.

Dave (the Israeli) didn't like that much. "How do you love someone but ignore what they want?" He asked, in a calmly condescending tone.

"Moses gave the Ten Commandments," they said, intuiting that Dave was a Jew. "But we follow Jesus..."

"Yeah, but Jesus was a Jew, right?" Dave interjected. "So, Jesus followed the laws of Moses, right? In the Bible, Jesus says, 'I come to uphold the law, not to destroy it," Right? So, if you love Jesus you should try to uphold what he tried to uphold: the ten commandments of Moses."

"Well, we do follow the Ten Commandments," they said.

I jumped back over the ropes into the tag team religion-wrestling ring. "The first commandment is 'thou shalt not kill', but you unnecessarily kill so many animals by eating meat…" My tone was less calm and more condescending than Dave's, for sure.

"This is our Bible study meeting," they eventually explained. "We would really appreciate it if you would let us do it our way instead of coming in here and trying to argue with us and convert us to whatever pagan religion you believe in."

As we left, we informed them, "By the way, its offensive to keep scripture on the floor."

Marianne is Not "Less Intelligent"

A few days later I wound up with Mark and Dave in the girl's wing again - this time to watch some kind of hippie movie. A hippie girl in her third year of school was there and we spontaneously decided that we were boyfriend and girlfriend. I wound up watching the movie with my head in her lap.

Thus, the three musketeers expanded to four: Marianne joining Dave, Mark and myself as the hippie-Krishna-vegetarian-philosophers of Cal Poly.

She was a Horticulture major who lived alone in a small house in the midst of all the campus greenhouses. A recovered alcoholic, she liked the straightedge idea and would come along with me to Inside Out shows. At first she was frightened by all the anger, but got used to it and would smile from ear to ear throughout the shows. She was also into my fascination with Hare Krishna, because she was a full-blown later-day hippie.

...Until she came across something she really didn't like towards the end of the first chapter of Gītā. Prabhupāda translated one of the verses:

> When irreligion is prominent in the family, O Kṛṣṇa, the women of the family become polluted, and from the degradation of womanhood, O descendant of Vṛṣṇi, comes unwanted progeny.

And added his comment:

> As children are very prone to be misled, women are similarly very prone to degradation. Therefore, both children and women require protection by the elder members of the family... According to Cāṇakya Paṇḍita, women are generally not very intelligent and therefore not trustworthy.

"What the hell, Vic?" Marianne protested. "I know Prabhupāda is supposed to be enlightened and everything, but this is just *sexist*. Women are like *children*? Women have to be 'protected' like children? Women are *not very intelligent*?"

I didn't like the sound of it either, but I was hooked on Krishna by now and felt there had to be some way to resolve this in a sensible, acceptable way. I brought up some other sections of Gītā that describe wise people as those who see everyone equally. "So this must not mean that women are *inferior*. They are just *different* from men."

"Yeah," she retorted sarcastically, "different in that men are adults but women are like children and need to be 'protected' from themselves."

"Well," I said, "maybe it's that women are more easily misled and deceived, because they are more naturally trusting and loving?"

She still protested, "Then why does Prabhupāda explain it by saying, 'Women are generally not very intelligent'? It's obvious that he thinks we are not intelligent. He says we are 'like children' so we have to be 'protected' so we don't have our evil ways and degrade society by having sex with everyone and making unwanted children. Come on, Vic, that is completely out-of-touch with reality. It's blatantly ignorant sexism!"

Ever since I was old enough to see straight, I saw sexism as one of the ugliest and stupidest things in existence, so I just couldn't accept the idea that the founder of the Hare Krishna movement was actually sexist. The fault must lie with us, I thought, with how we interpret his words.

I sat down and tried to work through it. "The Vedas talk about different kinds of intelligence," I said, slowly. "The most important kind is the intellect that discriminates between the soul and the body. When Prabhupāda says that women are 'less intelligent' he is talking about *this* type of intelligence, not school-intelligence or practical-intelligence."

"Do *you* think women are less intelligent then men in discriminating between body and soul?" she asked.

"Well," I offered, "I think it's said that in *kali-yuga* (she know that meant the modern age) everyone is less intelligent in discriminating between body and soul. Everyone in *kali-yuga* is a *śūdra*. But maybe in other yugas some men can become more intelligent about this?"

"Why?" she asked.

"I don't know, it seems sort of natural. I mean discriminating between body and soul means becoming detached from the body, but that is unnatural and even undesirable for women because women are the ones who can have children, so they are the ones who *have to* have strong attachment to their children, the products of their body."

She looked at me sideways, trying not to show her frustration at my obvious attempt to put a Band-Aid on cancer.

"Or maybe its some other kind of intelligence," I offered, "some left-brained / right-brained type of thing?"

She took a deep breath and sat down next to me. "Vic, let's be real," she said, sympathetic to my emotional need for seeing the Hare Krishna's as flawless, but unwilling to participate in any self-deception, "*Even if* Prabhupāda means what you say he means, it's definitely not what the Hare Krishna's think Prabhupāda means."

"What do you mean?" I asked. "How do you know that?"

"Come on, Vic!" she replied. "How many times have you gone to the temple? Have you *ever* seen a woman up on the altar? Have you ever seen a woman do the kīrtan? Have you ever seen a woman give the class? No, the women are always stuck in the *back* of the room like niggers at the back of the bus!"

I couldn't argue with that.

Proud to be Brains-Free

The next Sunday I went to the Los Angeles temple alone and approached a female devotee at random. She was maybe ten years older than me at most, beautiful in a very simple way, without a hairdo or makeup.

"In Bhagavad Gītā," I asked, "Prabhupāda says women are not very intelligent and therefore have to be protected. Do you believe that?"

To my complete surprise, she not only accepted the idea but was completely in favor of it. "Oh yes!" she declared, "Women are less intelligent then men! We are nine times more lusty and nine times more attached to our bodies than men are. That's why we are so obsessed with dressing nice and looking pretty."

Was I hallucinating? She seemed to *relish* the opportunity to declare her inferiority, and was completely unfazed and unimpressed with the disbelief and shock written all over my face.

"So," I asked, slowly and incredulously, "You're less intelligent than I am? Even though you are a devotee?"

"Probably!" she said, and laughed.

She noticed I wasn't laughing at all and offered a concession. "Well," she said, "Prabhupāda *did* say that devotee women are not less-intelligent like ordinary women."

"Then why don't women ever give class in the temple?" I asked.

"Well, devotee women are not less intelligent like ordinary women, but we are less intelligent than devotee men."

I stared at her and blinked, almost expecting her to disappear in between blinks, proving this to be just a bad dream.

She didn't disappear. Instead she got more intense. "You're brainwashed by the propaganda of the women's libbers," she explained. "Woman's liberation is a cheat invented by men. It claims to give women freedom and equality, but actually it only gives women the so-called freedom to be equally exploited by anyone and everyone. In Vedic society women are protected from exploitation, first by their father, then by their husband, and finally by their sons."

I left quietly - exhausted, confused, and disappointed; forced, for the first time, to see that Hare Krishna World wasn't utopia.

But I was *in love* with Hare Krishna, so I decided not to let this one black spot ruin the whole thing. Like a "less-intelligent" woman in love with a flawed man, I chose to believe that, if I stuck with them, I would one day be able to help the Hare Krishna's see Prabhupāda's words in ways that weren't so... well, *ignorant*.

CHAPTER TWELVE:

BY A THREAD

Can't Quiet the Undertone

The only thing that slowed down Inside Out's songwriting was how much we enjoyed playing the existing stuff over and over and over again in Alex's bedroom. Zack, Alex and myself *all* had a prolific knack for writing music and lyrics, and Sterling could pretty easily handle just about anything the three of us ever threw at him. It was like a creative soup; one person would put their idea into the pot, and everyone would stir it in their own ways and add their own spices. Though every song had a "mother" who initially birthed it, each one wound up being something the entire band had a significant part in creating.

After finishing Burning Fight and writing No Spiritual Surrender, we soon wrote Redemption (mostly Zack's song), By A Thread (Zack's music, my lyrics), and Undertone (mostly my song).

The lyrics to By A Thread were an intentionally "emo" way of expressing the feeling that I was stuck between "material life" and "spiritual life." With the whole world flowing like a rushing river towards materialism, my "spirituality" felt like something I had to cling to desperately.

> *Holding on, for my life.*
> *Hanging on, by a thread.*
>> *Cause I if I don't try,*
>> *I'm gonna fall into the hatred of this world.*
>
> *My hands are bleeding, this thread cuts through my veins;*
>> *But it's all I've got to hold.*
> *I hang and pray and struggle everyday,*
>> *to keep this spark of reality from growing cold.*
>
> *A tightrope balance;*
> *My very life hangs by a thread above the abyss of my despair.*
> *If I lose my grip again, oh if I snap.*
> *I will be lost again - a dark relapse.*

Undertone was our most "metal" song, and the lyrics meant a lot to me because they were about equality, and thus relevant to the whole ISKCON sexism issue I continued to grapple with.

> *We cannot separate*
> *We cannot cut the cord*
> *We can't deny to relate*
> *More ignorance we can't afford*
> *We cannot quiet the truth*
> *We can't quiet the undertone*
>
> *You're so eager to claim that we could never be the same*
>> *but you can't quiet the undertone*
> *It's just a stale superstition that puts compassion in remission*
>> *can't quiet the undertone*

Superficially we are all different - different shapes, colors, sizes, genders, talents, weaknesses, and so on - but there is an "undertone" beneath all the different melodies, an undertone that is the same in everyone. That undertone is life itself: consciousness, "Brahman." It is only the ignorance of old-fashioned, superficial, stupid ways of looking at things allows people to ignore this undertone and cling to hateful, divisive -isms.

Zack was into Rap music, so I also wrote a psuedo-rappy thing as a bit of a commentary on Undertone:

> *We still drawin' lines that divide*
> *An' we still takin' up sides*
> *An' hidin' behind false prides.*
>
> *We makin' up all these reasons to separate*
> *An' perpetrate the hate.*
>
> *Lie & try to set ourselves so hiiiiigh above*
> *An' deny the law of Love.*
>
> *But it's all in your fantasy-land mind.*
> *'Cause the undertone 'tween you and me*
> *Is our perpetual unity.*

Smoke Some *Prasādam*, Motherfuckers!

Inside Out played constantly in Southern California. I can't remember how many times we did San Diego's Che Cafe with Amenity, the Valley's Country Club with Insted, Riverside's Spanky's with Chain of Strength, or random churches and rental halls in Orange County with our friends in so many local bands. Occasionally we would venture up to The Barn in Santa Barbara to play Kent McClard's shows, often with Downcast. Sometimes we'd go all the way up to the motherland of punk rock - the Gilman Street Project in Berkley, and play with bands like Swiz. Once we even did a weekend of shows way up as far as Seattle.

Every show was memorable, because we treated every one as if the whole world would be changed by it. The Che was always so punk and raw - no stage, just a sea of sweaty bodies to slam into while playing guitar. Another nice thing about the Che was that it was close to the Krishna restaurant, and we could grab some Krishna snacks before the show. "*Prasādam*" became a household word in the scene; people would say it with such zeal! Mark Hayworth coined a phrase, "smoke some *prasādam*." Comedic Mike Madrid from Against the Wall would say it best in his surfer drawl, "Duuude, let's go smoke some prasaaaadam." "

The Country Club was like the polar opposite of the Che; so "rock-star" with its huge stage, mega sound system, rock and roll lighting, and huge capacity. I saw the Cro-Mags here on their Best Wishes tour. I expected a lot from the band that got me interested in Krishna, and moshed like a wrecking machine to We Gotta Know, Life of My Own, Death Camps, and The Only One, but overall the show let me down. Harley taunted us "motherfuckers" to "fuck shit up" nearly a zillion times, yet didn't even hint towards "Krishna" once. I think he even introduced The Only One as a song about his girlfriend. Come on, man! It was *obviously* about Krishna - "I'll never forget the way I felt when I first looked in your lotus eyes. When I hear your name there is no more fear." I didn't go up to him after the show to say, "Hi, you're awesome, you got me interested in Krishna." I didn't want to take the risk that his response would be less inspiring than his performance on stage.

Gandhi Core

On of the most memorable Inside Out shows happened at the "Backdoor," a pretty big venue on the campus of San Diego State University. A small scuffle broke out in the middle of our set, so we stopped playing to discover that three Nazi skinheads were threatening one of the straightedge kids.

Zack said something like, "cut the shit, assholes," but as soon as we started playing, assholes resumed shitting. Hitler's favorite trio was punching everyone as they goose-stepped and sieg-heil'd around the pit.

Zack was way into Mahātma Gandhi, so much so that he had the Mahātma's face tattooed on his arm! He was amazed by Gandhi's ability to accomplish political change through non-violent resistance. He brought Gandhi's inspiration to bear on the ugly situation at hand, and had everyone in the club sit quietly on the floor.

Of course the three lads from the SS didn't comply.

"Leave." He commanded them.

"Fuck you!" they shouted several times, in several variants, with several gestures.

"If you won't leave on your own we will remove you. We are not going to play another note until you leave."

The standoff lasted two or three minutes. That doesn't sound like long but its *forever* when you're in the middle of it. Eventually Hitler's best friends gave up, left, and were never heard from again. Mahātma Gandhi's approach worked, even in Hardcore punk!

The rest of the show howled with a level of energy never seen before. I picked up my nasty habit of throwing my guitar across the stage right here. Thus it was the last time my beautiful white Bich saw active service.

Sexism + No Sex = Fail

By the end of the school year the sparkle had faded completely from my relationship with Marianne, dulled to nil by the duo of sexism and sex. ISKCON sexism caused her enthusiasm for Krishna to decline steadily, while the ISKCON conception of sex ("none of it") short-circuited my enthusiasm for any physical intimacy. On both fronts it must have been painfully clear to Marianne that I loved the Hare Krishna's more than I loved her.

The relationship came to a close with her saying, in complete sincerity, "I want you to be able to pursue your spiritual dreams without feeling held back by me. You will do something wonderful for the whole world."

I felt bad, but admired her for it.

I remember walking back to my dorm from her place, noticing how grass grows much longer underneath windows that protrude from their buildings, or along the edges of garden-trim.

My Early Krishna Heroes

I spent the summer of '89 in Rancho Bernardo at mom and dad's house.

For a while now, Ray Cappo and I had been writing letters back and forth, making him my first steady mentor in Krishna consciousness. He wasn't so much a mentor who *taught* me things, but a mentor who inspired and encouraged me to devote myself more and more to Krishna consciousness. Earlier that year Ray had quit Youth of Today and put together a project named Shelter, whose every song was about Krishna consciousness. They had already recorded an LP, with old friend Tom Capone playing guitar. It hadn't come out yet, and wouldn't for a long time, but Ray was already envisioning the future of hardcore: Krishna-core, in which Shelter would spearhead a crop of bands with members who were into Krishna... bands like Inside Out.

I spent a lot of time at the San Diego Krishna temple that summer. It was even cooler than the one in Los Angeles. The inside was decorated and decked out, but the thing I liked best were the people. It was the headquarters of the Hare Krishna magazine, Back to Godhead, and I got along really well with the chief editor, Jayādvaita Swāmī. He was logical as folded laundry; thinking his clear thoughts and expressing them plainly and clearly, without caring a rat's ass for popularity or any bullshit like that. He was punk without the punk. I would go to the magazine's office now and then to vacuum, organize file cabinets, or whatever.

Dravida dās was another one like Jayādvaita Swāmī: more punk than punk - so absorbed in whatever it was he was absorbed in that he just didn't have time or energy to care about stupid, superficial things. He would sometimes hang out with me, recite Sanskrit poems, and answer my questions.

Another guy I loved was Mādhavendra Pūri, one of the three people involved in San Diego's branch of something called the Bhaktivedānta Institute - a group of devotees who were trying to explain Krishna consciousness in context of modern science. I was a huge fan of modern science — my dad had majored in physics, and I had been obsessed with astronomy for a few years as a young boy — so I'd sit with Mādhavendra for hours and ask him all sorts of detailed scientific questions.

"In a computer," I once asked him, "all the complex reality we experience on the screen is really just an interpretation of fantastic combinations of ones and zeros. So, maybe the so-called real world is like that too? Maybe the complexity of consciousness is really just an interpretation of a whole bunch of electrical and chemical ones and zeros in the brain?"

He answered the same way he always did: Light and cautious as the gait of a cat, but drifting into a mad-scientist's glimmer-eyed grin at every pause. "Well," he practically whispered in enthusiasm, "that *is* exactly the basic premise of mechanistic science. But *can* reality be broken down into ones and zeros? If so, what *are* those 'ones and zeros'? Science cannot seem to get to the bottom of subatomic particles, they keep finding smaller and smaller and smaller particles." His eyes lit up for a while as they gazed on the next idea formulating in his mind. "And even if reality is ultimately just ones and zeros... who or what is *interpreting* those ones and zeros as if they were the complex reality we experience all around us?"

Another of my early heroes from San Diego was Vaikuṇṭha dās, simply one of the gentlest, nicest men I had ever met. Once, my Yugo's tire went flat and, for whatever typical teenage-punk reason, I had no spare. He took me into his apartment a few yards down the street, where he lived with his wife, and made some phone calls. In an hour or two Triple-A showed up and fixed the flat. While we waited, I asked him questions and he explained that Paramātmā ("God," in a sense) is like the sun and all living beings were like water in pots. Just as the same sun reflects into many different pots, Paramātmā "reflects" into and exists within everyone.

Merry-go-Round of Majors

For my second year at university, my parents rented me a room nearby in West Covina (I called it West Govinda), from a single mom with two daughters who I rarely saw. We shared the kitchen, but I kept my own cooking pots (I didn't want to offer Krishna food cooked in pots that had been used for cooking dead animals).

Last year I somehow made the Dean's List without particularly trying at all. This year, I just zoned out - losing all interest in anything besides becoming a full-time Hare Krishna.

I did *try*, a little. I thought, "Maybe I would care about college more if it was a little relevant to what I'm actually interested in?" But what could California Polytechnic University possibly offer to a kid obsessed with Hare Krishna?

I declared myself a music major (at a polytechnic university...). My first class was "Sight Singing." The teacher handed out sheet music and we were supposed to just stand up one by one and *sing it*. I walked out, thinking, "This will be more embarrassing than peeing my pants, and has absolutely nothing to do with the kind of music I'm into."

I declared myself a philosophy major - another brilliant choice for a technical school. Those classes were interesting, but frustrating. Descartes was really hitting close to the mother lode, so why move on to Hume? For that matter what was wrong with Plato? He had a great understanding we hadn't even scratched the surface of. It dawned on me that I wasn't interested in *studying* philosophy; I was interested in *practicing* it.

I considered declaring myself a psychology major, since I had really enjoyed the Psych 101 course. It probably would have been the best choice for me, but by now I was just out of gas for anything in "the material world."

Enquirer

Back at my room, I seldom did any studying. Instead, I would either rock out to Cro-Mags' Best Wishes and Bad Brains' Quickness, or I would sit quietly at my computer using Microsoft Publisher 1.0 to put together a new zine called Enquirer.

In a week or two I was photocopying and stapling the first issue.

The graphics were drawn pixel-by-pixel or imported from Publishers "clip art gallery." The cover was a thicker, tan paper with two pictures of police brutality surrounded by a slew of question marks. Cro-Mags and Shelter were the featured bands. The Cro-Mags got two articles, one where I gave commentary on their song, Age of Quarrel, another where I told Bhāgavatam's story of Prāhlad and Nṛsiṁha to explain the painting of a bloody lion-man ripping someone's guts out on their Best Wishes album cover. Shelter hadn't released their album or played a show yet, but I printed an "interview" with "them" where both the questions and answers were written by Ray.

I wrote a detailed article on Vegetarianism, based on the intro to the Hare Krishna book, The Higher Taste. In another article I tried to establish a connection between Straight Edge and Hare Krishna:

> *Straightedge is actually a part of Krishna consciousness. Of course, you don't see devotees listening to Minor Threat with Xs on their hands very often; it's the ideals of straightedge that exist in a very pure form in Krishna consciousness. Devotees call these ideals "the four regulative principles of freedom," or "the four regs." No intoxication, no meat eating, no illicit sex and no gambling...*

On the last page, bordered by some awfully pixelated floral clip-art, I had an article entitled The Atheist, which typified the philosophy-in-fiction style I would use often in the Enquirer and elsewhere:

> *The parking lot was warm, but it felt like walking into a giant refrigerator when you came out of that sweaty club. Clusters of people huddled together here and there, gossip groups and yak packs. I heard some talk about the new Bad Brains album and drifted in that direction.*

> "There's too much 'Jah' and all that. I don't see how anybody could really believe all that stuff... I'm an atheist." There was an uneasy pride in his tone of voice, "I'm an atheist." Proud of it, as if it was the only good, intellectual thing to do.
>
> Feet shuffled. No one cared to speak up, but this one Kid looked surprised, "Whaddaya mean you don't think God exists? That's ridiculous... Do you believe in consciousness?"

With "The Kid" as my mouthpiece I tried to explain the Vedic origin of Descartes' fundamental argument: We know we exist because we are conscious, and this is the *only* truth that is impossible to disprove. All other truth, all of reality itself, exists *within* consciousness. Yet all our separate subjective realities are *synchronized*, demonstrating that there is a super-consciousness at the root of it all. That super-root-consciousness is the ultimate substrata of all consciousness and all reality, and is what people are really trying to talk about when they try to talk about "God."

I made a few dozen copies and sold them for a dollar each to my friends and to the people who came to our shows. Most people actually seemed more than willing to fork over the dollar to get a better idea what the Krishna thing was all about.

Chapter Thirteen:

Imperfections in Perfection

Garlic @ Govinda's

The first time I went to the Krishna's restaurant across the street from their temple in LA, a bottle of Mrs. Dash seasoning said hi from its spot between the salt and pepper shakers on my table.

Whaaaaat?

The Hare Krishna's made a *huge* deal out of how important it was not to eat onions and garlic, and I was stressing myself and frustrating the hell out of my Mom and Dad to observe this arcane principle. Yet, they put Mrs. Dash on their restaurant tables? I was pretty sure Mrs. Dash wasn't in the know on the "transcendental" principle of not eating onions and garlic. Checking her ingredients confirmed it.

I was pissed off.

Betrayed.

I carried the offensive bottle up to the devotees in plain-clothes who chatted while working at the cash register, pointed to the ingredients list, and said, "This has onions and garlic."

They said, "oh," and took the bottle.

Hare Christian

ISKCON Los Angeles had dinners on Wednesdays in the building right next to the temple. One night, a black devotee walked up the stairs to give the lecture while we ate, seated on the floor in front of our low tables. He looked incredibly cool with imposing muscles and smooth, jet-black skin contrasting dramatically with his saffron Krishna robes.

Sure enough he preached with charisma, confidence, and absolute conviction, and I felt like I was at the Vedic equivalent of a Christian revival. At a certain point he even turned the blast of his fire and brimstone upon the topic of abortion. In a booming, bass voice, he declared, "Anyone who aborts the unborn child in the womb will *go to hell and never again see the light of day!*"

Whoa, what? Yeah, Abortion is nasty, but eternal hell is a Christian concept!

I raised my hand, and he called on me.

"What about reincarnation?" I asked. "Won't they eventually be reincarnated and leave hell?"

"In Bhagavad Gītā," he said, "Krishna declares that he throws the demoniac into hellish births life after life. They will be reincarnated in hell, *and never again see the light of day.*"

It seemed to me that this guy was importing his biblical point of view and imposing it on his Bhagavad Gītā. "In Chapter Eight of Bhagavad Gītā," I countered, "Krishna says that heaven and hell are not permanent places. We go there temporarily and then get reborn again on earth after our rewards or punishments are done."

That made him really mad. Here was a sassy little 19-year-old kid, a guest at the Wednesday night FOLK dinner, trying to out-quote him and one-up his authority! I don't remember what he said next, but it was loud, and I shut up.

The Gangsta Pimp Guru

ISKCON San Diego was awesome.

ISKCON Los Angeles was hit and miss.

ISKCON Berkley was... madness.

Inside Out played at the Gilman in Berkley one Sunday, so I went over for their Sunday Feast... and walked away with the shivers. What I soon heard was that ISKCON Berkley was the former den of the infamous gangsta pimp guru, Haṁsadutta Swāmī, whose service to Krishna involved a stockpile of semi-automatic weapons, drug trafficking, and a harem of whores.

Oh... How lovely.

But I was beyond the point of no return. Nothing could break my fascination with this Krishna stuff, and ISKCON seemed to be the only venue in which I could pursue that fascination. "Yeah, there's a lot of crazy Krishna's and a lot of weird shit," I reasoned, "but there are also really amazing people, and what Prabhupāda teaches is amazing."

I had no idea that there might be a way to access the beautiful aspects of Krishna consciousness without having to merge my existence into the insanities of ISKCON. If a woman really wants a child and there is only one man on the planet, she will overlook all the warts on his face.

Tell it to the Straightedge Kids

For the second issue of Enquirer I used a typewriter to write "enquirer" in lower case. Then I enlarged it a zillion times on a Xerox machine before shrinking it again to the size I needed. This technique amplified the imperfections of the ink on the paper, making a really cool, grainy, rough-edged effect.

I put this logo sideways on the thick orange cover. Next to it, I border-taped a photo of someone moshing with a guitar at Che Cafe, below a drawing of Krishna holding a lotus flower while moshing on the hoods of a multi-headed sea-dragon. The guitarist moshing in the photo was me, but you couldn't really tell because the flash obscured my face.

The issue was mostly obsessed with the topic of equality, probably because I was still vexed by trying to accommodate the sexism in ISKCON. I had a three-page article called "Equality" explaining how spirituality provides a basis for equality without denying diversity. I followed this by printing Mantra Six of the Īśopaniṣad (with Sanskrit lettering I hand-moused pixel by pixel): "He who sees everything in relation to the Supreme Lord, who sees all entities as His parts and parcels, and who sees the Supreme Lord within everything, never hates anything nor any being."

I threw in a few cool lyrical bits here and there on the subject:

> Black power / white power
> What power is in your black/white skin?
> The skin that yellows in the grave.

> Equality,
> is a reality.

> Look within yourself to find the unity you seek.

> Not along the edges.
> Not in the skin.
> It's at the core of your existence, untouched within.

"Joe Hardcore: Open Minded Liberal or Biased Rascal Sap?" was a half-page rant about how un-punk it was to censor punk, even when the censored subject was traditionally un-punk, like religion. I followed this up with a full-page rant about how straightedge itself was nothing short of a secular religion.

In "Spiritual Life: A Cop Out?" I explained, "Just because 99% of so-called religion is completely bogus, that doesn't affect the fact that we have to find out who we are, and why we exist?"

In "The Truth" I explained that it's self-defeating to claim that there is absolutely no absolute truth.

Like the first issue, very little in this zine had much to do with Hardcore. I gave two pages to explaining the lyrics of Inside Out's No Spiritual Surrender and a new song called Land of the Lost. I also interviewed my friends in local bands, asking each one the same question, "What is the need for a spiritual dimension in life?" Sergio, the bassist of Amenity, said that people should discover the essential truths common to all religions and use that as a way to improve themselves, because all social change begins within. Mike Madrid, the singer of Against the Wall, answered that spirituality is much bigger than hardcore, but most of the best hardcore bands are spiritually motivated. Mike D, the singer from Amenity, answered that there is obviously truth beyond human conception, and human beings ruin themselves when their lives are out of touch with that.

Fall of the Perfect Lineup

Inside Out's lineup was almost perfect, but time did not fail to shatter it.

Alex was only fifteen, which is too young to drive, which annoyed the hell out of Sterling as he and Alex made the long drive back from Berkley after a show at the Gilman. He told Zack and I, "Dude, Chris Bratton keeps telling me he wants to play drums for us."

We weren't moved by the idea. Yeah, Chris was great, but so was Alex, so why mess with the lineup?

Soon, however, Alex's snare drum got stolen at the Country Club, and Zack didn't want to use Inside Out money to replace it. Their relationship went south, and Chris soon replaced Alex on drums.

Sterling's relationship with Zack also went south. His friend had committed suicide and Sterling was very uncomfortable with how Zack discussed it from the stage, in between songs. He told us he wished Zack would reduce his banter in between songs, which we interpreted as a sure sign that he wasn't really "into our philosophy." Thus, a few days after Chris joined, Sterling left, showing up at the Stompbox rehearsal studio in Anaheim to hand over all the Inside Out shirts he had and tender his resignation.

Zack replaced him immediately with Mark Hayworth.

The Apex of my Musical Career

Our show in Seattle was supposed to happen in a real club, but things fell apart at the last minute and it wound up happening in someone's single-car garage in Bellingham. The organizer, Ron Guardipee, got the help of a few local kids who donated enough money to make sure that at least the travel expenses would be covered for us and our San Diego friends, Forced Down.

It was one of the most incredible shows I ever played.

When a hundred and something people show up for a show at a big rock venue, it might feel a little empty. But when a hundred and something people pack into one-car garage...

Forced Down was at their best, legitimately close to being a contemporary Rites of Spring: musically complex, emotionally oriented lyrics, and a completely spastic, no-holds-barred live performance.

Then it was our turn. The first notes of Burning Fight roared, and the locals went at least as berserk as the dozen friends who had come up with us from San Diego. When my conquering lion of Judah shirt came off, it revealed the words "FALSE EGO" scrawled in thick, black marker across my stomach and chest.

Faces contorted without forethought. Bodies colliding without grace. Hair flying. Sweat dripping. Fists raised spontaneously in solidarity. Unparalleled intensity, unscripted sincerity, uncontrolled emotion, and wild, exciting desperation.

It was the apex of my musical career

Later that night I laid on a hammock in someone's backyard, drifting off to sleep while gazing up at the stars between the trees, chanting Hare Krishna quietly to myself.

Punk Discovers the Dark Side of Krishna

Krishna was pushing into the hardcore scene in a huge way, but in December of '89 the scene pushed back for the first time. Maximum Rocknroll, the biggest zine in hardcore punk, delivered an issue called "Inside Ray Cappo and the Krishnas" with a creepy infinity-mirror of Ray on the cover and 15 pages of no-line-spacing-tiny-font-exposé tearing Hare Krishna to shreds.

I bought a copy while at a show at the Gilman Street Project in Berkley. "Ray of Yesterday Meets Ray of Tomorrow: It's Enough to Make me Start Drinking!!!!!"

The more I read, the more I wanted to fall into a crack in the earth.

Ray's five-page interview was basically an argument between him and Tim Yo - the magazine's founder and chief editor. Whether honestly or by the magic of editing, Tim consistently came off as a lot more rational than Ray. For example, when Ray tried to prove that reincarnation was factual by explaining that our bodies constantly change, Tim embarrassed him for claiming that *growth* was evidence of life after death.

The interview was tough, but it was a piece of cake compared to what followed: a ten-page article called, "The Truth, The Whole Truth, And Nothing But The Truth, So Help Me Krishna?" This was more like several articles and interviews stitched together in a rambling Frankenstein of nausea. It started off with a woman's personal tale of intrigue about her husband Ed. He had become a brainwashed Krishna cult member, but she successfully rescued him. Tim interviewed her, Ed, and the ex-Hare Krishna's who had helped him "exit" the cult.

They depicted ISKCON as a deviant and dangerous branch of an otherwise admirable religious, spiritual, and philosophical movement.

I had to fight so hard to drown out the ring of truth in that.

They described ISKCON's deceitful fund-raising practices and a long list of serious crimes the Krishna's and their leaders had been convicted for: huge drug rings, illegal possession of firearms, murder, child molestation, and so on. ISKCON sexism also got a big spotlight. They said ISKCON had a hierarchy considering cows more important than women: "Man-Cow-Woman-Dog." ISKCON leaders, they said, encouraged physical "discipline" of women, quoting a former ISKCON guru, Bhaktipāda, who said (quoting, probably unknown to any of us, a much older Indian misogynist who Prabhupāda occasionally quoted, Cāṇakya Paṇḍit), "There are three things that get better when you beat them — your dog, your wife, and your drum."

I stood on the sidewalk outside Gilman, flipping from one emotion to the next with exhausting speed. One moment I was furious at MRR for giving such a "one-sided story." The next moment I was pitifully embarrassed to be a spokesman for such a circus of lunatics. How would I manage to explain all this to all these kids who were getting interested in Hare Krishna because of me?

I felt like vomiting. Maybe I should just get out and do something else with my life?

By the time we were in the car going home, I felt less like a human being and more like a growling wolf backed into a corner, bearing his fangs and posed for a battle to the death.

Over the next few weeks, however, I realized that nobody in the straightedge crowd seemed to really care much about what Maximum Rocknroll had printed. Maybe it was because they didn't really care about Krishna Consciousness that much? Maybe it was because MRR was just too *hard to read* - disorganized, rambling, and constantly bitching and moaning? Yeah, the issue affected people a bit. More than the drug-running, abject exploitation and mind-tyranny described in that article, what disgusted the straightedge kids the most, it seemed to me, was the sexism.

Some devotees assured me that the people behind MRR were "envious demons," and the ex-Krishna's interviewed were just "too weak to make it as devotees."

I didn't believe that, but it was just too late... too late for me to turn back. I was already married to ISKCON. If my spouse was having a hard time, I would have to try to help, not run away.

Devotees assured me that the vast majority of all the insanity MRR revealed was a thing of the past, and ISKCON was now making strides forward to "reform and represent Krishna and Prabhupāda more purely."

I believed that.

CHAPTER FOURTEEN:

NO SPIRITUAL SURRENDER

Kent or Jordan?

Initially, we were going to release a full-length LP to kick off Kent McClard's new record label, Ebullition, but when Revelation offered us an EP we decided to do a that first and then do the LP for Ebullition, to be called Rage Against the Machine - a phrase Kent himself had come up with on the pages of his popular zine, No Answers.

At the end of January in 1990, we went to Pendragon studio in Orange County, me with a notebook of codes and diagrams planning out all my guitar parts in fine detail: not two but *three* tracks, each with a different combination of guitars and amps, each playing the riffs slightly differently or breaking up the riffs into parts.

With the six songs done in about two hours, it was time for Zack to record vocals. We all sat in the control room, gawking at him through the big glass pane. He awkwardly did a few short passes and then asked, "Can we try a few with the lights turned off?"

We didn't turn the lights back on until the vocals were done.

About an hour later we walked out with the finished EP in our hands.

Rage Against ISKCON

I did a layout for the cover, and the band rejected it. Looking back, I don't blame them. It featured an ISKCON painting depicting reincarnation through species. I don't know *what* I thought that had to do with *anything* on the record. All it would do is identify Inside Out as a "Krishna band," which no one else in the band was comfortable with.

Speaking of Krishna bands, Revelation still hadn't released Ray Cappo's Shelter record, but he had recorded two more songs (with a completely different lineup) and wanted to release them himself on his own new record label, Equal Vision Records. He mailed me a top-secret cassette of the songs: Saranagati and Freewill.

It was Krishna-in-your-face. Saranagati even had a loop of Śrīla Prabhupāda chanting Hare Krishna over and over again, playing constantly through the whole song.

Ray wanted the first Equal Vision release to be a Shelter / Inside Out split 7-inch. I was positively giddy about it. When I told Zack and the others about it and played them the cassette, they went pale.

"I'm totally into the Krishna philosophy you tell me about," Zack said. "I can back that 100%. But I'm just not comfortable going out there as a band that supports ISKCON and the whole organized religion of Hare Krishna. If we do this split with Shelter, that's exactly what'll happen."

Deathbed & Empty Days

I was crushed that Zack and the rest of the band weren't willing to support my addition to ISKCON, and gradually started to come unglued from the band. Still, we were writing songs for the Ebullition LP, and they were coming out good.

Zack wrote a D.C. style song and I wrote the lyrics. It became known as Deathbed:

> I remember when you cried with your eyes on fire.
> With the gale in your lungs, screamed your throat red.
> Now it's getting colder, softer.
> What happened to you?
>
> I remember when you laughed with the sunlight on your lips.
> Sunrise energy in your early morning stride.
> But you're not waking up this time.
> Breathless cries over lifeless eyes.
>
> This thing that laughed with me, cried with me,
>   screamed with me, dreamed with me
>   lies before me on this deathbed
>
> But where are you?
> Who are you?

In spite of being straight outta Krishna 101, "You are not that body," it worked for Inside Out because the wording could apply to anyone or anything that had gone cold and lost its spirit.

A few months earlier, I had written another one called Land of the Lost. The lyrics had come to me while watching people walk around the sidewalks of Pacific Beach.

> Social robotics
> Mind manipulation
> Program me at will.

Clawing like cats to win the race of the rats.
Blind are lead by leaders blind as bats.

Lost in the Land of the Lost in the Land of the Lost.

The lyrics weren't a problem here either, but the music was. We played it at a few shows and then dropped it as "too metal." Zack said he appreciated the more complex rhymes and alliterations and started playing Public Enemy and other rap stuff for me. "This is all about the kind of rhymes you are doing!"

Then he wrote Empty Days. It's a shame we never wound up recording this LP, because that was probably the best Inside Out song we ever wrote.

Monotony grinds me down
   it keeps me down.
I've lost my faith in this haze
   these ways
   have led to empty days.

Now I struggle to find
   some love
   or some peace of mind.
Although I'm still in my youth
   I feel I'm running out of time.

Empty - the days they pass me by.
So Empty - time lost at the blink of an eye.
Empty - the feeling is gone.

Faster, Harder, More Insane

My song, Land of the Lost, had been dropped as being "too metal." My EP layout had been dropped for being too Krishna, and the opportunity to do a split 7" with Shelter had been canned for the same reason. So, I started a new band: Rage.

Alex, Inside Out's original drummer, played drums, Frosty, the hardest guy from Chain of Strength, played guitar, and Andy Alvarez from Against the Wall played bass. Our modus operandi was to be faster, harder, shorter, and more batshit crazy than any other band we knew of.

We claimed to be recording a demo, but that plan would fall off a cliff pretty soon. We did write and rehearse a handful of songs. Here's one, called *Māyā*:

> Illusion.
> Darkness.
> Leprous death breathing down our necks.
>
> Hatred.
> Fear.
> Leprous death breathing down our necks,
> > Wrapped around our throats.
>
> All this infection
> Because we keep on accepting
> > That which is not.

Zines for the Big Tour

Ray offered us a North-East summer tour with Shelter and Quicksand.

Zack and everyone else went for it.

With three new Revelation bands, the tour was certain to be huge. Revelation had released none of the three records, but so what? The entire straightedge scene in every city would be sure to turn out in droves to see Ray Cappo post Youth of Today and Walter Schreifels post Gorilla Biscuits.

I wanted to sell a boatload of Enquirers. So, in late April I combined the first and second issues and added new material to create 300 offset-printed copies of Enquirer #3. The cover had a picture of

Chris Bratton hitting the drums, although we had already switched him out of Inside Out and brought Alex back due to planetary misalignments and wardrobe malfunctions.

The issue explained the lyrics of Inside Out, Shelter and Rage. And I expanded the "What is the need for spirituality?" interviews to include Tim Amenity explaining how reincarnation, vegetarianism, and spiritual practices work in the context of Christian mysticism, and Rob Hardstance talking about eco- and animal- rights.

Towards the end of the zine I addressed the issue of sexism.

> *The philosophy is that regardless of bodily condition - black-white, man-woman, green, purple or orange - everyone is a part and parcel of God.*
>
> *Whatever discrepancies have snuck into the Hare Krishna movement in regards to women are mistakes. Devotees will admit that there have been mistakes, and currently there is a big reform program going on to insure that the movement is not deviating from the philosophy and teachings presented by Śrīla Prabhupāda.*
>
> *Women and men have the same basic roles in Krishna consciousness. Being a teacher, or a speaker, or a monk, or a priest, or whatever, is open to anyone who feels comfortable with that position. There are female priests, teachers, renunciates, farmers, career workers. There are male cooks, janitors...*

This was an accurate description of what I *wanted* ISKCON to be, or believed that it was. I wanted to believe that ISKCON could openly admit mistakes, and make big efforts to correct them. I wanted to believe that Prabhupāda had no flaw or blame in any of ISKCON's problems. I wanted to believe that women and men had the same career opportunities in ISKCON.

I *needed* to believe these things.

CHAPTER FIFTEEN:

KRISHNA'S TRIAL BY MOSH

Intentional Leftovers

As spring break approached, Inside Out flew to New York for the tour. There, I collected my guitar and bag from baggage claim and waved goodbye to Zack, Alex, and Mark. I was off to meet Ray at the Hare Krishna temple in Brooklyn.

It was a crisp Sunday afternoon. I rode the A train through the urinated subways. I walked past Black Muslims selling oils and incense on the street. When I finally passed the two sets of ordinary double glass doors at 305 Schermerhorn Street, the first thing I saw was a group of five or six straightedge kids huddled around Ray, who was explaining something to them with a big, energetic smile on his face.

Compared to ornate and colorful temples I had visited on the West Coast, ISKCON's temple in Brooklyn seemed like the cafeteria of a high school: cold, hard, and somehow empty.

Ray took me up the wide, square stairway. On the third floor he led me into a big, dim, windowless room, empty except for duffle bags stuffed into the corners.

"Are you hungry?" he asked, as I put my stuff down.

"Yeah," I said. "Starving!"

"Let's get some *mahā-prasādam*!" he said, walking towards a nondescript door. "There are three great souls in this room," he said. "If they are done, we can take their plates."

He was awfully over-excited about taking away someone's plate, I thought.

Inside the small, busy room sat three older men in shaved heads and saffron robes. Swāmīs. Ray introduced me as we took their industrial, rectangular metal plates, "This is Bhakta Vic. He is in one of the bands that are coming on tour with Shelter. He's really smart and writes a fanzine called The Enquirer."

There was quite a bit of food still left on the three plates, and we carried it all up to the roof and sat down.

"Taking the remnants of pure devotees is the greatest fortune," Ray told me. Then he recited some Sanskrit verse about *prasādam*, impressing me dizzy. I was slightly freaked out as he dove into the leftovers, but sounds of the Brooklyn hustle and bustle drifted up and mingled with the half-moon gracing the darkening twilight sky and I wasn't going to complain. I picked up a roll that had been left whole on the plate, and took a hearty chomp of it.

The Original Singer of the Cro-Mags is my Humble Servant

I woke up to the sight of two beaming smiles shining down on me in the pre-dawn darkness as I lay on the floor of that big, empty common room. "This is Eric Cassinova," Ray said, obviously experiencing a flow of ecstasy. "He's the original singer of the Cro-Mags."

As they probably expected, I practically wet myself in excitement.

Mr. Cassinova folded his hands and gently swayed his head from side to side, closing his eyes slightly. "I'm just your humble servant, Prabhu," he said sweetly. "Bhakta Ray has told me so many good things about you."

The original singer of the Cro-Mags had just told me that he was my humble servant... I blinked a lot, but when no one disappeared I had to accept that I was actually awake.

"The morning program will start in 15 minutes," Ray informed me with some authority in his voice. "Take a shower and come down to the temple room on the first floor."

The bathrooms were massively public. Yellow tile. Rows of sinks without mirrors. Rows of toilet stalls without doors or toilet paper. Rows of showers without hot water. There were so many guys in *gamcha* (Indian towels) that I had to wait my turn to use anything.

I got downstairs a little after the kīrtan had started, thrilled to be living the big life with the Hare Krishna's.

"I Like That He Farted"

We had a day or two to hang out before the tour started. I took Zack and Mark to an apartment somewhere in Brooklyn where the Hare Krishna's were having a "home program." A real live Indian swāmī would be speaking at the program, and I hoped it might be just the thing to give Zack and Mark the push they seemed to need to come on board with me and see how incredibly awesome this whole Hare Krishna thing really could be.

Come to think of it, it was the first time Zack had ever come to a Krishna function. Practically everyone else in the So Cal Straightedge scene had come to a Sunday Feast with me at least once, but not Zack. We sat around the apartment for what seemed like an awfully long time, chanting. I hoped that Zack might at least be intrigued by the cool two-headed Krishna drums.

Finally, the Swāmī arrived, and when he did, nearly everyone bowed their heads to the floor, including me - very self-consciously, though, because my mind was on what Zack must be thinking.

The Swāmī was incredibly small; even downright cute and lovable. He made his way straight to the chair set aside for him, one of those big round wicker chairs that look like a UFO landing on a mushroom, and sat down Indian-style on it. I was all atwitter with excitement; feeling almost like Prabhupāda himself had just walked into the room.

After a little more chanting, the swāmī started talking.

Mid-way through his talk a guest arrived with a big dog, causing something of a panic. Apparently it was a no-no to let a dog inside a house in "Vedic" culture.

It seemed like the dog and his master would be asked to leave, but the Swāmī laughed and said, "That's alright. He is Bhakta Dog. Come in, Bhakta Dog."

Everyone laughed.

While the swāmī talked, every once in a while he would let out an unrestrained burp. Once he even farted!

Eventually the swāmī was done and people started handing out paper plates. I took my empty plate and sat down next to Zack. "What did you think of the swāmī?" I asked.

"He's cool," Zack said. "I like how he ripped off a big fart in front of everyone. He's not self-conscious at all."

"What about what he said?"

Someone put some salad on our plates. Zack looked me straight in the face and said, "I don't know, Vic. When *you* tell me about Krishna, it all makes sense and I like it. But when anyone else talks about it, I can't even figure out what they are saying."

Your Intelligence is Third-Class

At the time I thought Shelter was the biggest deal of the tour, and it's true that this was the beginning of an era of "Krishna-core" that would dominate the US straightedge hardcore scene for a few years, but Quicksand would turn out to be much bigger. They were beginning a significant new genre: post-hardcore, which would influence major bands likes the Deftones and even Tool. Little did I know it, but my own band Inside Out was the most important of all three, for from the catastrophe that befell Inside Out on this tour, Rage Against the Machine soon arose.

The tour moved in a caravan of two vans, a motor-home, and a greyhound bus. The inside of the bus had been gutted and converted into a rolling "preaching center." It belonged to a Hare Krishna swāmī, Guṇagrahi Goswāmī, who captained it with a middle-aged single man as first-mate and a crew of three or four teenage boys, all practicing celibacy. A few straightedge guys, like Gus, Big Adam and Graham, joined them. Gus is the same guy who had told me, "don't worry, it's all illusion," a year or two ago when I had pulled away from the curb and made Beyond's Van of Suffering a bull's eye for some Guido's Mazda 280ZX. Adam was a massive and moral young man who served as a roadie and bouncer. Graham was the second guitarist for Shelter, an unknown guy from the Midwest who was into Krishna.

The rest of the people playing in Shelter were Sammy and Porcell from Youth of Today, and a devotee named Yaśo. It was the same lineup who recorded Shelter's 7" on Equal Vision Records, No Compromise.

Ray and I glued ourselves to the Krishna bus.

My old friends from Beyond, Tom Capone and Alan Cage were in Quicksand. They traveled in the van that always lagged behind and showed up late. I don't recall making any effort to speak with either of them more than once or twice, or for more than a grand total of three minutes. Maybe they used to be my dearest friends, but they weren't devotees.

There was an infinite chasm of total mutual disinterest separating the two groups: devotees and "non-devotees." The only exception was Shelter's bass player, Yaśo - a middle-aged Hare Krishna carpenter with no ties to punk rock at all. He was a tall, lanky, gentle angel; and a friend to everyone. He chanted with the devotees with just as much zeal as he chilled out and joked around with the non-devotees. Besides being the nicest Hare Krishna on the tour, he was also the only one who was married and had a child. That probably wasn't a coincidence.

Yaśo often drove the motor-home, which I called "the swāmī van" because another swāmī traveled in it (yes, not one but two swāmīs came on the tour). If Ray and I weren't in the bus, we were in the motor home. The motor home swāmī, Dhanurdhara Swāmī, just seemed cool and had a particular knack for being able to come down to earth and respond to all sorts of questions in reasonable, intelligent, and logical ways. So, Ray and I would orchestrate occasions to have people from the non-devotee clan ride in the motor home and talk with the swāmī.

I particularly remember Zack and Tom's conversations. We would sit on the linoleum floor in the back, the passenger's chair would swivel around, and the Swāmī would smile and laugh as he talked with us in detail about Krishna consciousness.

It was clear that Zack mostly conceived of spirituality as *feelings* and *emotions* and had no sympathy whatsoever for a hierarchically organized religious institution. The swāmī wasn't impressed with Zack or his "sentimentality."

Tom's conversation started out similar to the conversation we had years ago in my Dodge Dart. "Krishna enjoys life with the gopīs," he asked, "so why should his devotees have to renounce sense gratification?"

111

The swāmī tried to explain that sense gratification doesn't lead to true happiness, but Tom wasn't into it. "There *is* happiness in sense gratification. I've experienced it."

The swāmī explained that the happiness in sense gratification is mixed with suffering, "It's like sand in sweetrice," he said. "The whole cup is ruined by it."

Tom disagreed, "There's suffering in life," he said, "but that doesn't ruin it. It makes the happiness even more important, even better, even more special."

"You say that," the swāmī explained, "because you have no experience of happiness without suffering."

"Why should I even believe that there is such a thing as happiness without suffering?" Tom asked.

"Knowledge from beyond the range of the senses comes through revealed scripture," the swāmī said. "The revealed scripture speaks of *ānanda*, bliss without suffering."

"I have to believe it because it's written in a book?" Tom asked, unafraid to be honest.

They went back and forth a bit, and the swāmī finally said, "Well Tom, there are three kinds of intelligence. First-class intelligence hears, 'sense gratification causes suffering' and stays away from it. Second-class intelligence hears, 'sense gratification causes suffering,' tries it anyway, realizes that it really does lead to suffering, and then stays away from it. Third-class intelligence hears that sense gratification causes suffering, experiences it first-hand, but still holds on to the hope that he will somehow achieve happiness from it. It seems like you have third-class intelligence."

Tom was insulted. Maybe he had a different kind of "first-class intelligence" – one that doesn't believe in ideas that don't tally with experience?

Krishna's Trial by Mosh

On June 15th, 1990, Shelter, Inside Out, and Quicksand played the Anthrax in Connecticut.

It was intense.

On the one hand Ray Cappo was extremely influential, and Razor's Edge and my zine, Enquirer, had given Hardcore kids a lot of Krishna-positive exposure; but on the other hand, Maximum Rocknroll had exposed the dark side of ISKCON, and other voices were starting to speak up against us. The hardcore scene was still undecided about Krishna, and this show was the grand trial.

For some it a trial by philosophy, but for most it was just a trial by mosh. If we could make them mosh, they would accept us.

The plaintiff against Krishna was represented primarily by a band called Born Against. Just a few months earlier they had released a song called Eulogy, which voiced an extremely negative opinion of their ex-friend Steve Reddy, who, as the song name implies, they considered "dead" because he decided to become a Hare Krishna devotee. The plaintiff presented their evidence to the jury tonight, an assortment of anti-Krishna and anti-religion fliers.

When Inside Out was ready to play, Zack paced back and forth across whatever bits of stage weren't overrun with amps, drums, musicians or kids who somehow felt they had some business up there. "There's some really weird stuff going on tonight," he said over the mic to a packed, almost completely silent room. "I was checkin' out these fliers that they were passing around. One of them had this kinda comic-book picture of a Krishna devotee on it, along with a bunch of symbols - and one of them was a swastika... You might not agree with Krishna consciousness - I have my differences with it too, I mean, that's just how I am, it might not be for me - but, to put a swastika on a flier like that is *really fucking ignorant*, ok?"

Devotees cheered and howled in approval.

"I might not follow the beliefs of Krishna consciousness," Zack continued, "but I'll tell you what, I respect that these people make a lot of sacrifices in the search for the truth. That should be respected, man. We're all searching for something, so let's give it up to them."

Then I let the feedback rip, and Zack shouted, "THIS SONG IS CALLED *BURNING FIGHT!*"

I flailed through every single song so wildly that even at the age of 19 I felt close to the edge of cardiovascular collapse. After opening with Burning Fight we went directly into Unchanged, a very short fast song with lyrics that didn't say much more than the title. Then we caught our breath and did a song from Inside Out pre-history: Lost Cause. Next came two brand new songs intended for the LP we planned to record right after the tour: Blind Oppressor and (after an eternity spent replacing a broken snare drum) Turn and Face. We followed these with two songs from the Revelation EP: By a Thread and Sacrifice. Technically the EP wasn't out yet, but obviously it had leaked because people were familiar with the EP songs and unfamiliar with the others.

When Zack eventually said, "This is our last song." Someone in the audience shouted, "No! Spiritual! Surrender!"

Shelter played next. I was stagediving and moshing at max capacity. At one point, someone from the Born Against crew put on a Krishna ponytail wig and started tomfoolery in the pit. Gus Peña answered this with a foot-first stage dive on his head, I suppose illustrating one of Prabhupāda's statements about how we should deal with detractors, "kick on face with boot."

In the silence between two Shelter songs, the Born Against crew shouted in unison, "Go back to the airport!"

"Go back to the airport?" Ray replied. "I wish I could. It takes a lot of courage and sacrifice to go into public and stand up for what you believe in. I wish I had enough courage to go back to the airport."

I must have sold more than a hundred Enquirers that night. The jury had pretty clearly decided in favor of Krishna.

After the show I remember walking out the front door into the night, to find some straightedge Krishna's and some of the devotees from the bus standing near the door and debating some point, rather unsuccessfully it seemed, with some of the Born Against guys. "Man, what do you even know about Krishna consciousness?" I asked the antagonists, butting in. "You know a bunch of shit about how fucked up religion is, but what do you know about *Krishna consciousness*?" I hardly paused for them to answer, feeling pretty unstoppable. "Krishna consciousness isn't a religion," I continued, "it's a path of self-realization. All this shit on your fliers — pro-life vs. pro-choice, Spanish Inquisitions — what the fuck does that have to do with *me*? Krishna consciousness is totally different from all that."

"Oh come on," they argued. "You know you are in an organized religion just like any other organized religion."

"Oh, thanks for letting me know who I really am," I said, sarcastically. "You've never even met me before, but you know, better than I do, who I am and what I'm into. Thanks."

"I don't have to know you to know that you're in a fucked up religion."

"Ok," I said, switching from bad-cop to good-cop. "In a sense you're right. Hare Krishna is also an organized religion, and there are weird people and fucked up things it. But that not what *I'm* into, man. Just like in hardcore, some people are dicks do a lot of stupid things, but that's not what *you're* into, right? You're into something else about hardcore, not the bullshit that comes along with it, right? So why do you think I can't be involved in Krishna consciousness without being into whatever bullshit might come along with it?"

Maybe they gave the answer, maybe they didn't, but the answer was, "Because Hare Krishna is a religion and hardcore isn't. A religion demands that you believe *everything* they say, but Hardcore allows and even encourages us to critique one another."

Back then, I would have argued, "ISKCON is not a religion, it's a group of people on a spiritual path." I didn't yet realize they were right. ISKCON *was* a religion, a disorganized one, and I would be ostracized unless I adopted the whole party line or at least basically shut up about any complaints or disagreements.

I couldn't see clearly yet. I was still really high on the newness of it all. That's called *utsahā-mayī* in Sanskrit.

That night we slept inside the Anthrax. There were a few couches - but people claimed them pretty fast. The stage also filled up with bodies before I claimed a spot. I wound up sleeping on the "dance floor" in front of the stage. The video games wouldn't turn off, their lights and sounds echoed and reflected through the place all night long. The smell of piss drifted out from the doorless toilets. I had nothing but a sheet to sleep with.

Somehow I was still completely stoked.

A reporter had come to the show, a real reporter... from SPIN Magazine! The guy interviewed Ray, spent the night at the club, and rode back to New York City with us in the Krishna Greyhound Bus, while we all chanted our *maṅgala-arati* songs and Hare Krishna mantras on beads.

Chapter Sixteen:
Goodbye Friends

A Disneyland of Krishnacore

We expected every show on the tour to be as confrontational as the first one at the Anthrax, but they weren't. Not even close. After that show, it seemed as if the hardcore scene had tested the waters of Krishna-core, deemed it cool, and proceeded to mosh without protest.

The next day we all enjoyed the Rātha-Yātra celebration in NYC. The day after that we drove up to Buffalo, but one of the vans broke down so it took us 10 hours to get there. The club was a rundown bar in a rundown section of town, but I was happy to talk with the kids who were interested in Krishna. That night I slept in the van, woke up early the next morning and head over to the Krishna bus, where I took a shower. The water ran out just as the soap was getting into my eyes. It started *pouring* out, with immense thunders and epic lightning bolts. All of us Krishna kids sat with the Swāmīs in the bus, chanting Hare Krishna and clanging little hand cymbals - "ching, ching, *chaaang*... ching, ching, *chaang*." My heart was wide open, soaking the whole thing in.

The next day, our show in Rochester was cancelled, but I remember it as one of the best shows on the tour. Seventy straightedge kids met us on a lawn somewhere and we just talked about Krishna for a few hours. Then, about a third of them all went to a guy named DJ's house, where we cooked a Krishna feast, chanted, and talked even more about Krishna. Ray was completely in his element. He taught everyone how to cook Halava and Chapati, then taught them to use the picture of the pañca-tattva on the back of Shelter's 7" as an altar for offering the food to make it *prasādam*.

From Rochester we went to Boston, which was reputed to be violent and unfriendly towards vegetarianism. We were told to expect threats and meat thrown at us. I eventually worked up the courage to mingle in the crowd and try to sell my zines. To my surprise, the Boston kids were just as friendly and open as everyone else. I even met two kids associated with a local Buddhist temple. They weren't into our preachiness but were curious to hear our take on key philosophical topics.

I spent the night in the Boston temple, and did their whole "morning program" of chanting, dancing, discussing philosophy, and eating incredible amounts of delicious stuff for breakfast.

Don't Bother Us, We're Praying

Ray woke us up at 1:30 in the morning so we could chant together on beads while walking back and forth in a parking lot. While we are doing that, a guy rode by on a bike, then suddenly got off and started stumbling angrily towards us.

"You got a cigarette?" he said.

We gave no answer.

He repeated loudly, "Hey! You got a cigarette?"

"No," I said.

"*You* got a cigarette?" He demanded from Ray.

"We don't smoke," Ray replied, continuing to close the distance. I wished we would turn around and walk the other way.

"You laughing at me?" the guy demanded. "I heard you chuckling... you laughing at me?"

Now we were almost within reach of one another, and I was getting really nervous, trying to plan what I would do when he turned violent, since that was a pretty obvious probability.

"Hey!" he said. "I heard you chuckling. You laughing at me?"

"We're praying," Ray said calmly.

"What?"

"We're praying."

Suddenly the guy's anger disappeared. "What are you?" he asked in curiosity.

"We're Hare Krishna's" Ray explained.

"Hare Krishna's?" the guy asked incredulously. "Are you *serious*?"

Ray nodded and we continued pacing back and forth through the parking lot, chanting the mantra out loud. He followed us around. After a bit, he said, "I'm sorry to disrupt your prayer, but, how do you pray to ask for forgiveness for being drunk?"

"Like this," Ray answered, and just continued pacing back and forth, chanting away full speed on beads.

He paced back and forth with us for a few minutes, chanting the Hare Krishna mantra over and over again. Finally, he put one arm on Ray's shoulder and another on mine. "I have to leave now, but it was really nice being with you."

Then he joined his palms, raised them to his forehead, bowed his head, and said, "Hare Krishna."

Out of Inside Out

I was elated about traveling with Krishna's and the swāmīs, listening to explanations of Bhagavad Gītā and Śrīmad Bhāgavatam every day, visiting temples in city after city, chanting, telling people about Krishna consciousness.

I didn't want it to end.

Ray explained that it didn't have to. I could quit Inside Out and play guitar for Shelter.

Two days after Boston, we played to about six hundred kids at a huge venue in Chicago ironically named The Vic Theatre. Backstage, Zack, Mark and Alex were sitting around a table drinking soda or bottled water and eating potato chips. I walked in with Ray behind me for support. I can't remember exactly what I said. Something like, "I really want to become a devotee, and joining Shelter would really help me do that."

Later, Yaśo later found Zack sitting on a curb outside, crying. He sat down and put his arm around Zack's shoulder. "What's wrong?"

"My band is breaking up. I had so many plan's for this band, but now we are breaking up because Vic wants to become a devotee."

"Don't worry," Yaśo told him. "When Krishna takes something away, he only does it so he can give you something better."

Why Did You do *That*?

To play in Shelter I would live with Shelter. We weren't sure yet exactly where that would be, but it might not be in Southern California, so it might mean waving goodbye to mom and dad. Well, I was almost 20 years old, so it wasn't hard to convince myself that moving away from home was completely normal.

To play in Shelter I would have to quit college, perhaps limiting my prospects for mainstream employment and financial stability. Well, I didn't even have a major and never really even knew what I wanted to be when I grew up anyway.

To play in Shelter I would become a *brahmacārī* living in temples (and vans). "*Brahmacārī*" is a Sanskrit term Hare Krishna's mainly use to indicate someone who is celibate. Well, I had already given up Marianne in favor of Krishna and, to be honest, giving up girls was like giving up a million dollar bill I didn't have...

The hardest part of joining Shelter was quitting Inside Out. Yes, Ray Cappo was in Shelter, so it certainly wouldn't be a flop, but I had invested a lot of myself into Inside Out and it was already getting very popular. Also, I thought that Zack was a much better singer and songwriter, and Inside Out had members like Alex Baretto, one of Hardcore's all-time best drummers and all-around musicians, while Shelter was still trying to recruit permanent members. So, it wasn't like I saw this as a good "career move" for me as a musician.

In the end, I just didn't care too much about any of this. All I wanted was to be a Hare Krishna.

Since I was old enough to think, I didn't think much of the world that presented itself to my five senses. Lots of little boys get into dinosaurs, but most of them do so because dinosaurs are huge monsters with big teeth. I thought that was cool, sure, but the coolest thing about dinosaurs was that they didn't exist anymore. After dinosaurs I became obsessed with whatever might exist beyond the blue sky, out there in the stars, far away from this plastic and boring world of humans. After that, I became completely fascinated with high fantasy: Lord of the Rings or any half-decent knockoff thereof, and Dungeon's and Dragons and the emerging genre of mostly text-based computerized fantasy role-playing games. I never had much interest in anything real. To me, the world seemed spoiled by all our modern technology and culture, so nothing normal held much attraction.

I wanted to be different. Not because I was a silly and shallow teen, but because everything was silly and shallow. Hare Krishna appealed to me because it is hard to even imagine anything more different.

It might seem ironic, since ISKCON couldn't even seem to keep its own small world in order without serious social problems, but I really thought that Vedic ideas could change the world for the better. That sort of thing always mattered to me, ever since I can remember. When I was a kid, my parents took me into New York City for the first time and I started sobbing in the back seat of the car, looking out the window and the endless ugly, stupid nicknames scrawled all over the walls of beautifully carved buildings, symbolizing everything I instinctively knew made the world awful. The more we "progressed" the more we were turning a beautiful universe into something selfish and ugly. Krishna philosophy appealed to me because it seemed to have very deep solutions to this problem.

The real clincher for me was the *logic*. That might sound strange, since Hare Krishna's as a majority are hardly the most logical, systematic thinkers you'd hope to meet, but they exposed me to Vedāntic and Upaniṣadic culture - with its use of rigorous logic to communicate metaphysical topics so far outside the common purview of logic. This was just such a turn on. The idea of being able to answer existential questions was irresistibly tempting.

Sanskrit and the wizard robes didn't hurt either.

This is why I was addicted to the idea of "becoming a Hare Krishna." This is why I couldn't see ISKCON's flaws as being as serious as they truly were. This is why I was willing to give up just about everything to join ISKCON.

Ten-Thousand Dollar Lamps... for Krishna

Two days after playing to six hundred kids in Chicago, we played to only thirty in Detroit, but I sold an Enquirer to almost every single one of them. Youth of Today played four songs.

After the show, we drove over to the ISKCON temple. I was surprised to discover that it was a palace built by an auto-baron in the late 1920s, "Fisher Mansion." I soon found myself, with just about everyone else in the bands, walking through decadent room after decedent room with our devotee tour-guide in slacks and shirt proudly pointing out the ridiculous price tags that would be hung on any and all of the lamps, couches, and light-switches.

There was an indoor swimming pool with jillion-dollar tiles imported from Italy. Marilyn Monroe swam in it. There was a huge boathouse, lined in marble of course, for the rich guy's ridiculously large yacht. Elvis was here.

Zack was looking at everything, and I felt I could hear his thoughts. They were identical to mine, "What the hell is spiritual about this?"

I asked Dhanurdhara Mahārāja, "What's the *purpose* of this? It just seems to glorify some *karmī* and his materialism."

"I have my own doubts about it," the swāmī replied.

That was a relief.

When our tour of the palace ended, Mahārāja asked for something we could all eat. What they brought was cold, which seemed to really bother him, and he called for someone in charge.

"These are important guests, musicians in popular bands," he said to the man in charge. "You can't bring warm *prasādam*?"

The man apologized.

"Some of them also have questions. They are confused about the mansion." Then he turned to me, "Vic, go ahead and explain your doubts."

"Well," I said. "It just seems so *materialistic*."

"Prabhupāda wanted us to buy this mansion," the man explained, "to attract people to come hear about Krishna."

"OK," I replied, "but when they come they *don't* hear about Krishna, they just hear about how expensive the lamps and couches are."

"It's *yukta-vairagya*," the man said. "We can use everything in Krishna's service. Even very fancy material things. This is Krishna's temple. The money people pay to tour the mansion pays for Krishna's temple and feeds Krishna's devotees. So they are doing devotional service, unknowingly. During the tour they see paintings of Krishna, diorama's of Krishna, and they even visit the ballroom, which is really a temple, so they get darśan of Krishna on the altar, and they get *prasādam*, and hear recordings of Prabhupāda chanting Hare Krishna."

"That must just *weird people out*," I said. "They must feel like it's a 'bait and switch.' They come to see a historic mansion, but wind up in a Hare Krishna temple halfway through it? Why not make the whole thing a temple, like a Vedic museum. People would still be attracted to see the opulence, but it would be so much more legit."

Dhanurdhara Mahārāja seemed to be on my side in the debate, and that made me feel great. I felt that even if there was stuff in ISKCON that made me very uncomfortable, at least this Swāmī was cool and might be on the same page as I was about it.

This is what I wrote in my diary:

> *The Detroit trip did not do wonders for my faith in the current structure of ISKCON, but I did gain a great deal of respect for Danerdar [sic] Maharaj. I think that the present ISKCON is not anywhere near perfect, but if it is being helped into the future by great devotees like Maharaj, then there is good hope and bright times ahead.*

When we retired to individual rooms for the night, Ray and I went with the two Swāmīs. Dhanurdhara Swāmī seemed proud of me. "You are a Vṛndāvana devotee, Bhakta Vic," he said. "You are not interested in majesty and opulence, you are interested in sweetness.

You should come to Vṛndāvana in October. We will have the Vṛndāvana Institute for Higher Education. It's perfect for people like you."

(Don't Need) Friends (Like Me)

"You've changed so much, man," Zack told me, confidentially. "We used to hang out and joke around and laugh. But now you are so serious all the time. You never hang out with us. It's like you've become a totally different person than the guy you were when we started this tour."

In my diary I explained to myself that Zack's dissatisfaction wasn't my fault. It was *his*. He was just to shallow. His idea of friendship, I told myself, was evaluated simply only on the basis of how much you can waste one another's time laughing over meaningless things. I was proud of being incredibly serious about my life.

Judging from my diary, I was also quite proud of my "preaching." Oh, I could really stump the atheists, for example, by asking them to explain the difference between a living body and a dead body, and then asking why they couldn't just reintroduce whatever was missing from the dead body and bring it back to life. And I could really "preach" to agnostics too. In Minneapolis, for example, a skeptical agnostic asked me to prove logically that there was such a thing as a soul. I explained that the soul is consciousness, a thing that proves its own existence.

I was not as interested in having good friends as I was in being incredibly serious, and having all the answers to all the big questions.

I was quite impressed with Dhanurdhara Swami, and filled my diary with notes from the classes he would give on the road or at different temples we stopped at. I really liked the class he gave on chanting. He read from Harināma Cintāmaṇi, explaining that we need to overcome three things — distraction, laziness, and lack of taste — before our chanting would result in love of Krishna. He gave practical suggestions for overcoming each obstacle. Overcoming distraction would be made easier, he said, by chanting in a place that wasn't distracting; one that was clean and dedicated to chanting. Overcoming laziness means taking chanting more seriously, so at least don't talk during the round. Wait till the round of beads is entirely finished, and then talk about whatever else, or do whatever else distracted you. Overcoming lack of taste, he suggested, could be done by chanting more. The more you chant the more you get a taste for it. We could start by chanting more on certain days, like *ekādaśī*.

This is the kind of stuff I was interested in! Not joking around with friends.

Thus I was slightly dumbfounded one day, when Dhanurdhara Swāmī was simply being friendly with people without doing any "preaching" about Krishna. Sammy Siegler from Shelter and Mark Hayworth from Inside Out rode in the "Swāmī Van" with him, forcing me to ride with my old friends in the "Vrinda Van." (My diary describes this as an "austerity" for me.) When we stopped to get gas I poked my head into the Swāmī Van for a breath of fresh air. To my surprise, Mahārāja wasn't talking about Krishna; he was talking about astrology and just being friendly.

Later on I asked him why. "If someone isn't interested in Krishna," he told me, "it won't matter what you say. First you have to establish a friendly relationship with a person like that, and later it can naturally develop into talking about Krishna."

300 Bucks... So What?

On the drive from Minneapolis to Gītā-Nāgarī (a Krishna farm in Pennsylvania) I realized that I left behind a bag with my wallet, Walkman, and cassettes. Losing the wallet meant losing my driver's license, a bankcard my dad had given me, and about three hundred dollars I had made from selling zines.

It wouldn't have been too hard to go back, or even call the people from Minneapolis to see if they might have found it and could send it to me, but I just didn't care. My head was totally elsewhere.

We arrived at midnight and spent the next two days chanting in the temple and watching bulls knock over old trees. I interviewed Zack and Porcel for the next issue of Enquirer, and also interviewed the devotee in charge of the cows.

We'll Handle This

At Gītā-Nāgarī, Dhanurdhara Mahārāja invited me on a walk. He kicked it off by saying, "OK Vic, bring on the questions."

All of my questions were about ISKCON.

He explained that ISKCON had almost collapsed after Prabhupāda left because young western men with hardly a few years experience in spiritual life suddenly assumed big positions as the spiritual leaders of society. As a result, ISKCON's focus shifted from preaching to making money "by hook or by crook" to fund huge projects that would supposedly be great for preaching. The assets and resources of the movement grew as a result of the influx of money, but everything fell apart when these leaders "fell down." Huge numbers of people left the movement, leaving a very understaffed ISKCON with huge properties to maintain and pay for.

That answered why most of the temples we visited were falling apart, but it didn't answer why a lot of devotees left in the temples were nuts... or maybe it did: the insanity sieve must have filtered out everyone else. Only the most incredibly dedicated or the most incredibly cracked would have been able to endure the madness inflicted by these big bad leaders.

I asked what I could do to help.

He assured me that a reform movement was already underway and things would be OK. I could forget about all that and just concentrate on chanting Hare Krishna and learning the Krishna philosophy. "Become a brāhmaṇa," he said. "Always study and preach. Make a definite program for reading Prabhupāda's books and writing about them."

I told him about my idea of doing a verse-by-verse Bhagavad Gītā study diary. "Do that!" he encouraged. "And write to me in Vṛndāvana."

The End of Innocence

Our DC Safari Club show was cancelled, so we headed to the Hare Krishna temple nearby. This what I had to say about it, in my diary:

This temple is falling apart at the seams. Everything is dismal. Some nice devotees are here, but they number only about 10 and the temple property is large. It requires at least 30 people to maintain, in my opinion. Still, even for having only 10 people, the place is filthy. I can't even imagine what Prabhupāda would be saying on seeing it. It's a wreck. Kṛṣṇafest needs to inspire these places to get their acts together.

The tour ended in New Jersey on the first of July with a huge show at a huge club called City Gardens. Ironically, the only thing I remember about the last show I ever played with Inside Out is that I sold out of Enquirers.

The Shelter Era

Chapter Seventeen:

Mom and Dad

600 Bucks in the Seat Pocket

I sat next to Zack on the plane back to So Cal, counting money. Even after losing $300 bucks, I still had $600 in my hands. I put it all back in its envelope and put that envelope in the seat pocket in front of me. We were all pretty jazzed that we had made any money at all from doing something so fun.

I fell asleep.

When we landed in LA, mom and dad picked us up at the airport, and we drove Zack back to his mom's apartment in Irvine. On the way, dad asked if we made any money.

"He made a lot more than me," Zack said. "You should've seen him selling those zines. He was really hustlin' out there."

While everyone laughed, I was busy checking every pocket and looking again and again through my big Indian shoulder bag, trying to find the envelope with the cash in it.

I remembered the seat pocket.

"Oh fuck," an eloquent summary.

"What happened?" dad asked.

I didn't want to say. I just said, "...shit..."

"You lost the money?"

"I lost the damn money."

"You left it on the plane?"

"I left it on the plane... in the freaking seat pocket."

Everyone groaned.

"How much was it?" dad asked.

"Six hundred."

"Six hundred *dollars*?"

"Six hundred dollars."

"Wow. I'm impressed," he said.

"You're impressed that I lost six hundred dollars?"

"No," he said, "I'm impressed that you *made* six hundred dollars."

Zack started laughing.

There was silence for a few moments.

Then Zack cracked a joke, "Hey, now *I* made more than *you!*"

Everyone laughed, even me.

I didn't really care that much about the money itself, but it was embarrassing to be so obviously distracted and irresponsible. I wasn't thinking about anything in the present, I was thinking about how to tell my parents I was becoming a Hare Krishna. In a few weeks Ray would show up in San Diego with a van and some musicians, and then I would become one of them and make my exit. How could I possibly focus on anything else? My head was flying a holding pattern up in the clouds, and there was no schedule for it to land.

I'm Going on Tour With Shelter

"How was the tour?" was, of course, the first question from dad and mom.

"It was amazing!" I said. "So intense. I decided to join Shelter and go back out on tour with them in a few weeks, starting out here on the West Coast."

They were shocked.

"What about Inside Out?" Dad asked.

"I quit."

He was confused. Inside Out was an awesome band, and I had been so *into* it. Why would I quit? But he told himself it was probably a smart career move, since Ray, after all, was famous.

"What about college?" He asked.

I lied. "I'll just take off for a semester, or if the band goes really well, for a year."

I intended to go away *for good*, all the way to a "spiritual world;" a mystical place from which there would be no return, and no contact with outsiders like parents. I wasn't joining Shelter; I was joining the Hare Krishna's. The whole Shelter thing was candy coating for the castor oil.

Promise Me You Won't Join a Cult

Mom was particularly terrified. She came up to my room one day in tears, saying, "I'm so worried that you are going to wind up in a cult."

I lied. "I'm just joining a band, mom. Don't worry."

"Promise me that you won't join a cult." She asked.

I promised.

I had heard from devotees that it was OK to lie for Krishna.

How Can You Serve God?

Dad tried to reason with me, or, more accurately, tried to defeat my reasoning.

In one of his more memorable arguments he asked, "You say you want to dedicate yourself to serving God, but how do you even know what God wants? Maybe God wants you to finish college, not join the Hare Krishna's."

Even if God did want me to finish college, *I* didn't. I wanted to do something *exciting*!

"How do you know it's even a good idea to 'serve God'?" he continued. "So many people were completely convinced they were serving God while they did horrible things, from holy wars in the Middle East to the Spanish Inquisition."

I replied with the answer I had learned from Prabhupāda and ISKCON: a guru would tell me what God wanted. "Krishna explains what he wants to very spiritually advanced people," I said, "and those people explain it to others, and those people explain it to others. It's a system called *paramparā* and it's how an ordinary person like you or me can learn what God wants from us."

That scared the crap out of dad. "Come on, Vic!" he replied in frustration, "The only thing you'll find out that way is what *that* person *thinks* God wants! And what if that person is not as pure and 'spiritually advanced' as you think? What if they use the idea of what 'God wants' as a way to get what *they* want?"

I replied that a person's level of 'spiritual advancement' is not something I would accept on faith. It would be demonstrable through tangible character traits and behavior – like renunciation of power and wealth.

"Well," he said, "the gurus of ISKCON hardly seem to have positions of power and wealth."

How Can You Love God?

In another debate, dad asked, "How can you love God? He is not here, like you or your mom."

I replied with an answer I had learned from Prabhupāda: we could dedicate our work to serving him. This was another mess though, because it goes back to the question, How do you know what would serve God?

I eventually gave another answer, "Well, expressing love is simple, all you have to do is focus your *attention* on those you love. That's what chanting Hare Krishna is all about. It's a simple way to focus our attention on Krishna by focusing on his names."

Dad grimaced. "Why focus your attention on someone that's not even here? We should love *each other* and focus on *each other*! That's how we should love God."

"That's backwards," I argued, giving another answer I learned from Prabhupāda. "God is the root of everyone, so if we love God we love everyone. It's just like watering a plant. If you water the root, all the leaves are nourished. But if you try to love people independently from God, it's like pouring water on a leaf: neither the plant nor the leaf benefits."

"What are you talking about?" He blurted out. "I can 'pour water on you' and you will 'grow.' I can love you, without needing to love you *through* someone else who isn't even tangible!"

Dad had a single, obvious motive: to talk me out of becoming a Hare Krishna. Reciprocally, I wasn't much interested in whatever truth he was expressing to me.

A Bhagavad Gita Diary

While at home that summer I would wake up early to chant Hare Krishna on beads and read Bhagavad Gītā, writing and self-publishing a pretty thick book called A Bhagavad Gita Diary. In it, I went through each verse in the Gītā's Second Chapter, giving Prabhupāda's translation and then quoting section by section from his "purport," giving my own thoughts on the main points he made in each.

I printed 25 copies, gave them to my favorite San Diego devotees, and mailed a few to my Hare Krishna heroes and Hardcore pen pals.

Editorial Tricks & Homophobia Makeovers

I also used the "down time" in San Diego to put together the fourth issue of Enquirer, featuring interviews with Zack and Porcell. This is where I started going overboard with selective editing; obscuring interviewee's opinions that I didn't like, in favor those I did.

For example:

> **Zack:** "I think leading a spiritual life means casting away and putting aside the physical nature in life, and the intellectual nature in life. But actually it's using all three of them... And spirituality   like..."

I knew what Zack really wanted to say, but I hid it. A real editor would have written it like this:

> **Zack:** "I don't think leading a spiritual life means you have to cast away or put aside the physical and intellectual nature of life. I think it means combining all three — physical, intellectual, and spiritual."

I didn't write it like that, because I didn't *want* the meaning to be clear; it contradicted my agenda of absolute dedication to Krishna consciousness. I didn't want to integrate physical, intellectual and spiritual. I wanted to sacrifice the physical and intellectual aspects of my life for the sake of the spiritual. The weird thing, though, is that Zack's message is exactly the same message Krishna himself delivers in the third and fifth chapters of Bhagavad Gītā. At the time, I didn't realize it because my knowledge of Krishna consciousness was still more influenced by ISKCON than by Krishna. ISKCON's battle cry, at least so far as I could hear it, was simple, "Shave up now and join the temple, whatever you've got, give it to us (we'll give it to Krishna for you)."

Another interviewing trick up my sleeve, which I used quite a bit in both Porcell's and Zack's interview, was to steer the conversation clear of controversy and keep it on subjects I knew we had no disagreements about. To illustrate this strategy more clearly, imagine a Martian writing a fanzine to attract Earthlings to Mars. The Martian could passionately interview famous Earthlings on a subject that everyone in the universe agrees on, giving the impression that Earthlings and Martians are bosom buddies who agree all the time.

Thus almost all the interviews in Issue Four revolved almost entirely around a subject that practically any punk in the world would agree on: modern television-culture is totally jacked, and pressures us to conform to its hollow, self-serving norms. The unspoken message: "Super cool hardcore dudes like Zack de la Rocha and John Porcelly believe so many of the same things we Hare Krishna's do. They love us. You want to be like them, so love us, too."

In my zine I seemed to be a representative of ISKCON, when in fact I was just a hardcore kid who never even lived in a temple. I gave *my* views about homosexuality and sexism, for example, as if they were ISKCON's.

About homosexuality, I said that we Hare Krishna's believe that *who* we relate to doesn't matter as much as *how* we relate to them. If we relate to one another primarily for sense gratification, it's not a spiritually positive relationship, regardless if it's with a man or a woman.

Yeah, that's nice, and some people in ISKCON would probably agree, but overall this was not how ISKCON as a whole addressed the issue of "demonic" homosexuality.

When the angel on my right shoulder told the devil on my left about what I was doing, the guy in the middle had a good excuse: my agenda was not to get kids to join ISKCON and bring new blood into the almost bled-out society. My agenda was to help people comprehend the *true* spiritual concepts of Krishna consciousness.

Both the devil and the angel were happy with this smokescreen.

CHAPTER EIGHTEEN:

IS THAT OUR SON?

Barfi Bags

Ray rolled in to San Diego and I started spending every day down at the Krishna temple, hanging out with my new band and practicing in Amenity's rehearsal space.

I slept at the temple. "It's just more practical," I told my parents.

When not doing "hardcore band" stuff, we would Krishna-out, attending the regular daily functions in the temple early in the morning and in the evening, or going out on the Pacific Beach sidewalks with cymbals and drums and chanting Hare Krishna without looking at college girls in bikinis.

There was a very small house on the temple property that they used as their school. We used it off-hours as a place to hang out. I remember sitting on the floor with three or four huge trays of *laḍḍu* - a Krishna treat made from chickpea flower and lots of sugar, and *barfi* - Krishna milk-fudge. We were packing them into plastic bags, which we intended to hand out to people while we chanted on the beach-town's sidewalks.

I don't think we ever made it out to the sidewalks that day. Ray was in a particularly humorous mood, so the whole effort just turned into a party. We ate at least as many *laḍḍus* as we packed.

The Psychopathic Transcendentalist

Nothing had ever come of Rage — the band I sang for with Frosty, Alex, and Andy Alvarez. We had postponed recording our demo till after the Shelter tour, but by the time I got back from that tour I was too busy packing my bags for the spiritual world.

There would be no Rage demo, but at least we played one show.

It was a huge show at Spanky's a few days before my 20th birthday. Judge and Shelter were the big names, headlining. It would be the first time I played with Shelter.

Rage opened.

We had only a few short songs, but I talked in between them for at least as long. It was my first chance to have a microphone to myself, and I took full advantage of it. Donning a fairly true-to-life psychopathic-transcendentalist persona, I climbed in my socks over amps and strangled myself with microphone cords while ranting and raving at the top of my lungs to the spastic, fast and heavy music.

"Yeah, you know," I said to the shocked crowd. "I was walking home the other day and something weird happened. I got hit in the head by a soaking wet Nerf football. Yeah, It knocked me out, and when I came to again, I could see the future."

People were silent, waiting for the rest of the story and wondering if I was on PCP.

"Yeah, man, I'm not kidding. I can see the future... So, who wants to know their future?"

No one did.

"No one wants to know their future?"

A couple of people shouted for me to tell them.

"Well, I'll tell you *all* your future... YOU'RE ALL GONNA DIE! This next song is called Leprous Death."

Hair Falling on Porcelain

It was a Saturday.

It was inevitable.

There seemed no way to become a true Hare Krishna without it.

It happened in an empty bathtub, in that small house on the San Diego temple property. Wielding the electric razor was one of the guys from the greyhound bus that had come on the tour with us: a Latin teenage *brahmacārī* with a Krishna ponytail that would reach down to his knees when he untied it.

We stepped into the tub wearing *gamcha*.

I looked down at the whiteness of the porcelain.

He set the razor to my head.

Clusters of hair fell, each one removing another bit of my former identity, sending it to the porcelain where it tried to cling to my feet, desperate in the final throes of hopeless abandonment.

After the buzzing, we stepped over to the sink and used a razor blade. Buzzing just wasn't enough, you see. It should be a "Schick shave," right down to the skin.

Guṇagrahi Swāmī, the man in charge of that same greyhound bus, had given me permission to shave up and dress in saffron. So, when I stepped out of the tub I changed into the orange-pink Hare Krishna robes.

Now I was 100% committed, and there was no way to hide it.

There was no turning back.

I was bald.

I had a Krishna ponytail.

I wore the robes.

I *was* a Hare Krishna.

Vic DiCara was gone. All my nicknames dispersed, unable to apply to this new being. The only name that now fit was *Bhakta Vic*. And even that was on the chopping block.

I looked out the bathroom window. Across the yard I saw Umāpati Swāmī walking out of the temple and up the steps to the men's ashram.

His head was bald. My head was bald.

He wore orange robes. I wore orange robes.

He was a swāmī. I... would be one soon! Maybe it would take two or three years, but soon I would be walking around with one of those awesome staffs.

Then I would be perfect.

In Our Own Little Bubble

That night, as they did every Saturday night, the San Diego devotees went out to La Jolla to walk and dance up and down the busy sidewalks chanting Hare Krishna amidst rich locals and happy tourists. I had done this before, of course, but, till now I had always been the cool guy with the Krishna's; the adventurous and handsome young man with an open mind and elevated interests in everything from punk rock to Hare Krishna.

Not anymore.

Now I was just another baldhead in the crowd of baldheads. I had merged my identity with theirs. We had the same strange hairstyle. We wore the same strange clothes. We were one with one another, and different from everyone else on the sidewalks, everyone else in the city... everyone else in the world.

Until now I could say to myself, "ISKCON is like this or that, but I'm different."

Not anymore.

Now I was one of them, included and implicated in any strange thing anyone else with my strange clothes and strange haircut might say or do on the sidewalk tonight, or might have already done in the movements curiously under-discussed mysterious past.

We chanted in a bubble. Most of these La Jolla people — indeed most people in the world — looked at us as a danger, a nuisance, or a freak show. The bubble insulated us from that. To form the bubble mostly looked at each other, or looked nowhere, certainly not at the people in the restaurants or stores, or on the sidewalks.

But, for me, the bubble wasn't perfect. I looked around.

One restaurant looked very familiar. My parents had taken me there once or twice. A fear came over me. What if they were here right now, at that restaurant? They would *flip out* to see me for the first time in a bald head and pink bed sheets dancing with the Hare Krishna's in front of their expensive restaurant!

It must have been ESP.

As we got closer, I saw them. My mother and father were coming down the steps from that restaurant.

I stared straight ahead. Surely they had had a few drinks. Maybe they wouldn't be all that alert? Maybe they wouldn't notice me?

Time dilated as I walked past them, standing to the side of the sidewalk, letting the imposing caravan pass, looking though it to see if their son was tagging along.

At any moment, I expected to hear them call my name in some never-before-heard mixture of disbelief and indignation.

Their eyes passed right through me.

They couldn't recognize me?

Parting Gifts

The next day, I called my mom. Shelter would be hitting the road tomorrow, and I asked if she could drive me back down to the temple after I dropped my car off at home.

I pulled up to the house in shorts and a T-shirt, but with my shaved head and Krishna ponytail glowing in the sun. She was outside the front door talking to a neighbor, so I parked at a distance and waited for the lady to leave. I knew she was going to freak out and wanted to at least spare her the embarrassment of freaking out in front of her next-door neighbor.

I have no idea why I didn't just wait to shave up till after my mom dropped me off at the temple. I guess I really didn't think about it too carefully.

"Victor," she cried, "You *promised* me..."

"Don't worry mom," I said, as if it was incredibly common for every 20-year-old son to shave his head and join the Hare Krishna's. "It's just a haircut. Everyone in the band has the same haircut; it'll look really powerful."

She drove me down to the temple. The 30 or 40 minute long trip took forever.

"We saw the Hare Krishna's chanting in La Jolla, last night," she said. "We were looking for you. Were you there?"

"Yeah! I was there," I said, in the cheeriest, most nonchalant tone I could manage. "I was looking for you, too, but didn't see you."

Why did almost everything have to be a lie?

When we stopped in front of the temple she handed me Kitty, "*Promise me you'll keep this.*" Kitty was a small stuffed animal she had made for me when I was a little kid, a replica of a doll my dad's mom had made for him.

My promises to my mother were obviously worth about as much as a presidential candidate's on a campaign, yet she kept asking for them.

I was about to sail off on the high seas of transcendence. What would Kitty be but another anchor on the boat, another symbolic bit of former identity, another reminder that she had actually *made* me, and she and my dad had actually *raised* me for 20 years? What would Kitty be except another reminder that I was abandoning the two people who loved me more than anyone?

I don't remember what happened to Kitty.

CHAPTER NINETEEN:

SHELTER TEMPLE TOUR 1990

Pink Socks

San Diego was one of ISKCON's finest temples, but I was glad when we got on the road again. In the back of my head I knew I was really messing with my parent's sanity, and I wanted to get some distance from them ...so I could forget about it.

We all got in the van: Ray and I, Eric Dailey (our bass player — a totally non-hardcore guy Ray had recruited from the Chicago temple when we rolled through on the last tour), Kevin (our drummer - a hardcore kid Ray recruited from somewhere), and Chris Interrante (our tour manager - who had nothing to do with hardcore but was about our age, and very organized and businesslike).

The first show on the tour was a sparsely attended outdoor show in Santa Barbara, organized by Kent McClard. I was self-conscious and felt weird. Even my clothes were a little embarrassing. Everyone in the band wore Krishna-pink shorts, Krishna-pink T-shirts, and even Krishna-pink socks.

What few non-musicians know is that 80% of touring in a small band is spent cramped in a van, and another 18% is spent waiting around. It's physically exhausting and mind numbing. Surely, this is a big reason so many touring musicians get hooked on drugs. My drug was a pen and paper. I spent practically all my time writing a diary, or keeping Gītā study notes, or writing poems about things I saw outside the van window.

Only the Berzerkly Gurus Fall Down?

We played the Gilman Street Project in Berkley. Some of the Berkley punks protested with an anti-Krishna flier, but Ray pretty convincingly decried it onstage as being one-sided and stereotypical. As we played, one of them held up a mirror pointed towards us, while continuously pogoing up and down. I think his point was that we claimed to be against material things, but here we were in a band, on stage, like rock stars - so we should look in the mirror and see how hypocritical we were. When he left, Ray asked him to come back, saying it was a big help to decrease his false ego.

Right after the matinee show we headed over to the temple for the Sunday feast, taking eight or nine kids with us.

We spent about a week in Berkley chanting on the streets here and there. The temple still had the frightening post-gangsta-guru vibe I had felt last time I was here. A nice man named Hari Vilas was trying valiantly to make it a functional āśrama. He told us not to be deterred by all the gurus who had "fallen down" in such catastrophic ways. He said we should, "Have faith in Krishna, Prabhupāda, and the disciplic line leading to Prabhupāda... other people might fall down, but they never will."

But wait... these gurus who fell down *were* the "disciplic line leading to Prabhupāda."

My First Bhāgavatam Class

In the van, we arranged our own program of spiritual practices, which meant that we would be giving our own classes on Śrīmad Bhāgavatam. I was excited about that! I gave my first Bhāgavatam class in a van rolling down the highway towards Seattle on September 7th of 1990. I picked text 8 of Chapter Two, in Canto One:

> *dharmaḥ svanuṣṭhitaḥ puṁsāṁ viṣvaksena-kathāsu yaḥ*
> *notpādayed yadi ratiṁ śrama eva hi kevalam*

"The occupational activities a man performs according to his own position are only so much useless labor if they do not provoke attraction for the message of the Personality of Godhead."

As musicians, our natural occupation *(sva-dharma)* was to make music, but unless we made our music in such a way that it attracted us to Krishna, our music making would amount to nothing more than ordinary work *(śrama eva hi kevalam)*. I got into quoting and explaining the Sanskrit, which was possible even though I didn't know Sanskrit because Prabhupāda's books had word-by-word translations from Sanskrit to English.

Straightedge Kīrtan Fest

In Seattle the temple was just a simple, small house on a large plot of somewhat rural land, with a handful of devotees and a big altar built into what was once someone's living room. The deities looked absolutely gigantic because they were so close. I liked that the Krishna deity was black.

Everything felt small and simple, but beautiful.

On the first night, we played a converted garage in Olympia to a small but receptive crowd. The next night was a much bigger show. On Sunday we played a relaxed midday party at a house near the temple, then took about 30 kids with us to the Sunday Feast. We gave cymbals, tambourines or shakers to just about every one of them and had a rip-roaring kīrtan for about an hour and a half, jumping and running around like mad.

Desperate (for) Drummers

Everyone in Shelter was practically high off the excitement of spreading Krishna consciousness to so many kids, everyone but Kevin, our drummer. The more temples we went to the less he wanted to be a devotee. After a few days in Seattle he developed kidney stones, checked himself into a hospital, and we decided to kick him out. I don't remember the details clearly, but suddenly we had no drummer.

We had a tour manager who could play bass, but that didn't solve the problem.

Then, Eric had an idea: he gave the tour manager his bass and volunteered to learn drums. Chris would become our bassist, even though he was a new-age synthesizer-man and businesslike briefcase wielder, and Eric would become our drummer, even though he also wasn't into heavy music and had never played drums before.

We started practicing a few hours a day, and within two or three days it started to seem like it might be plausible, a testament especially to Eric Daily's musicianship and flexibility.

"Plausible," however, is not "great."

Bogus Anti-ISKCON Devotees

Many of the Seattle kids had been going to Gauri Dasa's Wednesday kīrtan in town. Gauri had been kicked out of ISKCON because he was part of a group of people who reacted to ISKCON's guru-fall-downs by deciding that no one but Śrīla Prabhupāda should be a guru from now on. ISKCON didn't agree and, like any institution worth its weight in conformity, banished them.

I had never met, spoken to, or even read a single word written by Gauri or any of his "ṛtvik" camp. Nonetheless I accepted the premise that he was "bogus," because he wasn't in ISKCON.

My diary from Seattle is full of obvious rivalry:

Everyone was blown away by the Sunday Feast kīrtan. They had only known Gauri dās' "boring sit-down kirtans," and "didn't even know you ever danced in kīrtan."

Everyone confided in me that, now that they had been to ISKCON, Gauri dās' Wednesday program was obviously inferior and bogus. I encouraged them to go to the ISKCON temple feasts always.

Wednesday came and we launched into a protracted debate on whether or not to attend. Apparently it was fine to chant Hare Krishna on the streets with total strangers, but debatable if you should do it with devotees whose opinions are slightly different from yours.

We finally decided to go, *for the kids*.

Then Chris brought up the issue of *prasādam*. You see, if you were to eat something that hadn't been offered to Krishna, you would be "eating lumps of sin."

But wouldn't Gauri offer the food to Krishna?

Yes, Chris explained, but it's not enough to offer food, Krishna has to accept it.

Why wouldn't Krishna accept Gauri's offering?

Gauri was "offensive," Chris explained, and Krishna doesn't accept things from offensive people.

What was his offense?

The worst kind: offense to the guru.

To whose guru? To our gurus! Well OK, we didn't even have gurus yet, but to our potential gurus, to ISKCON's gurus.

And, what exactly what his offense to our potential future gurus?

His claim that they weren't qualified to be gurus, which objectively speaking was not a claim I should have seen as outlandish, judging by what had just happened in ISKCON.

Anyway, Ray and Eric decided to risk eating potential lumps of sin. Chris and I resolved to fast.

At the kīrtan, everyone sat down, which we thought was boring and bogus. We and stood on the side, dancing mildly. Gauri then stood up to join us, after which everyone stood up and started dancing. Kīrtan went off the hook for a good long time.

We all wound up eating everything.

Gold Mines in the Great White North

We drove up to Vancouver with Undertow and a host of Seattle kids to play a show at the ISKCON temple there. They had set up a stage outside, under a huge statue of Śrī Krishna Caitanya dancing in kīrtan. Devotees mixed with hardcore kids in the small crowd, curious, confused and amazed by what they were hearing and seeing. A middle-aged, somewhat overweight, executive-looking man in saffron robes took photos. His name was Vipramukhya Swāmī.

It started raining right before we started playing. We did five songs in the cold rain and then high-tailed it, along with everyone else, into the temple room to sit in rows on the floor and have a Hare Krishna feast.

After a day or two of drab, Vipramukhya Swāmī took us to a nearby farm named Śaraṇāgatī: 160 acres of off the grid land in a valley between Nowhere and Nowhere Else, on Vancouver's side of Canada.

We put our sleeping bags in an empty log cabin and went out to pick vegetables. I put my hand into the cold dirt and it came back out with a real potato. I felt like an extension of the dirt, which formed a unit with rain, sky, and sun. Everything, including me, was part of a whole; a distinct yet integrated part of a cooperative, unified reality.

We chopped wood, cooked the potatoes on a wood-burning stove, and ate them while the Swāmī told humorous stories. The stars in the sky were vivid and sharp. It was the first time I had ever lived without grocery stores and electricity. The whole world was so much more *real*!

The next day we went up to the farm's abandoned gold mine. Parking the car at the ruins of an old gold-miner's house, we walked up the steep mountainside, stopping at the foreboding mine entrance. Shale vomited from its mouth all over the mountainside. Ancient support beams cracked and jutted in different directions like rotten teeth. Barbed wire clung to everything like a vine.

The inside of the mine was enormous. Rats ran here and there, but they looked more like hamsters than the filthy things you see in a city. A huge shaft was flooded with crystal clear water - probably very close to freezing cold. "Bleeding rocks" were everywhere with minerals oozing out of them. Towards the front of the mine they oozed white minerals, like cake icing. Deeper in, reddish oxides leaked out and pooled on the floor like blood. Even further into the heart of mountain, the colors turned purple.

Girls in the Back, Please

We returned for a while to Seattle. A young lady from the straightedge scene, Cassandra, had a shaved head except for a tuft of blue hair in the front. She came to the temple early on Sunday to help cook the feast. It was awkward when someone told her she had to stand at the back of the temple during the kīrtan, because she wasn't a man.

I had been working on a letter addressed to the Governing Body of ISKCON, protesting how women were treated in ISKCON. I read it to her, hoping to pass on the same illusion I had - that ISKCON leaders would listen and things would change soon.

A Wall Between Us

Knowing my tour schedule, my parents could send letters to the temples ahead of us, kind of like how a quarterback throws the ball where he knows the receiver will be by the time the ball gets there. We wrote back and forth pretty often. They were going through hell trying to deal with what I was doing with my life. They knew, and so did I, that ISKCON pressures its members to move away from family and cut off contact with them and other "*karmīs.*"

Mom had given up hope of "getting me back," but dad still tried to convince me that I was going down the wrong path.

He would have had better luck inventing a Star Trek transporter.

He didn't try much to discredit the basic idea of searching for God; he mostly tried to help me see ISKCON as a faulty representation of a great idea. I knew ISKCON was faulty, but I didn't yet comprehend just how faulty. I still lived in the dream that ISKCON's leadership were "reformers" who would be responsive, willing and even eager to improve. Thus I refused to admit that ISKCON's faults outweighed the value of its core content, and I refused to admit that its core content could be accessed without having to merge myself into its institutionalism.

My parents complained that, "A wall has arisen between us," but they weren't willing to come very far towards my side of the wall. That was odd because they had gotten very involved in everything else I ever did. When I was into BMX freestyle, my dad became a contest judge and helped me make a Freestyle zine. When I was into straightedge, he became straightedge. But Krishna? Apparently not even the pain of losing an only son was enough to motivate them towards *that*.

Get Serious

From Seattle to Denver to Utah... we went from city to city spending several days in each temple getting all the local straightedge kids as hyped on Krishna as we possibly could.

I no longer thought of myself as a straightedge kid or a musician, I was now a budding guru and swāmī. I kept diaries, as if the world was just waiting to read them, and carefully wrote letters to the fans I secretly saw as disciples, eager to elaborately answer their inquiries about Krishna, half because I sincerely loved Krishna consciousness, but half because I sincerely loved acting like a guru.

Trying to be as worthy as I could of my grand daydream, I focused on eating less, waking up earlier to chant better, and trying to thoroughly learn the philosophical details of Krishna Consciousness by studying Gītā, Bhāgavatam, and my photocopy of Hari-nām Cintāmaṇī - keeping careful notes and trying to memorize the Sanskrit.

My uber-serious attitude caused tension between Ray and I.

Ray had as much or more ego as I, but, to his credit, he never seemed to envision himself as the new swāmī on the block, or the guru in the batter's box. He seemed content just to get people interested in Krishna, get them to the temple, and get them in touch with someone who was more advanced and experienced with Krishna consciousness. My aspiration was different; I wasn't so interested in getting a zillion people into Krishna. I was more focused on helping the dozen or so who were already very serious about it. And, of course, I would help them by *being* the more advanced and experienced person... the guru.

I wanted Shelter to become more grave and serious. Ray wanted to be more ebullient and popular. I was gradually becoming more and more frustrated with this, and he was gradually becoming more and more frustrated with me.

Destination: Philly

As we neared the Atlantic, we all started wondering when and where we would stop and settle down. Would we turn around and tour our way back towards the Pacific, making our home base at ISKCON's San Diego temple? Half of me hoped so. San Diego was so much better than any of the other temples we had visited; and maybe being close to mom and dad would help ease the pain I knew I was putting them through.

But the other half of me wanted to go somewhere far from San Diego, where the canvas would once again be blank, giving me more freedom to sketch and paint my new self-image as the serious, advanced devotee I dreamed of being.

One day, Ray announced that he had found a permanent home for us: ISKCON Philadelphia. Ravindra Svarūpa Prabhu, the president there, was welcoming us with open arms.

CHAPTER TWENTY:

A Crumbling Mansion

Bhakta Uncle Fester

Pulling into 41 West Allens Lane was like pulling up to the home of the Addams family. It was a sprawling, ornate mansion... that was literally falling apart at the seams.

Up the broken porch steps and into the window-walled passage that connected two large three-story buildings and rattled in the breeze, we eventually found our way to the temple room just as devotees were carrying *prasādam* out of it. In an empty room with nothing but a podium standing near a wall-phone, almost all of the temple's half-dozen residents gathered for breakfast.

One of them introduced himself as Shyamānanda.

"What?" I gasped. "Did you say Shyamānanda?"

"Yes?" he said, uncomfortably.

"Oh my God!" I shouted in uncontrolled enthusiasm, "Last night, in the van, on the way here, I *dreamt* I would meet someone named Shyamānanda in this temple!"

No one seemed even a tenth as amazed by it as I was.

Ravindra Svarūpa Prabhu himself came down to greet us, looking like the archetype grown-up geek with round glasses hung on ears that uncommonly protruded from a very round face graced with an unreservedly goofy smile. He was a famous hero in my eyes — a crucial figure in the all-important "guru-reform" which allowed me to maintain hope that ISKCON wasn't going to keep being what it was in the '80s. The Prabhu was an intellectual, deft with pen and paper, an actual PhD! Perhaps here was an ISKCON leader even my dad would find intelligent, legit and respectable.

The temple room itself was well kept; a bit bear, but beautiful. Wooden Jagannāth deities were on the main altar. Gaura Nitai danced with their arms raised on a smaller altar to the left. Rādhā Krishna stood on the right. Krishna played his flute as Rādhā raised her right hand to bless all her guests. "Rādhā Śaradbihari" — the Love Queen and her Autumnal Enjoyer — a reference to Krishna's autumn *rāsa-līlā* dance with the girls of Vṛndāvana, my favorite of all Krishna's "pastimes."

Porn-āśrama Dhrama

Ravindra Svarūpa gave us two big rooms at the end of the third floor hallway in the main temple building. We turned one into our sleeping quarters, and the other into Equal Vision Records' very first office.

The sleeping room had three exposed walls, each with windows. A lot of glass had fallen out of their squares, replaced by sheets of plastic. Even in autumn the room was cold. It would be an icebox in the winter.

There were two or three large wooden bunk beds, with drawers built-in beneath the bare plywood platforms. I selected one as my own and opened the drawers to unpack my stuff.

Bright pink pussy lips greeted me from between dark black spreading legs. Yes, here in a drawer in a bed in the last bastion of celibacy, the pristinely monastic Hare Krishna temple's *brahmacārī-āśrama*, I found someone's porn.

Infuriating.

I was putting my parents though hell because their "materialistic association" would supposedly be counterproductive to my "spiritual advancement." I had given up everything to dedicate myself to Krishna in what was advertised as the most favorable spiritual environment: the Hare Krishna temple. And what did it turn out to be? A freezing room with broken windows in a semi-abandoned building with a stash of hardcore porn magazines.

"There's porn in the drawers of my bunk." I told the rest of the band in the EVR office.

A long, awkward moment of disbelief and embarrassment.

"Should I tell Ravindra Svarūpa Prabhu?" I asked.

Another long, awkward moment of disbelief and embarrassment.

"Just throw it out," Ray finally answered, decisively. "*I'll* tell him about it."

Welcome to Philly

In all the excitement, we had neglected to immediately move all our equipment out of the van. While we slept on the first night, someone broke in and made off with as much of it as they could carry.

Tape a Crystal to your Forehead

Śyāmānanda turned out to be a puppeteer. During Sunday Feasts he would bring out his Kermit the Frog puppet, spiritualized I guess by being dressed in a devotee-robe (*"dhoti"*) and bearing a devotee-mark (*"tilak"*) on his froggie green forehead.

Two Latinos sold flowers at stoplights, and apparently made significant contributions to paying the bills by doing so. They didn't speak English so I never got to know them very well, but it was unnerving to see a surviving holdover from the "selling flowers" era.

I made a point not to take much note of the two young women who lived across the breezeway in the other building. One of them, exceedingly quiet and timid, got engaged to a 70s-rock musician-prabhu whose retro-hip swagger lost its curiosity when I found out that their engagement ended because he had *pushed her down a flight of steps*.

The all-star inmate, however, was Bhakta Richard, whose all-star moments would occur at random when he would enter the temple-room for the pre-dawn kīrtan with a purple crystal (made of plastic, I think) scotch-taped to his forehead, and aluminum foil donned like armor. During the kīrtan he would dance like an American Indian. During breakfast he would talk incessantly about ghosts, UFOs and aliens, brainwaves, and the end of the world.

He was black.

So was the porn I had found in my bunk drawer.

I put two and two together and felt relieved: At least some of the madness could be consolidated to a common source.

Ravindra Svarupa was sane, though. "Smart," even. I kept reminding myself of that. He just seemed impossibly detached from everything that surrounded him, *too* detached. His wife, "Mother Sudamani" was very kind and seemed quite advanced in her devotion, judging by how well she took care of Rādhā Śaradbihari. The two had a boy in elementary school, Rūpa, who was totally into the idea that a rock band had just moved in.

There was also a hardcore kid amongst the sparse temple population: Bhakta Rob. He used to sing for a straightedge band called Release, and had a brooding, darkly introspective personality. We got along well.

Sinful Grains

They kept Krishna warm with a propane heater in the temple room, but the rest of the place became dazzlingly cold in the winter. Hot-water radiators occasionally turned on, but their effort to beat the frigid wind coming in through so many unsealed doors and plastic windows was doomed to failure. One night, I sat next to the warm radiator in the hall outside my room and sketched it lovingly on paper, an illustration for the booklet of poems I was working on. It had become for me an icon of comfort.

A huge snowstorm blew in on the night before *ekādaśī*. That word literally means "eleventh," and marks the eleventh lunar day after every full and dark moon. It's a particular day in Vedic culture, and ISKCON devotees observe it by "fasting from grains and beans."

I asked around but no one really knew why.

Some said, "Sin enters grains on *ekādaśī*, so it's sinful to eat them."

What? Sin enters grains for a day, and then leaves?

Dhanurdhara Swāmī had told me that what is really important on *ekādaśī* is to reduce my eating and sleeping, and increase my hearing and chanting.

It seemed logical to conclude that *ekādaśī* was a day set aside for fasting because occasional fasting has significant physical, mental, and emotional merits, which would improve the sharpness of mind for meditation and chanting. Abstaining from grains and beans was not the ideal; it was the minimum that could still be considered a fast.

Most devotees, though, preferred the more fantastic and hocus-pocus explanation, and saw the lack of grains/beans simply as a change of menu, not as a way to reduce their eating. Instead of pigging out on farina-halava we would pig out on tapioca pudding and dairy-drenched potatoes.

The Wise Don't Lament for their Mom

Rob and I decided to spend this snowy *ekādaśī* the *right* way: not eating at all, and chanting 64 rounds of "Hare Krishna" on our beads.

"64 rounds" was one of those magic numbers. Super pure, super serious devotees chanted 64 rounds. The rest of us small fries only chanted 16. It was exciting to get up on that super pure, super serious level and be able to say, "(Ahem) I'm chanting 64 rounds today, please don't bother me."

We woke at 2am, chanted 16 before the pre-dawn kīrtan, another 16 during the standard time set aside for it, and started on our next set of 16 at about 9am while everyone else was busy "fasting" on tapioca pudding and Gaurāṅga potatoes.

My stomach was empty, but it wasn't uncomfortable. In fact, it felt great to be so much better than everyone else!

We were over 40 rounds when Rob got a phone call. It was from his father. His mother, who had been extremely ill with severe Lupus for many years, was dying.

Rob immediately left, but the storm made a four-hour ordeal out of what should have been a one and a half hour train ride. His mother had already passed away before he arrived at the hospital.

He didn't return to the temple right away. People thought it odd.

A week or so went by.

"He is in *māyā*. We have to help him."

Devotees called him. Their idea of sympathy was to say things like, "It's her *karma*. The wise lament neither for the living nor the dead. Come back to the temple right away, don't fall into *māyā*."

He finally returned, for fifteen minutes, to pick up his belongings.

Writing Letters > Playing Pop Punk

In the big backyard behind the buildings was a smaller, simpler one-story house, now used as headquarters for the recently founded Hare Krishna mail order: Krishna Culture. They graciously let us use two small rooms at the back of the house. In one, a square about eight feet on either side, we set up drums and amplifiers. The other, a rectangle maybe eight feet on the long side and four on the short, became my own personal office! I had my dad ship out my computer and printer, and made this room ground zero for all the writing I was doing.

I didn't have much fun in the square room. Shelter wasn't working out the way I had hoped. Ray wanted to take the band in a more "pop" direction, and I just couldn't relate or write the kind of music or lyrics he was looking for. I become completely uninvolved with the creative process, while he collaborated with others to write riffs I didn't really like, ringing with twangy strings to support nasal vocal melodies instead of the howling screeches he was really good at.

During my entire time with Shelter, the only artistic contribution I could make was a particular syncopation on one iteration of the main riff to Quest for Certainty.

My office, however, was my safe haven. I could be alone there and write. I began by producing a batch of pamphlets about Krishna consciousness, with titles like The Core of Equality, and Individuality.

EVR2: The Core of Equality

The Core of Equality was a fiction based loosely on a romanticized version of the relationship between Ray and I in the early days, except that this character talked more like me or Zack than Ray. Here is a shortened version:

> "First of all," he told me, "anyone who thinks there's any equality in this society is crazy."
>
> His right hand rested on the shallow stage. Casual.
>
> Contrast his compelling voice: "I mean, you can't so much as set your big toe on the sidewalk without instantly being labeled up and down, stereotyped, and neatly filed away under everyone's preconceptions and prejudices. Ain't that right?"
>
> Of course I had to agree.
>
> "But why?" His words were punctuated with deep enthusiasm. "Why are we so totally lacking any living equality in this society?"
>
> I mumbled, "Uh... I don't... I guess... you know..."
>
> "Because this society is based on bodies."
>
> Pause: Dramatic effect.
>
> "If you want to get right down to the hard reality, in their eyes you ain't nothing but a lump of flesh. They have no scientific understanding of the spirit soul, and that's why there's not a single shred of equality in their world."
>
> I protested: "Are you really trying to tell me that people are prejudiced because they don't believe in some kind of soul? I can't see how a 'soul' has anything at all to do with equal rights."
>
> "All right, OK," he said. "Let's just say there is no such thing as a soul and we are nothing but bodies... Is there any equality on the bodily platform? No two bodies are the same. No two bodies have the same skills. Like the kid I used to sit next to in elementary school, he was the best superhero drawer in the whole wide world.

And me, I could barely draw a stick figure. Or that girl sitting behind me, the soloist for the glee club, or whatever it was. Her mouth could open up wider than her whole head and hit the highest notes you'd ever imagine. Meanwhile, they shoved me and my lousy voice wa-a-a-ay in the back. They practically had to bribe me to quit.

I got a kick out of his stories, and he seemed to make sense, so I kept quiet and let him go on.

"My mom told me everyone was equal," he said, "and deep down inside I knew she was right. But if we were equal, how come I couldn't draw or sing as good as those other kids?"

"Well, you know," I said, "different people may be good at different things, but we're all the same on the inside."

"On the 'inside'!?" He said, eyebrows arching over wide eyes. "What 'inside'? We are nothing but bodies, what the heck is so special about the inside of a body?"

"Come on," I said. "You know what I mean. I'm talking about the real person inside."

"That's it!" His face lit up. "You got it!"

"I did?"

"Yeah. You just hit the nail right on the head. That's the 'soul' and that's where true equality lies - in the soul, not the body. And as long as the masses believe they are the body, they will think they are white or black or man or woman, or human or animal or insect. As long as people think like this, there will only be exploitation and inequality. Every living being is a spirit soul, part and parcel of the Supreme Spirit Soul, the Personality of Godhead. That's real equality. And if we sincerely want to do something about it, we have to smash all this false materialistic propaganda of modern society, and we have to educate, on a massive scale, about spiritual reality. That's the whole purpose of this Krishna consciousness movement. That's what we're all about."

My dry mouth hung slightly open, speechless.

> "So please," he implored, "do something to push on this movement. In whatever way you can, do something to advance this revolution."

EVR3: Individuality

The other pamphlet, "Individuality," was framed as an answer to a semi-fictitious letter from an angry hardcore kid. "Matt" writes:

> Let's face it, man, you joined a club just like everyone else. You all dress the same. You all have the same bald haircut. You all believe the same things. You totally gave up your individuality, man. Sheep. You're no longer a person. You're just another Hare Krishna, like all the rest. Let's face it, you lost it.

Here's a short version of my reply:

> What you wind up saying in your letter is that people have to be made into individuals by the clothes they wear, the hairdo they have, etc. - we are all just blank slates who have to go out and buy our personhood, and wear our "individuality." So, although I'm sure you think of yourself as someone who holds individuality very dear, you've turned it into something bought from a thrift store and a hair salon.
>
> I don't subscribe to your opinion. Sorry.
>
> In Krishna consciousness we say that true individuality is not in the clothes you wear or the style of your hair. It's deep inside the self, an inalterable reality. Krishna consciousness, believe it or not, is intended to uncover the true self, the real individual. Behind all the masks. Beyond all the acts. Krishna consciousness doesn't take away individuality. On the contrary, it gives individuality the freedom to expand and express itself to its fullest potential.

We treated these little Xerox-and-fold do-dads as if they were actual releases on Equal Vision Records, stamping them with the "EVR" logo and giving them catalog numbers as is usually done for records. We handed them out to hardcore kids by the dozens.

EVR4: Blueprint for Socio Spiritual Revolution

Eventually I set my ambitions higher than 3-fold pamphlets and began writing a booklet. Blueprint for Socio Spiritual Revolution would express the social relevance of Krishna conscious ideology in terms that subversive and rebellious young punks like myself could relate to.

A summary of the Introduction:

> To keep us in our place, and keep themselves in power, the establishment skillfully provides us countless diversions to drain and squander the life force of our youth: the power of rebellion. We mice run faster and faster on tailor-made treadmills: changing fashion, corporate ladders, "the drug experience," "the sexual revolution..." Finally, we collapse from exhaustion — the force which could have been used to overturn the corrupt system quietly and fruitlessly spent, we retire into the deadpan complacency of adulthood and middle age. The power structure remains intact. We remain pawns. And the businessman turns a mighty profit extinguishing the fire of youth.
>
> In these times of hatred, no sane person can deny the absolute necessity of widespread progressive change. The people with the vigor to change it are us: the youth and the youthful. But along with our enthusiasm comes a full supply of naiveté. The youth naturally lack the wisdom born of practical experience in the real world, and so are easily misled. Thus even in our attempts at rebellion we play right into their hands. Our potency for effecting change is diffused and nullified, and the system remains safe and sound.
>
> But if the power of the youth could somehow be allied with sound and steady wisdom — focusing our revolutionary zeal to a single, concentrated and precise point — the result would be a unified

force of social reformation with unstoppable might unmatched in all the pages of history. The purpose of this booklet is to provide such a focus and direction.

This book presents a clear and detailed outline for wide-sweeping reform and revolution. It borrows needed wisdom from the Vedic texts — literature of gigantic antiquity that reveal a complete blueprint of a society based on simplicity in material life and intense dedication to spiritual realization; a society based not on mutual exploitation and ego-centric profit, but on cooperative progress towards the common cause.

CHAPTER TWENTY-ONE:

THE KRISHNACORE EXPLOSION

Temple to the Hardcores, Hardcores to the Temple

Shelter toured so frequently and played so constantly that Hare Krishna's had become as common as stage dives at hardcore shows in the North East. But besides taking the temple to the kids, we were taking kids to the temple.

On South Street in downtown Philly, a devotee named Hariyāśva had a vegetarian restaurant named Govinda's. It was on the ground floor of a multi-story building, the fourth floor of which served as a temple room for kīrtan and Krishna conscious gatherings. Bhakta Rob had been using this space for Wednesday night programs. Shelter took it over and expanded it with zeal, cooking multi-course vegetarian feasts in the apartment-sized kitchen for a few dozen hardcore kids who would pack in wall-to-wall, week after week, for months on end. I specialized in cooking the halava - a sweet treat made from farina. I tried to make a different flavor each week: blueberry halava, strawberry halava, banana halava, raisin-walnut halava... even peanut butter and chocolate halava!

To be honest, that halava was crazy delicious, and I would eat mountains of it.

The similarities between traditional *khol-karatāla* kīrtan and the more familiar hardcore mosh pit became evident on those sweaty and blissful Wednesday nights. Older but eternally jovial, Hariyāśva himself would often join us and gracefully leap around the kīrtan with a huge, effulgent smile, reminding me of a prancing black horse, erasing the border between "hardcore kid" and "non-hardcore kid." So many people were jumping up and down in that small fourth-story room that the floor literally moved like a trampoline, and the pictures and *mūrti* figures of Krishna tottered in danger of falling off the shelves!

Out in the suburbs, the temple on West Allen's Lane was also bustling with an influx of new full-time residents moving in from all parts of the country, eager to become a part of the Krishna Consciousness movement swirling thrillingly like a new hurricane around Shelter. Antonio Valladerez, Norman Brannon, Glen Burns, Dan Davis... these and many others brought new life into a temple that had been practically deserted just a month or two before.

Texas Krishnacore

Many of the straightedge kids in Texas had taken strongly to Krishna Consciousness, and Ray decided to make one of their local bands, Refuse to Fall, the next band on Equal Vision Records. Shelter spent a lot of time down there (along with Guṇagrahi Goswāmī and his KrishnaFest greyhound crew, coincidentally) while Ray worked out his first Equal Vision Records experiment, coaching them on how to write better songs and lyrics.

I wasn't interested in helping them with music, but was happy for any opportunity to answer their questions about Krishna conscious philosophy and practice.

Hi Dad, Can I Have Money?

Ray booked his flight to Vṛndāvana, India - the motherland of Krishna Consciousness.

I wanted to do the same, but I had no money.

Neither Shelter nor KrishnaFest nor ISKCON was able to pay for such a thing. Seemed I could give my life to the institution, but it couldn't give me a plane ticket in return. Guṇagrahi Swami suggested that I ask my parents for the money.

Everyone seemed to think it was a perfect idea. "It's Krishna's money," they said. "Be merciful and engage them in Krishna's service."

I didn't think it would be smart. I had written them letters, but hadn't called since I left San Diego, and I knew they hadn't yet even come to grips with what I was doing. Yet I found myself dialing the temple payphone anyway, with the Swāmī and everyone else sitting around me, listening.

I'm not particularly good at small talk. "Can I borrow about a thousand dollars?" I asked.

"What for?" My dad asked.

"To study at the Vṛndāvan Institute for Higher Education, in India." Wow, it sounded good! This might work!

My dad was not impressed. "We haven't talked to you in months," he said, "and the first time we do you only call to ask us for a thousand dollars so you can go to *India*? No. I'm sorry, Vic. I don't even *want* you to go to India, it's a dangerous place."

The devotees consoled me. My parents, they explained were just, "too attached to their money."

Friends in High Places

One of the benefits of joining ISKCON in America in 1990 is that new guys like me didn't really have to "start at the bottom." There were plenty of vacant positions, and Ray and I seemed pretty well qualified to fill them.

Ray was just a natural born leader. His presence in a room was like the presence of the sun in the sky. And me, I guess I was turning out to be a natural born writer and philosopher? We never really experienced what it was like to be "rank and file new recruits" washing pots and going out all day trying to extract donations from people in parking lots. We were given almost full autonomy to run our own "Shelter program" in the Philly temple, and that included often being given the "guru seat" to give lectures about Krishna consciousness in the temple.

Of course some devotees hated us, but who can blame them for being annoyed by a bunch of wet-eared new kids stepping into the scene like self-appointed saviors of ISKCON? These people had been though a lot of really difficult times in ISKCON and had plenty of sensitive scar tissue as a result.

Most devotees, however, liked us, even loved us — especially the really important leaders in North America.

I was surprised how close I became with many of them. While rolling through Texas I had met Tamāla Kṛṣṇa Goswāmī, who had been one of Prabhupāda's long-time personal assistants, and was one of the eleven people appointed to "succeed" Śrīla Prabhupāda as spiritual leaders of ISKCON. He came with us to an outdoor Shelter show at a festival in Austin. During a break in sound-check, he shouted loudly from where he was standing at a short distance in front of the stage, "Turn up the guitar! Much louder."

Yeah! That's an order from a guru, Ray!

Another leader I had been close with since the very beginning was Jayadvaita Swāmī, Chief Editor of the Hare Krishna magazine, Back to Godhead. He and I would sometimes talk about J.D. Salinger's writing, and he recommended that I read Strunk & White's Elements of Style, and a collection of essays called Radical Chic & Mau-Mauing the Flak Catchers.

Though we never met in person, Satsvarūpa Mahārāja was also close and very supportive. Like Jayadvaita Swāmī, he was also from the very earliest wave of people who began to follow Śrīla Prabhupāda, and like Tamāla Krishna Goswāmī he was also one of the eleven successors to Prabhupāda. The author of Śrīla Prabhupāda's biography, he was my favorite ISKCON author by far (come to think of it, he was almost the only ISKCON author at the time; the only one that wrote and published frequently, at least). I sent him just about everything I wrote, and he would always write me back with encouragement. Once, he said:

"I think you are a talented writer, with a strong, personal voice that is fresh and enthusiastic. I must admit that I rarely find creative writing from contemporary Krishna conscious devotees that I like — they tend to write in a stilted, old-fashioned way — but your writing is alive and I can hear a real person in it."

Straightedge Goes Back to Godhead

While passing the Chief Editor's baton to Jayadvaita Swāmī, Satsvarūpa Mahārāja recommended that he give me a regular column in the magazine. Jayadvaita Swāmī agreed, and decided to launch it with a huge feature article.

The September 1991 issue had only one headline on the cover: "Straightedge Youth - Finding Shelter in Kṛṣṇa."

Whoa! We were blown away! We had only just joined the Hare Krishna's *last year*, and now we were the sole feature on the front cover of Prabhupāda's own magazine!

Here is an excerpt from the first part of my article:

> Last year I joined the Hare Krishna's. And as if that wasn't enough to drive any respectable American mother to tears, these weren't just any Hare Krishna's: they were punk rockers.
>
> Yes, I joined a punk rock Hare Krishna band.
>
> If you want to get accurate about it, "punk" isn't exactly the right term. Nowadays it's called hardcore, specifically, straightedge hardcore. Straightedge is a youth movement whose adherents pretty much follow the four regs (well, at least three of them). All around the world there are hundreds of thousands of straightedge kids who don't take intoxicants, and most of them don't eat meat or gamble. They all look down on casual sex, and some of them are even strictly celibate. No lie.
>
> That was last year. Today I'm sitting behind a computer at ISKCON Philadelphia. On my right there's a desk that has a constant supply of at least fifteen letters from unbelievably intelligent and sincere people all over the world. I spend at least an hour and a half every day writing replies to their inquiries about Krishna consciousness.
>
> Upstairs is the office of the record label we run, Equal Vision Records, which is a showcase for the growing number of Krishna conscious hardcore bands. Through Equal Vision we sell Srila Prabhupada's books and other Krishna conscious music and literature.

Towards the end my persona switched from the down-to-earth conversationalist to uber-humble pure-devotee poet:

> This hardcore arm of Srila Prabhupada's movement has expanded beyond my ability to describe. And it's continuing to expand exponentially. I only hope that more and more devotees will come forward to lend a hand in this wonderful opportunity to give real shelter to souls wandering homeless and aimless through the life-threatening Age of Quarrel.
>
> The best part about the whole thing is that I've been blessed with the constant association of the members of Shelter and Equal Vision, who are such sincere and fired-up devotees. By their mercy, I'm managing to stay in Prabhupada's revolutionary

movement for spreading Krishna consciousness. I pray that they'll continue to treat me so kindly, despite my constant flow of offenses.

Dear Straightedge Guru,

In that issue, BTG[1] also published the full text of my "Equality" pamphlet, followed by pages and pages of the letters I had exchanged with straightedge kids.

Chris from Maryland asked, "Is hiding from my mom that Krishna is the way for me wrong?" I answered:

> When everything is said and done I would say yes, it is wrong. But you have to be careful not to blow her out of the water... Make it gradual, and don't be defensive or self-righteous about it: 'Mom, you're a materialistic demon!' Be open and honest... One of the four pillars of spiritual life is honesty.

He also wanted to know, "When I'm 18, what needs to be done so I can move into a temple?" I replied:

> For now become Krsna conscious as far as possible in your current situation. When 18 comes then we'll worry about 18. Temple life is dead serious and is a big step. My advice is to begin preparing now by following a Krsna conscious life as far as possible. You may not be able to go the whole nine yards right now, but whatever you can do, do it without fail, every day. Then, if and when you move into a temple, you will be able to do it right.

Erika from New Jersey asked, "How do Kṛṣṇas feel about homeless people? Why are they homeless? Did they do something wrong in their past life to deserve being homeless, diseased and ill? Why?" I replied:

---

[1] Almost everyone called the magazine "BTG." ISKCON has a fetish for acronyms.

> A devotee is compassionate to everyone. In reality, everyone is homeless. We can't stay anywhere permanently, not even in our own bodies. At death all of our flimsy, makeshift shelters get torn away. We're kicked out, evicted, homeless.
>
> Yes, homeless people are homeless because of their karma. So, yes, it's their own fault, when you get right down to it. But the spirit-soul doesn't deserve to have anything to do with karma at all. So a devotee doesn't become cold: 'Oh, you deserve to be homeless!' Instead, the devotee realizes, 'You're a spirit soul. You deserve happiness, not suffering.' So a devotee's mercy goes out to everyone. He or she tries to give everyone a home under the shelter of Krsna's lotus feet. That's real welfare work. And that's the real way to take care of the homeless.

Tom from Salzburg, Austria said, "I think it's real hard to control sex."

I replied by saying that it would be hard for a hungry person to give up a piece of pizza, but it's not very hard to give up the same slice if your hunger is already satisfied.

Dan from Pennsylvania brought up a similar topic, "I'm seeing this girl, and we have sex. I don't view it as illicit, though. I love her, and she loves me." I replied:

> Would this 'love' keep going if either party didn't get what they wanted? Try it as an experiment for a month or so. If the relationship is true love, you'll find that by stopping sex your relationship will deepen and become more intimate and exciting. And, if it isn't real love, things will start to fall apart as soon as the bed isn't bouncing.

Emil from New Jersey asked, "I think Krishna's are supposed to be against sense gratification. Correct? But if you believe in not gratifying your senses how can you go to shows and dance and sing along and stuff like that? Isn't that gratifying your senses?"

I replied that sense *activity* is not the same as sense *gratification*. "Gratification" is a selfish thing. Sense activity doesn't have to be selfish. We use our senses to serve others and to serve God. That is sense activity, but not sense gratification.

I sounded like a real guru! And now all the readers of BTG could hear me chirp! My ego felt like a kid waking up on Christmas morning.

CHAPTER TWENTY-TWO:

TROUBLE IN PARADISE

By Hook or By Crook

In the very early years of ISKCON, devotees had spent most of their time dancing on the sidewalks chanting "Hare Krishna, Hare Krishna" while passing out fliers, pamphlets, and small paperbacks in exchange for small donations. During the Christmas season of 1973, however, a few devotees put on wigs, dressed like regular people, and stayed out until the wee hours selling tons of Prabhupāda's books to the throngs of Christmas shoppers.

This radically changed the face of ISKCON. Within months almost everyone had given up on chanting in the streets and dedicated themselves instead to selling more and more books with more and more deceptive and aggressive techniques. They adopted a misappropriated mantra: "By hook or by crook, distribute that book."

By the '80s, "crooks and hooks" had eclipsed the "books," and most ISKCON members found themselves on the streets every day hawking bootlegged Snoopy stickers and various bargain bin brick-a-brack, or short changing *karmīs* on surreptitiously solicited donations to charlatan charities.

It was a far cry from the original Hare Krishna lifestyle, and the whole thing came down in flames around 1986.

By the time I got involved, ISKCON's survivors were trying to rebuild the ruins by returning to a focus on selling Prabhupāda's books. I've often wondered why they didn't think of returning to the *original* ISKCON focus, the original focus of the original Krishna Consciousness movement of Śrī Krishna Caitanya: chanting.

Run a Mile in Santa's Shoes

I hated book distribution.

I could never say that out loud. ISKCON had zero tolerance for negative opinions about book distribution, their sacred cow. "Prabhupāda said book distribution was his heart and soul! Trying to stop book distribution is like trying to stop Prabhupāda's heart! To be against book distribution is to be against Śrīla Prabhupāda!!!"

I didn't hate it because I wasn't a salesman. Even if I was a salesman I doubt I would ever get behind the idea that annoying the public with aggressive and deceptive salesmanship was a great way to represent a spiritual movement. I couldn't comprehend why we should focus on this so strenuously when we could just as easily display the beauty of Krishna consciousness through chanting and dancing, and allow that beauty to attract people.

I stayed as far away from book distribution as I could, but during my first Christmas in ISKCON, they got me. They got us all, the whole Shelter party.

We all relocated our sleeping bags downtown to Govinda's fourth floor, and banged our heads against the brick walls for a week trying to sell books all day to random passers-by in downtown Philly. None of us were any good at it, so at least we could look each other in the eye with sympathy. Most of the time I wandered around inside 30th Street Station, failing to figure out how to stop people from rushing to their trains long enough to convince them that a book about "yoga and meditation" was exactly what they wanted to spend a few bucks on.

Ray vs. Vic

Things were tense between me and the material world. Things were tense between me and my family. In areas like book distribution and sexism, things were tense between me and ISKCON. And now things were getting tense even between me and Ray.

Much of the problem was rooted in artistic discord and my lack of creative input in the band. Some of it may have been rivalry. Most of it was just a result of the fact that our personalities were simply incompatible: He was the archetypal extrovert and I was a textbook introvert.

His approach to preaching seemed so external to me, as if our ultimate goal was to make the whole world move into a temple, shave up, and wear robes and Tarzan-Krishna underwear, giving up toilet paper for good. In his eyes I probably seemed like an incurably stubborn and abstract pessimist, an ideologically elitist wannabe-bookworm and self-made know-it-all self-appointed guru.

We didn't hate each other, but we couldn't seem to work together.

I Have a Dream

"Guṇagrahi Swāmī is on the phone," Bhakta Tony told me, "He wants to talk to you."

Ray was there, he had just returned from India with the enviable new name Raghunath. *Everyone* was there, trying not to look like they had something else to pay attention to as I walked in and picked up the phone.

"Mahārāja?" I said.

"Bhakta Vic?" he said.

"Yes, Mahārāja. Please accept my humble obeisances."

"Glories to Prabhupāda." He replied. "Bhakta Vic, I had a dream."

A dream?

"In my dream," he continued, "there were two Krishna conscious hardcore bands."

Oh...

"Why don't you come down to D.C.," he concluded "and start a second band?"

On one hand, I thought this was ridiculous. I didn't need a "swāmī's dream" to sell me on the idea of getting out of Shelter and doing my own thing! On the other hand, I thought it was endearing, "They made an effort to be gentle about kicking me out."

The 108 Era

Chapter Twenty-Three:

Banned to DC

Instant 108

Immediately after the swāmī's phone call, I sat on the floor with the guitar Bhakta Dave had donated to me, and wrote a song called "Holyname." It took about fifteen minutes.

Bhakta Jay Holtzman used to sing for a straightedge band named Fed Up before he joined Guṇagrahi Swāmī and KrishnaFest. We decided he could sing for the band, so he came up to Philly for a while to brainstorm ideas. The first thing we needed to brainstorm was a name.

Everything I thought of seemed so corny. The best thing I could come up with was "catharsis."

Jay suggested a number.

Yeah! Why bother with words, when we could just use a number and be done with it. And what better number than 108?

There are 108 principle gopīs. I was particularly fascinated by the gopīs, the infinitely beautiful and artistic goddesses who are Krishna's immediate companions, expansions of his intrinsic bliss-potency. We chanted on a strand of 108 beads. The Vedas had 108 principle philosophical books, called Upanishads. The earth was 108 times closer to the moon than the sun, while the sun was 108 times bigger than the moon. There seemed to be an endless supply of mystical things numbering 108.

It was decided, then. The band would be called 108, pronounced "one, oh, eight."

Now that I had a name, I could use the next issue of Enquirer, the fifth issue, to announce the band:

> *direct expression. bypass mind. bypass intellect.*
> *unbroken connection - self to sound.*
>
> *Io8 Io8 iO8 IO8 1O8 108 108 108 108 108 108 108 108*
>
> *against the dead trend. the robot me.*
> *against the polyester person. the modern social entity,*
> *stripped of color and vibrancy.*
>
> *not philosophy. not religion. not interested in public opinion.*
> *the struggle for the real emotion of soul.*
> *not philosophy. not religion.*
> *true self expressed in sound.*

Veganism - The Next Level of Purity

Hare Krishna had been "taking straightedge to the next level of purity," but one day straightedge knocked on our door, offering to take us a rung or two higher on the purity ladder. Yesterday we preached, "It's morally wrong to make animals suffer unnecessarily, *so don't eat meat.*" Today that message echoed back into our own ears, "It's morally wrong to make animals suffer unnecessarily, *so don't drink milk.*"

How did we react?

Defensively.

When the scene produced people even more "cruelty free" than we were, instead of honoring and applauding them, we tried to shoot them down. Maybe we didn't really care about animals so much as we cared about being recognized as the holiest dudes this side of CBGBs, in the holiest cult this side of the Ganges?

Thus began the war between "Krishna-core" and the "Hardline Vegans."

In Enquirer #5 I wrote an attempt at a truce. It was titled, "Mother Cow, Father Bull - Honor Thy Parents."

The main idea was this: To be sustainable, cruelty-free agriculture can't remain dependent on the steel and petroleum machines that are cruel to the environment. To do agriculture without machines, however, we would have to return towards a symbiotic relationship with animals like the bull and cow. So, the best cruelty-free solution would not be one that tries to totally negate any interdependence between humans and animals, as the vegans in hardcore were proposing.

In the article, I responded to several "arguments from the Hard Line." The first argument was: "It's cruel to make bulls work."

My reply: They like it. If you don't believe me go check out the bulls in India and on Hare Krishna farms.

The next argument: "Milk is not good for humans."

My reply: Modern milk might not be healthy, but Vedic culture has, for centuries, venerated the effect of natural milk on human health.

Another argument: "Cow's milk is for calves, not you."

My reply: This is the wrong way to look at nature. Nature is symbiotic. Species are interdependent.

The last argument: "Milk from protected cows is ok, but most milk involves cruelty."

My reply: I agree, milk from modern farms involves cruelty, so it's better to avoid it.

Hardline vegans, however, went overboard in how much stress they placed on avoiding milk: as if vegetarians were evil because they don't. A zealously strict boycott of milk is not the only way to do the best we can against cruelty. It's just as important to make a practical demonstration of a positive alternative: natural, sustainable agriculture based on the cow and bull. And that's what the Hare Krishna farm projects were trying to do.

I think this article helped begin a trend that eventually made a much more tolerant, and sometimes even cooperative and friendly environment between the Straightedge Krishna's and the Straightedge Vegans.

Another Sprawling Mess

Glen and Tony were both like me, in very different ways. Bhakta Glen was introverted and good with a pen, but no good with any musical instruments. DC was close to his hometown, so he flew the Philly nest with me. Bhakta Tony was dark and serious like me, and he could play bass. I enlisted him to play for 108 and took him along with me.

The DC temple was still a sprawling dilapidated mess in the middle of a clean and tidy upscale neighborhood. A huge plot of land, it had been a summer camp before ISKCON bought it in the early '70s. A few small houses were scattered here and there. Prabhupāda had actually lived in one for at least a few days. A narrow horse-stable had been converted into a storage building, as was a tiny, house-shaped shed that used to be the camp's hotdog stand. What used to be the cafeteria were now a kitchen and an unusually simple and spartan temple room. The two-story building next to it probably used to be the campers rooms. Upstairs, small dorms lined either side of the long hallway, with a shared toilet and shower room. Downstairs, a big open space with a stage was probably used by the camp for assemblies. Shelter had packed this place with straightedge kids just a few months ago. The photo on the cover of Quest for Certainty was taken at that show.

Outside one of the houses was a greyhound bus. *The* Greyhound bus. Guṇagrahi Swāmī lived in it, and the KrishnaFest men lived in the house. They would set up their synthesizers and drum pads on the "mall" in front of the Smithsonian museums, where one or two would dance, one or two would sell books to onlookers, and the others would play 70's-pop tunes while singing "Hare Krishna, Hare Krishna."

A Prayer for Me?

The three of us got two of the dorm rooms. I took one for myself, since I was the "party leader." Glenn and Tony would have to share the other one.

My room had a low table with my computer and my stereo. On the wall I hung two big, matt-framed photos of Rādhā-Śaradbihari from Philly. I pushed two pins into the wall below Śaradbihari, to hold his flute — Mother Sudāmani had given it to me as a gift just before I left Philly. On either side of them, I had photos of Rādhārāṇī's closest two friends, Lalitā and Viśākhā, taken of their brass deities at the farm in Pennsylvania. Below, I had a smaller painting of the Pañca-Tattva - Śrī Krishna Caitanya and his four primary associates, flanked on one side by a photo of Prabhupada's face, taken before he left Vṛndāvana, and on the other side by a photo of Dhanurdhara Swāmī sitting in the dirt in front of Govardhana Hill in Vṛndāvana, smiling and gesturing with a cane as he described Krishna's pastimes here.

At night as I lie in my sleeping bag, an uncommonly palpable nightmare overtook me. I wasn't in dream land, I was right there in my room, lying down in my sleeping bag — but I wasn't awake either. From down the long hall, a terrifying cloaked figure very slowly inched towards my room, dry and scraping.

Being asleep, all I could do was lie there and wait.

Drawing near, it began to speak. They were silent words, slow and full of sarcastic malice. "Bhakta Vic," it named me, mocking the word bhakta. Arriving at my door, it removed its hood to reveal the horned skull from Samhain's logo! "Bhakta Vic," it hissed again, gripping the doorknob, "do you have a *prayer* for **me**, Bhakta Vic?"

I woke up!

Proud Owner of a Shack

Within a week or two Tony and Glenn were at each other's throats, so I got permission to move into the camp's former hotdog shed, allowing them to take separate rooms. It was nothing but a decaying shack, its frame slanting towards imminent collapse, but when I moved in, I felt like a homeowner.

I considered it a "two-story building," since I could get into the attic via a ladder. I closed the empty window up there with some trash bags and made the tiny "second floor" my bedroom and storage area. Downstairs became my workspace. I set up my computer, stereo and pictures and made the place fit for human habitation.

When my parent's visited I showed them my "house" like it was a major accomplishment.

They pretended not to be depressed.

Bhakta Zac 108

108 had a name, stickers, articles in the Enquirer, and even a bunch of songs, but we were missing something fairly important: a drummer.

The drummer from World's Collide had taken an interest in Krishna, so... Clearing out one of the rooms in the former horse-stable, we invited him over to jam. He turned out to be pretty damn good, so we changed his name to Bhakta Zac 108 and felt like we had a complete lineup.

He and I practiced every once in a while. I don't really know why the other guys didn't. Maybe it was because we didn't have a bass amp or a PA? Zac and I used a boom-box recorder to make a demo of the songs, so Tony and Jay could practice on their own without needing amplification.

109 Inch Nails

Without playing a single show or even practicing once with a full line-up, we went into the studio to record an EP for Equal Vision Records.

Raghunath was still in charge of EVR at the time and felt that 108 needed a producer. What's really odd is *who* he chose for the role: Shelter's bassist, Chris, the guy with no hardcore background at all, the synthesizer and briefcase guy.

Chris' first task was to find a studio. He found The Station; which, like him, had never heard of hardcore before. It was an 8-track quarter-inch-tape studio built into a basement in Maryland, manned by a newly middle-aged engineer, Trip, and his assistant, Rich. We booked 108 for two weekends in December of 1991.

Zack set up his drums and began discussing the drum sound, using words like "big," "tight," and "powerful" to describe what he wanted.

The engineers and producer were puzzled.

"Like cannibal corpse," Zack suggested helpfully.

It only confused them more.

"The best way to get that sound here," Trip suggested eventually, "would be to use your drums to trigger drum samples from our sampler."

"Well, who knows," I thought, naively, "maybe it'll sound like Nine Inch Nails or something. Let's try it out."

Chris thought it was a fantastic idea, and when he saw the studio's electro-gadgets he knew he had to leverage his extensive experience in that department by putting synthesizers on the record. Again, I thought, "Sure, why not?" So we recorded samples of rivers, chirping birds, and a flute - over which Chris chanted a few Sanskrit verses from the Bhagavad Gītā.

Zack did his tracks with me playing guitar. Then I overdubbed the real guitar tracks, and finally the bass. I played bass because I knew the songs much better than Tony.

He didn't even mind.

I wanted to make a sonic statement that this record was transcendental, an offering to Krishna, so I brought a bell and conch shell, two sounds that begin *ārati* offerings in temples, and recorded them as the intro to the opening song, Holyname.

A Chance in Atlantic City

We recorded all the music that weekend, leaving us the next to record the vocals and do the mix. Before returning to The Station, however, we jumped unexpectedly onto a bill with Ressurection, Worlds Collide, and No Escape.

That show was my first chance to see Bhakta Rob in action for the first time, singing for his new band, Ressurection. Damn, he was good: scary, moody, and loud as hell.

After them, Zack set up his drums, and Worlds Collide set up their equipment. Before they played, they let us play two or three songs. Tony wasn't around, so Eric played Bass.

"You jump around too much," I told Jay after the show. "108 aren't Youth Crew. We're not a posi-straightedge band. 108 is heavy ...and dark. Don't run and hop all over the stage like a bunny, just stand in one place and be hard, heavy, intimidating and intense."

I didn't say it, but I was thinking, "...like Rob."

Vocals

The next day, we went back to The Station to record vocals. For the first time I could actually *hear* what Jay's vocals sounded like.

I wasn't psyched.

"It has to be a straight downbeat," I told him from the control room, as he stood behind the glass in front of a mac, with his headphones on. "It has to be like this, 'I - have - no - e - mo - tion, I - have - no - de - vo - tion, it's - em - pty - mo - tion.' You know? Like that. It's all gotta line up. Like a drum. Like a march. Like a machine, a relentless machine."

I mean, I had already told him (via letter) to do the vocals the same way I did them on the demo. So... WTF?

He tried it again. "I have no emotion! ...I have no devotion! ...It's all empty motion!"

"No," I said bluntly, and repeated the previous demonstration more emphatically.

He tried it again and eventually sort of got it, but it sounded uncertain, unnatural. "That's the idea, but now do it with a lot more intensity, and more growl."

It didn't seem to be working.

"Why don't you take the rest of the day off, and go over the demo and try to get the feel for it," I said. "We can record it tomorrow. I'll just do the vocals for the parts of songs like this where I really want it to be an exact way."

Jay agreed and went back to the temple to study the demo more carefully. I recorded 60% of the vocals, and then called Rob.

"I've got a bunch of vocal parts left," I said, "and I don't feel like Jay fits the band. From what I saw of Ressurection, I think you *do*. You want to do the vocals?"

"Yeah, that's cool." He said. "If it's cool with Jay."

"Yeah," I said, "I'll work on that."

I called the Guṇagrahi Swāmī. "Mahārāja, Jay's mood is just too positive and bright, it doesn't fit what we are trying to do. I'm going to do the vocals with Bhakta Rob."

He called Jay and told him the bad news.

CHAPTER TWENTY-FOUR:
VṚNDĀVANA! VṚNDĀVANA!

Out of the Recording Studio, Into the Holy Land

Right after recording Holyname, Glenn, Tony, Ekendra (Eric from Shelter) and I found ourselves bound for India for a three month extended stay in Krishna's hometown: Vṛndāvana.

Exiting the plane at New Delhi, the first thing I saw on the airport walls was a huge modernistic bas-relief of Viṣṇu lying in the ocean of causality, generating all the "bubbles" of worlds from his pores. I stopped in my tracks and kissed the airport floor!

The weight of the air, and its smell... It seemed like the fragrance and sweat of a lover: not clean or rosy, but better — saturated with identity and intimacy.

In front of the airport, signs warned us not to accept a ride from anyone who didn't have an official taxi license on display. Dhanurdhara Swāmī had already briefed me on this, adding, "Make sure the driver agrees on the price before you get in, and don't let him change it."

Vṛndāvana is about two hours from the airport by taxi. I spent all of it in awe. India was in almost as much disrepair as ISKCON. Everything seemed dangerous, real, vivid and alive.

Besides awe, the ride was saturated with a good bit of white-knuckle fear. The roads had almost nothing in common with the roads of America. "Sanskrit" letters were everywhere, on every traffic sign and billboard. The vehicles were decorated and painted with devotional slogans like "Jai Maaa," "Har Har Mahādev" and so on. Trucks and busses shared the narrow roads with cars, motorcycles, scooters and three-wheeled motorized rickshaws - all of which held at least twice as many people and goods then they were designed for. All this motor-traffic zigzagged around the non-motorized traffic: rickshaw's pulling people on three-wheeled cycles, bicycles, walkers, buffalo and bulls pulling carts, herds of sheep, roaming dogs, and occasionally even a plodding, thorn-chewing camel or a gigantic elephant!

If the big traffic carried twice as much as they should, the smaller vehicles must have carried five to ten times of what any sane person would attempt. I gawked at entire families — husband, wife and two children — traveling on a single motor scooter! What prevented this from imploding in mass destruction must have been nothing less than a constant succession of miracles, or maybe it was a magic incanted by the ever-blaring cacophonous symphony of all those horns?

By the will of providence, our taxi was not smashed by a bus or truck, nor stepped on by an elephant, nor run off the road by a bull. We actually made it alive out of Delhi and its suburbs and gradually entered a much more rural tract, with fields stretching off either side of the road for acres in either direction, small temples popping up here and there amidst the crops.

We were all chanting intently the entire way, half in fear for our lives, half in the delightful anticipation of entering Vṛndāvana —

the place where everyone was Krishna's devotee, the place where Krishna had displayed his most intimate affairs, the most spiritual place in the universe!

And, suddenly, we were there.

I knew because we had stopped under an archway with an inscription that read, "Bhaktivedānta Swāmī Marga." Someone had lowered a gate, like those at railroad crossings, and was probably collecting a dubious tax from the driver.

I immediately got out of the taxi, bowed flat in the dirt at the roadside, and rolled around in the dust until my self-consciousness caught up with me. I was here! I was in Vṛndāvana! And I was covered in her dust!

Rasa-Līlā Tonight

The taxi had let us out in front of ISKCON's Krishna-Balaram Mandir - an absolutely gorgeous thing built in traditional Vṛndāvana style. Tony, Glenn, and Ekendra went to get their rooms, and I went directly into the gurukula building, an international boarding school annexed directly to the right of the temple itself. I had Dhanurdhara Swāmī's room number, and his instruction to come see him as soon as I arrived.

He was delighted to see me and gave me a room a few doors down from his own very cool Gurukula Headmaster office. My room was just an empty concrete rectangle with a heavy door and metal latch, but to me it was as good as a mansion in heaven.

I shared the room with a Bengali who was about my age. "Tonight is rās-līlā at Rādhā-Dāmodar," he said. "You should come with me!" He beamed with a smile that shone like moonlight against his night-dark complexion. I had no idea what "rās-līlā at Rādhā-Dāmodar" was, but it sounded like the most exciting proposition in the world. I entertained the idea that I just might actually wind up seeing the rāsa-līlā - Krishna's dance with the gopīs.

As the sun set on my first day in Vṛndāvana, I left the gurukula with my Bengali roommate, following him into the street. We approached a small herd of rickshaw drivers who sat around on their bikes, shooting the breeze while waiting for customers from the wealthy "foreigner's temple." As we approached they all snapped to attention like pigeons sensing bread crumb, "Yes, hello! Hello!" they called. "Where you are going, sir?" followed by a string of possible destinations I couldn't make out.

My friend was a veteran with this. He bargained one to a price he wouldn't accept, but kept insisting until another driver stepped in and accepted the offer.

The rickshaw moved leisurely down a magical road, Bhaktivedānta Swāmī Marg. Burning wood and leaves saturated the twilight, like musky incense. Lines of sturdy trees screened mysterious temples and *āśramas*. *Sādhu's* walked quietly. Locals cycled. A few three-wheeled motor-rickshaws occasionally passed, beeping, usually carrying quite a few local ladies into the bazaar district. Nothing was clean; all was saturated in dust - a most beautiful haze, making the air simmer like the cinematic effects of filmmakers.

A dense town gradually built up, and the roads gradually became older and bumpier. Finally, we stopped at Rādhā Dāmodara, Jīva Goswāmī's temple, where Śrīla Prabhupāda had lived for 11 years before coming to the West. Across from the temple was a big, walled field, full of bushes and clearly owned entirely by monkeys. "That is Seva-Kuñja," my roommate told me with that same smile. "That is where *rās-līlā* takes place. The *real* one."

The sandstone temple's courtyard was festooned with flags, cloth, tinsel, and an incredible abundance of flowers sewn into strands and hanging everywhere like curtains and streamers. It was packed with people sitting on the marble floor in front of a large, empty stage. Most of them were locals - old men and women with leathery skin, younger *sādhus* with beards and intense glances, semi-portulent proprietors in flashy yellow attire, and one or two westerners.

Eventually, musicians came and sat at the side of the stage, followed shortly by a troupe of children, about 12 years old I'd guess, dressed to the hilt as Rādhā, Krishna and the gopīs. Swirling and twirling, they danced and played their parts.

Somehow, by intuition and basic knowledge of *rāsa-līlā* I could make out some of the Hindi. At one point Krishna was circling the gopīs by twirling around at higher and higher speed, on his knees. The dancing and drumming was amazing.

The whole thing wasn't over till close to midnight. That was new for me. "Temple life" for me meant "lets go to sleep ASAP and wake up ridiculously early."

"There are no more rickshaws," my Bengali friend said to me. "We will walk."

Vṛndāvana was even more profound late at night. The moonlight multiplied her mysteries a thousand-fold. The streets were calm but for the sounds of animals: peacocks sometimes, or a cow here and there, but mostly dogs. "Take this stick," my friend said. "If dogs come, you don't have to hit them. Just raise the stick over your head and say, '*hut!*'"

I had a pretty strong fear of dogs, having been bit on the eyelid as a kid, and mildly traumatized by my mom's short-lived attempt to keep a poodle who hated my 7-year old guts. As we walked, dogs often came sniffing, sometimes barking in a pack. My 'hut, hut' didn't do much, but the '*hut hut!*' from my roommate got rid of them.

Every now and then Vṛndāvan had a streetlight. It would make the trees incredibly gorgeous, like green jewels against the black-velvet sky.

I was in love.

The Inside Out of Kīrtan

Raghunath had told me, "There is a devotee in Vṛndāvana you have to meet. He does 24-hour kīrtan. He is like the Inside Out of kīrtan, with mosh-parts and everything."

I didn't have to look for him; he was almost impossible to miss.

He looked nothing like the others, sitting in the temple with a handful of people around him, unconcerned with his appearance, wearing thick woolen socks and all sorts of brownish rag-like cloth wrapped around him here and there in a completely unique way, some of them looking almost like burlap. One of his legs stuck out around the side of his harmonium, with a huge strand of bells wrapped around the ankle. From time to time, when all else failed, he would enforce the tempo by stamping that belled-foot on the ground.

I sat down to join him.

He acknowledged by looking straight into my eyes without hesitation or pretense. Those eyes were intense, piercing, powerful things that simultaneously delighted and embarrassed with their attention. He used them constantly, the same way most people use their hands: to gesture, get things done, and even pull people in closer. They kept pulling me closer. They told me to play karate. They told me to sing louder. They told me I had a place here, in this sonic realm, with him.

Raghunath was right. He *was* hardcore.

The drummer next to him played with an expertise and authority light-years beyond anything I had heard in the West. The karatāl too sounded completely different from the "cling, clang, shrang" they produced in the West. Here they played the karatāl on their edges, with intricate trills between crystal clear bell-like accents.

The kīrtan tempo rose up to D.R.I. speed, and suddenly crashed down into slow mosh parts as epic as Slayer. The melodies changed constantly and almost every note had some specialty to it, some ornament or nuance, which his eyes told me to pay attention to.

Compared to this, the kīrtan in the West seemed like a concert of elementary school students or a painting made with crayons. His kīrtan was so far above and beyond all others I had ever heard, yet not for a millisecond was he or it ever "sophisticated" or self-conscious in the least. Nor was it calculated, it flowed naturally and was easy to relate to and *feel*.

When he sang his eyebrows furrowed and he often stared intently at something I couldn't see. His head, and sometimes even his whole body, shook with the intensity of his expression. The whole thing was as raw, real, and desperate as Negative Approach.

> Hare Krishna, Hare Krishna
> Krishna Krishna, Hare Hare
> Hare Rāma, Hare Rāma
> Rāma Rāma, Hare Hare

Over and over again, twenty-four hours a day, every day, year after year... Nothing else. No filler.

This was the real thing!

This was what the "International Society for Krishna Consciousness" was supposed to be. I realized that I was finally sitting in a real kīrtan with a real devotee. Instantly, he became dear to me. I felt proud of this westerner who actually got it right. In him I found someone I could truly admire.

His name was Aindra, and he had just released a new kīrtan recording, Vṛndāvana Mellows. I eagerly bought it from the temple bookstall, and it completely changed the way I experience life.

Yet, although he came to mean everything to me, I would never once say a single word to him.

I've often wondered why.

One thing is that, when someone means a great deal to you, you become shy and worried about doing or saying something that might change the relationship. Another thing was that there never a reason for any words between us. I would come to his kīrtan, sit down, give him my energy, and he would look into me and communicate with his eyes. What need was there for words? A third reason: he was dangerous. I instinctually knew that if I got any closer to him my already insane life would go completely out of control.

Nectar of Devotion

My main reason for being here was the Vṛndāvana Institute for Higher Education, and I spent a few hours each day in courses, especially in Dhanurdhara Swāmī's Bhagavad Gītā and Nectar of Devotion classes. Mahārāja's personal copies of those books were impressive; almost twice as thick as they should be, brimming with post-it notes stuck to almost every page, with his study notes scrawled on them and overflowing into the margins.

Studying intently with teachers like him, who had seriously scrutinized the books, chanting everyday with Aindra, the greatest kīrtaniya in the world, and going here and there around and about Vṛndāvana... How could I leave this? Vṛndāvana was everything I had dreamed Krishna consciousness would be. Here, "Krishna" wasn't just some adjunct to straightedge and vegetarianism, it wasn't just a checklist of mandatory conformities, it wasn't just another religion where a "search and replace" had been done substituting "Prabhupāda" for "Jesus." Here in Vṛndāvana Krishna was *real*, and *completely uncensored* in all his fully wild, mind-bending, unconventional, thrilling, raw, pleasure-bomb uniqueness. Here in Vṛndāvana I could almost *hear* Krishna's flute still echoing from the trees, and the peacocks still answered his song in the midnight moonlight.

I told the Swāmī that I wanted to stay for good.

He appreciated the sentiment but said, "Krishna consciousness means to please Krishna, and we do that by adhering to the order of the spiritual master. Śrīla Prabhupāda wanted us to spread Krishna consciousness in the West, and the preaching you are doing there is too important to stop. But you should come back to Vṛndāvana regularly, maybe every year, and spend more and more time here."

I decided that Dhanurdhara Swāmī should become my guru, and I asked him to accept me as a disciple. He gravely suggested that we try out the relationship for a year.

Time Won't Dye My Substance Pale

The only place in India I really cared to be was Vṛndāvana, but Dhanurdhara Swami did take me to other places as well. In the suburbs of Delhi we stayed for a day or two in the impressive home of the wealthy owner of Surya light bulb company. In Bombay we had lunch at the Birla's beachfront mansion, a very wealthy family who gives lots of money to ISKCON.

Our most significant trip was to Māyāpura, in West Bengal. Vṛndāvana is Krishna's hometown, and Māyāpura is said to be Krishna Caitanya's. Śrī Krishna Caitanya is the personality who opened the door to Vṛndāvana, revealing Krishna as the most intimate, personal, vulnerable and spontaneous core of divinity, and providing a path of similarly spontaneous, personal, and intimate devotional practice, which can bring our own consciousness into unreserved contact with Krishna's. He was the original founder of what was not the Hare Krishna movement.

Vṛndāvana has been a place of saints and *sādhu's* for hundreds of years now, with thousands of temples crammed into every nook and corner. Māyāpura, on the other hand, has relatively few. In Vṛndāvana, the ISKCON temple exists amidst a well-established Krishna conscious culture. In Māyāpura, however, the ISKCON temple dominates the culture. It is a huge, sprawling town unto itself, and there seems to be almost nothing else besides it and its very near uncles from the Gauḍīya Maṭh.

Māyāpura is the headquarters of ISKCON management, and I was there in March, when all the managers of the world would converge for their yearly management meetings.

Dhanurdhara Swami arranged for me to get away from it all. Thanks to him I stayed in the gurukula — a peaceful complex of thatched-roof mud huts nestled among palm trees. It was nice to live like that for a few days, showering outside in the morning with water from a hand-pumped well, eating incredible food from banana-leaf plates.

Mahārāja also took me on the *parikrama*. In Vṛndāvana, *parikrama* was among my favorite things to do, walking from one sacred place to another. But this was very different. Hundreds of people were involved, including dozens of the international managers from the international management convention atmosphere I thought I would be escaping.

I felt out of place where I really wished I didn't. All the big leaders seemed to have their own thing going on, their own inter-personal world, and the rest of us seemed like spectators at their event. I watched them doing kīrtan and heard them speaking about the events that happened at these holy places, but I felt removed from the whole thing — distant, like I was only permitted to admire it all from afar.

Nonetheless I did get the inspiration to write the song Pale. Here is how I described it on a flier that explained the lyrics:

> I had been walking around Śrī Māyāpur for the past four days, barefoot, with my Guru Maharaja and hundreds of other devotees. All day long we would walk and sing Hare Krishna, sometimes stopping for a gigantic chanting and dancing party, lasting for hours and hours.
>
> These parties happened at least twice a day. Everyday. And everyday these 40-50 year old devotees would be jumping around like little kids - smiling and singing and rolling in the dusty sand. They looked completely stoned, dancing with each other and cracking everyone up - for hours on end.
>
> Here were these middle-aged people partying down like no tomorrow — twice a day everyday — without the crutch of drugs, alcohol or sexuality. My mind was blown.
>
> I mentioned it to my Guru Maharaja, as we laughed in the Indian sun. He said, "We're the only ones who made it through. All the people from the '60s, all the rebels and hippies, got regular jobs and families and live boring lives in the suburbs now. Out of all my friends, only the devotees were able to stick to their philosophy and never give in and become normal like everyone else."

CHAPTER TWENTY-FIVE:

BROKEN HOMES, FORGOTTEN FATHERS

108 House Usurped

Henry was a very wealthy devotee in DC who was a big fan of what we were doing with our bands and had become quite involved with us, especially Shelter. Before I had left for India, he promised to renovate the old horse-stables, and have them transformed them into a "108 house" with a front room for living and working, and space in the back for rehearsing. I wasn't thrilled to have left Vṛndāvana, but at least I could look forward to returning to a place we could call our own, a place to consolidate and focus our efforts.

It was about one in the morning when the taxi from the airport dropped us off in front of 10310 Oaklyn Drive. The temple property was very dark, but we walked over to the house and were psyched to see a new sliding-door at the entrance, with address numbers beside it spelling out, "108."

Wow, we really had our own place!

Opening the door, however, the smell of half a dozen or so sleeping men leaked out, wilting our smiles. I walked inside to find that KrishnaFest had occupied the building, and was sprawled in sleeping bags across our would-be living room!

One meek devotee was awake and greeted us cheerfully. "Welcome back to the West, prabhus."

I was in no mood for being nice. "What the hell is going on here?" I said, "This is temporary, right?"

He, of course, had no answers. It wasn't his decision.

I returned to my former hot-dog shack and Tony and Glenn to their rooms in the Samhain-haunted dorms. It irritated me, and I wondered why the man who paid to renovate the building didn't seem to care that the place was being used for something totally different from what it seemed he intended. Guṇagrahi Goswāmī explained something to the effect that 108 was a branch of KrishnaFest, so the facility belonged to KrishnaFest.

And this and that, and that and this…

Whatever.

I didn't feel like fussing about it. Devotees are supposed to be tolerant and unconcerned with external circumstances, right? Maybe I had misunderstood Henry's intentions.

Forgotten Father's Day

Part of being an "important" or "advanced" Hare Krishna devotee was to be as busy as a business executive. I emulated the swāmī's by getting my own "Day-Timer," and reading "Seven Habits of Highly Effective People." I was that busy with my "preaching." I was *that* important.

I made a careful point to schedule a call to my dad on Father's Day. But I missed it. Then, after trying to call, I wrote him this letter:

> I'm totally sorry for screwing up on father's day. I mean it - I'm sorry.
>
> There's no excuses, but I just want to say that I was totally busy that entire weekend - traveling all over the North East, between Philly, New York, and Potomac - and there were a million and two things going on. I had even wrote down in my "day timer" to call you on that Sunday; but the weekend was so busy that I never even got around to opening up my day timer that day.
>
> That's not an excuse but it's just so that you know it's not because I never think of you or something but because of extraordinary circumstances.
>
> I'm really sorry. When I woke up on Monday morning I realized that yesterday was father's day. I called you a few times when I thought you would just be getting into work, but you were never at your desk and the answering machine wasn't on either.
>
> I'm sorry.

But he had already mailed me his letter, which poignantly expressed a lot of pain and frustration:

> We are writing this letter because the events of this Father's Day require explanation. From your point of view this was probably just like all of the other trivial non-Krishna holidays, and missing by one day wasn't such a bad performance. For us, however, this was not an isolated incident, but just the next in a long line.
>
> You are our only child and we focus all of our "parenting" attention on you: this is neither your doing, nor will you undo it - it is so. Always we thought you would be an important part of our family. At this time of your life it is easy for us to understand that family doesn't come first and that you are very busy trying to establish yourself professionally. Unfortunately, we feel we are being crowded out of even a minor role in your life, and that your religion is doing this to us.

> Mark my words: I am not talking about 5000 year old Vedic teachings; I'm talking about the ISKCON organization. Their rules and practices have slowly but steadily removed us from your world. Yes, we are allowed into your circle if we follow your rules, even if only for a few hours. We are free to go in your direction, but you cannot move in our direction. Slowly all non-devotees are pushed out of significant roles in your life. Apparently it is a goal of the ISKCON policies.
>
> We have had some success in accepting your choices and affiliations, but are still without a clue as to what you think you are doing. When you missed Father's Day a black mood overtook us and we thought that our efforts are in vain; the wall stands as tall as before. We realize that you were and are still a headstrong, willful boy who will do what he pleases. This is a very sad realization, but we see it clearly now.
>
> Therefore our relationship has passed through a doorway; and it is impossible to retrace our steps and return to the other side. That time is forever gone. There are only memories, sweet dreams and the dark, unknowable future. Present is prologue to the future; our hopes and spirit ride on a very low tide.

Three days later, he sent another:

> I was thinking about the letter we just sent you and imagined your reaction. I hope you're not too put off - I think it's time we are as honest as possible with each other.
>
> I also thought that you are probably asking a question like "Just what do they want from me?" A good question. I want to be in your thoughts, I want you to think about me and feel good inside. I want to be important to you just as you are important to me. I want to feel you returning my love - I don't want to love the void.
>
> In order that we may remain in each other's thoughts we need to share. That's why I read your books and eat prasadam and cook for Krishna. I'm trying to be a part of your life. I have no need for any of these things except that they bring me closer to you.

> When love is a one-way street it is very sad and depressing. If this is a one-way street please let me know so that I can abandon false hope and make the best of what I am left.

My reply to these two letters mostly did exactly what my dad expected, defended myself. But after that ugly reflex was spent I wrote:

> I want to share. What do you want me to share? I try to share your stuff too. I look at your pictures, I read the articles you send, and I ask you about Grandma Mindy and all of that stuff. I try.
>
> For your information, you are very often in my thoughts. 90% of the time it is very positive.
>
> How should I return your love? By changing back into jeans and long hair? I thought I was returning your love - I'm sorry it didn't reach you.

A few days later, my Mom called and we talked through it.

Dad then sent a much brighter letter, clearly articulating his valid concerns and critiques:

> My Dearest Son;
>
> I'm proud of our family (the three of us)! I'm proud of Mom for being so direct and calling you to communicate so directly. I'm proud of you for standing up to your father with such strength. I always wanted you to think for yourself, If I had a goal in your upbringing, that was it. So now I must accept the results of your thinking. I do.
>
> The robes and haircuts and chanting and dancing aren't the problem - it's the distance (not physical, but mental) between us. I know that the distance is inevitable, and that with other choices you may have made the distance would be also there. It's one of the difficult parts of having a child reach self-sufficiency, and become a man.
>
> "Learn about me from me." That's it. Exactly what I want! I want to learn about you from you; that is what has been denied me. I

> don't know what you are thinking, or were thinking when you
> made your decisions, or when you make your current decisions. I
> know, the decisions are yours to make, I don't want to run your
> life, I want to understand what I can and be a part of what I can.
> Mom tells me that you said that you believe I have an ulterior
> motive to everything I say or do: that I'm always trying to
> disprove, or belittle or somehow get the advantage over you.
>
> It's true I do have a motive to much of our communications: I am
> opposed to your membership in ISKCON (notice carefully - no bad
> words or thoughts about Krishna or anything Vedic). I try to show
> you other avenues or sources that have merit and value. Why? So
> that you won't restrict yourself to only the ISKCON stream.
>
> My dislike of ISKON is based on my belief (and experience with
> you alone) that it is an isolationist framework. They want to
> separate you from the (purportedly) evil world. Mom and I are on
> the wrong side of that barrier. It will take a lot to convince me
> that isolation is good for you. It may be a way to solve some
> problems, but on balance I think it is not the proper avenue for a
> lifetime.
>
> I learned the 4 phases of life from a book that you gave me for
> Christmas: Readings in Vedic Literature by Satsvarupa dasa
> Goswami. I see the four orders to be a reasonable prescription for
> a social and economic order. During the second 25 years, one is
> working and supporting those in the other ages of life. Without
> the work done in the second period, all of the other periods would
> not be possible. Why are you excused from this important
> contribution to society? If the 4 orders of life have been found
> effective and useful over the 5000 years of Vedic tradition, why
> would you want to discard that knowledge and tradition? Could
> you be missing out on something that is really important to life
> which you have not recognized yet?

I already knew ISKCON was messed up, but I didn't see a better alternative to achieve Krishna consciousness.

As for the four orders of life, frankly, I thought of myself as being beyond all that. I was already practicing pure devotional service, so what would be the point of doing things that help bring one to the point of practicing pure devotional service? I knew my father was very intelligent, but I wasn't ready to accept that he might have a leveler view of the issue than the swāmīs who were guiding me. They were encouraging me to skip the second order of life (marriage and any modicum of normalcy) and jump straight to the conclusion: renouncing everything, cutting off the world, giving up family and so on - in favor of "pure devotional service."

CHAPTER TWENTY-SIX:
LET'S TALK ABOUT SEX, BABY

Discussing Celibacy with Hot High School Girls

Now and then, on unusual days, I would wind up out on the DC Mall in front of the Smithsonian with the electro-mantra-synth-rockers of KrishnaFest. High school kids on field trips would always wander by and occasionally stop for a minute or two to get a book or ask a question. A very cute, perky, and friendly little blond and her taller, thinner, brunette friend somehow strayed away from their field trip to discuss Krishna consciousness with me for a very long time.

The topic was sex.

"Are you guys allowed to have girlfriends?" they asked.

"Some devotees marry," I said, "but I've accepted a vow of lifelong celibacy."

"That's terrible!" the blonde said, emphatically. "Come on. You're missing out on one of the most amazing, beautiful things in life!"

I could take two angles in response. I could either try to explain that sex wasn't so amazing, or I could try to explain that it is amazing, but it's amazingness is a reflection of something far more amazing. I decided to start with the first and try to segue into the second.

"Sex isn't so amazing," I set out to explain, "even insects do it."

She looked at me in a way that is hard to describe, one of those looks that expresses four or five different, contradictory things simultaneously; a look that only women know how to do, and men find it hard to even comprehend. "If you're not having sex," she said slowly, "how do you know it isn't amazing?"

"Do you have to put your hand in fire to know that it burns?"

"Oh, come on," she protested. "Haven't you ever had sex?"

When they heard my answer they gasped in shock. "You've never had sex and you are going to be celibate for the rest of your life? Why are you throwing your life away like this?"

"I must be crazy, right?" I said, laughing. They also laughed in agreement. "Sex really is a very universally important thing, a special, amazing thing, the greatest pleasure in the world. I want to give that up? I am still a young man, why would I want to give up sex?"

"Because you're crazy," they suggested.

"Do I really seem crazy?" I asked.

"No, you seem smart, but..."

"Then maybe there is some other explanation. Maybe there is something better than sex. Maybe sex, as great as it is, is just a reflection of something even better, something even more pleasurable and blissful."

"Well, what would that be?" the blonde asked.

"Well," I said, feeling more like a member of their gender than they realized, "What if sexual intimacy is just a reflection of our intimacy with God? What if you could have sex *with God*? If sex is great, imagine how great it would be with the *supreme* lover."

They didn't expect to hear that.

"500 years ago, Śrī Krishna Caitanya came to share that with the world; to share the idea that the supreme sexual impulse can be satisfied only in relation to the supreme lover, and that the way to begin to establish that relationship with God is by singing his names. Which is what we are doing here right now."

As I gestured towards the band, I noticed that they *were all staring at me*.

They seemed extremely concerned that I had been talking intimately to two very well endowed high-school seniors for about half an hour straight. The Swāmī sent someone over to inform me that I was needed elsewhere.

I excused myself from the girls and gave them a magazine and book as a parting gift.

Guṇagrahi Swāmī sat down with me and tried to explain that women just want to get inside my *dhoti* and inside my head, and I really should avoid spending so much time talking to them.

There is Indeed a Punk Among Us!

ISKCON sexism was a non-stop issue for me, bothering me at every step. I had never sent my letter to the GBC; one of the Swāmī's had probably assured me it was unnecessary. But now, by late 1992, I decided it was time to make a more concerted effort about this problem that no one seemed to be in a rush to fix or even address honestly.

I sat at the computer at my desk in my converted hot-dog shack of a home, and started writing a 4 page pamphlet called Anartha-Nivṛtti.

That title means "The Process of Purging Worthless Things." It is a phrase used by Śrī Rūpa Goswāmī for the stage that should immediately follow after one begins devotional practices. This title was outlandishly bold, for it meant that ISKCON's policies towards women were as worthless as all the other things that a spiritualist must purify: addiction to sense gratification, false-ego, disrespect of guru and Krishna, and so on.

Rather than tackle the issue in an abstract, philosophical way, I decided to be very specific and concrete. I identified a few specific instances of sexism in ISKCON daily life: women have to stand in the back of the room at any temple function, women are not permitted to give the morning classes on Śrīmad Bhāgavatam, women are not allowed to lead kīrtans when men are present. Then I then laid out the desired changes, including floor-plans detailing how to arrange men and women in the Boston, Brooklyn, Philly, and DC temple rooms to maintain āśrama decorum without putting women into the offensively inferior positions.

With several dozen photocopied pamphlets in my shoulder bag, I traveled to the four temples I was focusing on and handed my pamphlet to the residents, or slipped them under closed doors.

I didn't exclude the doors of the Swāmīs and Temple Presidents, either.

They *flipped*.

They complained to Dhanurdhara Swāmī who relatively sternly instructed me that criticism of the policies of superiors in ISKCON cannot be done so boldly and tactlessly. He asked why I didn't consult with him before doing this, and said something that would rattle disturbingly around my head for years, "Maybe I agree with you, but what if I don't? By writing this and distributing it like that, without even consulting me first, you may have inadvertently been making a statement that your own guru is full of Anartha and needs to be purified by you."

The only people who were happy about Anartha-Nivṛtti were a few grateful ISKCON women (not all) and the majority of hardcore kids who had become involved over the last year, almost all of whom had similar perplexions on the subject as I.

The unwelcome reception bothered me, but not as much as the content of the objections, focusing nothing on what was said and everything on how it was said and who said it. This kind of inability to conduct intelligent self-scrutiny was one of the only things about ISKCON that I liked less than sexism.

My pamphlet changed nothing, but in hindsight I like to believe it contributed to the momentum that, decades later, eventually started to achieve these changes.

Prior to writing Anartha-Nivṛtti I had carefully nursed and even propagated the idea that all of ISKCON's flaws were the result of spiritually immature madness in the early '80s. Now that we had great reformers in place, I reasoned, everything weird would be repaired. After seeing how these "reformers" reacted to my pamphlet, however, I began to doubt the practicality of this optimism. I had thought I could help create a positive change in ISKCON, but now I began to see that it is almost impossible to help someone who doesn't want your help. I had pictured ISKCON as a community striving nobly for reform, and therefore open to critique, but this experience very clearly showed me otherwise.

But I still didn't give up.

I couldn't.

You can't just fall out of love.

I was like a woman married to a man she thought she could "change." Even if my eyes clandestinely wandered on occasion, they could find no better destination. *How else* could I achieve Krishna consciousness if not in the International Society for Krishna Consciousness?

I Only Watched...

A few weeks after the failure of Anartha-Nivrtti, I got a call to attend a private meeting with a swāmī who I knew fairly well and who was in charge of many important projects.

When I arrived there was no one else in the room, which was unusual. He asked me to sit at a table with him, which was also strange - a *sannyāsī* usually sat in a higher seat. Something was obviously up, and the air felt tense.

"The GBC instructed me to meet with everyone who serves under me," he said, "to explain and apologize for an unfortunate incident I was involved in recently."

The air got a lot more tense.

"Over the past few months I fell into a very unfortunate habit of watching pornography."

I forgot how to breathe.

"All I did was watch," he said, escalating the surreal discomfort. "I did not want it to go any further, so I brought it to the attention of my Godbrothers, who instructed me to bring it out in the open. So I am letting you, and everyone who serves with me, know about it. I apologize for this weakness."

I didn't know what to say or do.

"Do you have any questions about it?"

How can you ask questions about something that has paralyzed your brain? Um... "How could anyone *just watch* porn *for a month*?" Um... "Where did you get the tapes?" I wouldn't really want to know the answers, so I didn't bother to ask. I just wanted to leave the room as quickly as possible and get somewhere I could breathe.

My dismay over this incident is not about porn, it's about *sannyāsīs,* swāmīs feeling the need for it.

I'm not "against" pornography or associated trades, although I must admit that the modern forms of these things almost always wind up extremely exploitive and unattractive. I speak from experience because, in the role of a computer programmer, I worked with some of these companies for a few years at one point. 90% of it or more is anything but sexy.

Vedic culture is *far* less Victorian than you would probably imagine, especially if your only exposure to it is through conventional ISKCON channels, or through post-Muslim, post-Christian India. Ancient sculpture and Sanskrit texts reveal that Vedic culture was shockingly straightforward and liberal about sex. Gender concepts and sexual practices that our supposedly modern and liberal culture find very difficult to comprehend and deal with in healthy, productive ways — like homosexuality, third gender, polygamy, "prostitution," and pornography — were integrated parts of Vedic society. If you find this doubtful, pause for a minute to remember that this culture produced the Kāma Sūtra and has *explicitly* hardcore erotic pornographic sculpture adoring the exterior walls of many of their *temples.*

In Manu Saṁhitā, Manu says, "There is nothing wrong with sex and other vices, these are natural, but there is great virtue in curtailing them and giving them up."

I have nothing against sex, or even pornography in theory, but this man was a *sannyāsī*. The primary trait of a *sannyāsī* is supposed to be their renunciation and absolute abstinence from any sexual behavior at all. On that basis, they were given immense power and respect in ISKCON. People bow when they walk in a room. People sit on the floor and put them on a couch. People follow their orders and serve their needs and demands. If one could be a *sannyāsī* in ISKCON yet watch pornography behind the scenes... then, *what the hell was going on here with all this bowing and respect and so on?*

More importantly, much more, *what the hell was going on with the viability of becoming Krishna conscious?*

Was the whole thing just a facade? A month or two earlier, I had tried to convince those hot high-school chicks on the Mall that chanting Hare Krishna gives access to a pleasure greater than sex. What about that? The swāmī's had been chanting for decades and were supposedly the most advanced devotees. If they were still getting hooked on porn, was the bliss of Krishna consciousness even real?

I had my armor to protect my dedication to ISKCON from assaults, but even with armor, if you get smashed on the chest with a mace it hurts like hell.

And, if you smash it hard enough, enough times, even armor breaks.

I relied on the Gītā verse, *api cet sudūrācāro*, wherein Krishna says, "Even if one slips into very bad habits, he will quickly be reformed because his heart is sincerely fixed on attaining me." I decided to try and admire the bravery and honesty it took for a *sannyāsī* to call people in one by one and admit to watching porn.

No one even talked about it.

Sexist Things Krishna's Say

> *Aren't you sick of being seen as just a piece of meat? An exploitable toy? I want the Hare Krishnas out of hardcore, and I'll tell you why: blatant sexism. Sexism has no place in our scene. Female domination and male subordination must end!*

That's how I opened the "Sexist Things Krishna's Say" article in Enquirer #6, which was attempt to unexpectedly flip the tables and show a plethora of Prabhupāda quotes about the *superiority* of women.

> *[Prabhupāda] belittles the male's role in marriage by repeatedly describing the wife as, "the better half of the husband." (SB 1.7.45)*
>
> *A man is portrayed as spiritually incompetent. The "foolish" and "hard-hearted" man is said to be completely dependent on the*

mercy of his "good wife." Without her help he cannot be elevated. Prabhupāda says, "the wife is considered to be the source of all liberation." (SB 3.14.17) Thus, "Husbands as a class cannot repay their debt to women, either in this life or in the next." (SB 3.14.21). "The wife is mentioned here as ishta, which means 'worshipable.'" (SB 4.13.12)

> The spiritual master of Śrīla Prabhupāda's guru instructs that the wife should always be seen as the greatest exalted devotee. The husband should respectfully place the dust of her feet on his head, and serve her like a menial servant. He is to serve her every meal, taking for himself only what she leaves behind. And what fate awaits a husband who won't do all this? Surely, he falls down into hellish existence. (Bab., part 1)

Next to this I had a painting of the Hera Pañcamī festival of Goddess Laxmī, showing the goddess on a throne surrounded by women who were forcing men with bald heads and pony tails to bow down in supplication, threatening them with sticks.

> Women are advised not to be allured by men, who are death-like representatives of Māyā [illusion and lust] "A woman foolishly looks upon māyā in the form of a man, her husband. A woman, therefore, should consider her husband... to be the arrangement of the external energy of the Lord for her death, just as the sweet singing of the hunter is death for the deer." (SB 3.31.41-42)

> Women, on the other hand, are to be seen as embodiments of divinity and the representatives of intelligence (SB 4.25.21). Krishna himself declares all these good qualities to be feminine, "Among women I am fame, fortune, fine speech, memory, intelligence, steadfastness, and patience." (Gītā 10.34) Even the ultimate source of intelligence, the Vedas (the body of knowledge on which the Hare Krishna movement is based) is treated as being of feminine gender. (SB 3.24.15)

> Hare Krishna's claim that their movement is based on spiritual equality. The truth, however, is that women are awarded absolute superiority, even in the realm of the soul. "The soul... is supposed to be originally a woman." (SB 3.31.41) Hare Krishna's boldly assert that the highest spiritual perfection is exclusively in the domain of the female (Cc. Mad.8.79). Without serving those most

perfect women, a man has no hope of entering the spiritual world (Cc Mad.8.223). It is absolutely impossible, they say, for a male to attain that level of perfection, he must first become a woman (Cc. Mad.8.225).

Obviously this article was a parody, but by giving this glaringly one-sided interpretation I hoped to demonstrate that the male chauvinism in ISKCON was based on similarly one-sided interpretations.

> *Female chauvinism is a distorted view of Krishna consciousness. Male chauvinism is an equally distorted view. Both positions are based on hasty, unwarranted conclusions deduced from isolated quotes taken out of context.*

Women are More Intelligent

Sexism was so hard to root out of ISKCON because Prabhupāda himself had definitely said a lot of things that were quite negative about women. The more deeply I studied Gītā and Bhāgavatam the more I realized that these were not the primary source material for such statements. Some of his statements were easy to trace to Cāṇakya, a misogynist political strategist. Others seemed related to his own less-than-satisfying experience in marriage. Others seemed traceable to the way he was educated by the British at Scottish Churches University in Calcutta.

Some of his followers claim that inferiority of women as a gender is a Vedic concept, a "tradition." This memoir isn't really the place for a thorough examination of their specific claims, but after years of research under the guidance of scholars, my opinion is that the Vedas do not conclude that women are "less intelligent", "more lusty" or "inferior" to men. Quite the contrary, Krishna makes a very direct and obvious statement in Gītā (10.34) that women epitomize many superior human qualities, including intelligence and forbearance:

> *kīrtiḥ śrīr vāk ca nārīṇāṁ smṛtir medhā dhṛtiḥ kṣamā*

"Among women I am the goddess Kīriti - the epitome of venerable reputation, Śrī - the epitome of beauty and opulence, Vāk - the epitome of excellent speech, Smṛti - the epitome of memory and contemplation, Medhā - the epitome of intelligence, Dhṛti - the epitome of forbearance, and Kṣamā - the epitome of forgiveness."

So, were Prabhupāda's teachings colored by the circumstances of his nature as an individual?

An ordinary person would consider this an obvious given — *everyone* speaks from their own perspective. Most members of ISKCON, however, considered it a cardinal blasphemy. For them *everything* Prabhupāda said was *absolutely* perfect *absolute* truth. The fact that Prabhupāda often said contradictory things in different circumstances didn't seem to trouble them. The fact that Prabhupāda said that *śāstra* alone points to the absolute truth also didn't seem to register.

CHAPTER TWENTY-SEVEN:

108... SLOW OUTTA THA GATE

Weirder Than You Crew

108 was going nowhere, and wasn't getting there very fast either. We told the world we were a band almost a year ago, and recorded a record about half a year ago — but the record still wasn't out, and we hadn't played a real show other than jumping on stage in between other bands. We didn't even practice with a full lineup.

That wasn't going to change anytime soon either, because Tony and I would be spending a few months playing guitar and bass for Shelter, on their first European tour.

We decided to think of it as a way to advertise the promise of 108 over there in the other world across the sea. We dubbed a few dozen copies of the 108 "spoken word" cassette — a wild bit of hardcore psychedelia with kīrtan by Yamunā devī, short sound bites from

Prabhupāda lectures made into strange loops, and me reading 108 lyrics with corresponding guitar riffs looped in the background — and took them along to sell on the tour, as evidence of the weird spiritual scariness we hoped 108 would become.

Shelter came down to ISKCON DC to pick us up. I remember the rocks in the gravel under my feet in the parking lot as I got into the van to leave. It was a relief to get away from the weird atmosphere created by the porn-confession, and it was exciting to leave the country with a band.

Steve Reddy and John Porcelly were on the tour too. Steve had decided to commit to being a temple-dwelling Hare Krishna, and Porcell decided to take the plunge too. When kids saw Porcell playing guitar for Shelter, with beads, ponytail, and shaved head, they were amazed. "Whoa, is everyone in America going Krishna?"

Steve got a kick out of saying, "Yeah, everyone in America has gone Krishna. Henry Rollins, too. Even Jello Biafra."

It wasn't clear whether or not the European kids knew he was pulling their legs.

My countenance was intense and downcast. I wore dark clothes riddled with strange bleach splatters, violently pummeled my guitar on stage, and head banged with a shirt tied to my head in lieu of hair. Tony's aura was icy and hard. In Italy he decided that some of the Shelter fans were undeserving of their Krishna neck beads, and proceeded to rip them off their necks.

Tony and I wanted kids to leave the show more excited about 108 than Shelter. To do that, we needed to steal the spotlight from the rest of the band.

Karmī Grains

The Hare Krishna world in Europe was quite different from the one I was used to. The '80s hadn't devastated it as fully as in America. I guess that's because their main post-Prabhupāda guru actually managed to "keep the dream alive" and continue acting as their unquestionable divinely anointed leader.

One of the first things we heard on arrival in Germany was, "Śrīla Viṣṇupāda says you are not bonafide."

Śrīla Viṣṇupāda, a.k.a. Harikeśa Swāmī, made awful rock albums, and the fact that his disciples listened to them made me really believe in brainwashing. Despite being a rocker himself, had he really declared Shelter an affront to Śrīla Prabhupāda?

Some of the ISKCON's most prolific booksellers were here amongst his disciples. When we walked into the temple room in Germany they seemed to welcome us with their backs.

If we were real devotees, I guess, we would be selling Prabhupāda's books on the streets, not rocking out on stage.

Unfortunately our lack of bonafidity didn't stop them from coming to our shows. Somewhere in Germany, we pulled into a club. They were already there, somberly eyeing the peculiarities of our decidedly un-bonafide selves. They hadn't brought anything to eat, but, as usual, the person in charge of the show had cooked us a vegetarian meal.

The devotees sat along the wall, glaring as we sat at the table.

It was exceedingly awkward, so I made a plate and carried it over to offer it to them.

"We eat only *prasādam*," their spokesman said, renouncing my offer with a German accent that was almost cartoonish.

"This *is prasādam*." I replied, already a bit insulted. "I offered it to my deities." I was referring to the box I carried with an altar to a picture of the pictures of Rādhā Śaradbihari that hung on my wall back in DC.

"No. This food is cooked by the *karmīs*," he declared. "We do not eat *karmī* grains. Krishna does not accept *karmī* grains."

223

I handed him an apple from a basket of fruit on the table.

He refused it, "We do not eat fruits that have been washed by the *karmīs*."

Devotees all over the world are guilty of fanaticism, but this was just beyond imagination. Had they completely lost touch with the fact that they were supposed to be working toward bhakti, love? Did they think they could get closer to divine love by insulting people and refusing food?

Suddenly I realized how my parents must feel, about me. To them I must look exactly like these devotees: critical, unwilling to compromise, damning. My mother had wanted to cook for her son. First I said, "No, I don't eat meat." She cooked without meat. Then I said, "No, I don't eat it if it's not offered to Krishna." She even went along with that. Then I said, "I can't offer it to Krishna if you use onions and garlic." I realized now that I had treated her exactly the way these people were treating me. My stipulations and demands must have sounded as obnoxious and absurd to her as "We don't eat fruit washed by the *karmīs*."

I sat down and ate as much *karmī* grain as I could.

You Know the Center of a Circle by its Circumference

In other European countries the devotees were so different: kind, generous, and helpful. The parents of the straightedge kids whose homes we sometimes stayed in didn't seem so terrified by the "Hare Krishna sect[2]," either.

I remember sitting on the grassy hill of one of the Krishna farms somewhere out there in I-forget-where, twirling a dandelion flower

---

[2] "Sect" is the European equivalent of "cult."

between my fingers, wondering how Viṣṇupāda could be the leader here, were everyone was so sweet, and over there too, where everyone was so mean?

I realized that, unless we are personally very close to a person, we can only experience that person *through* those who are close to him or her. *The center of a circle is perceived mainly by its circumference.*

I could imagine the non-*karmī*-fruit-eaters from over there approaching their guru saying, "Shelter is coming, but is this punk rock bonafide?" I imagined their guru saying something relative to their mood. Something like, "Well, Prabhupāda stopped Viṣṇujana from doing the same thing..." Then, I could see them coming away with the conclusion, "Our guru says you are bogus."

On the other hand I could imagine the simple, down-to-earth people from over here approaching the same guru saying, "What should we do to help Shelter when they come?" Responding to their mood, the same guru might say, "Bring them *prasādam* and see if you can coordinate some book distribution and harināma."

Then I thought of Prabhupāda. He was so different during the very early years of ISKCON, when his circumference was so much smaller and women were also an important part of it. Later, the circumference became so different, and he too seemed very different. I began to realize that what ISKCON accepted as "Prabhupāda's Mood" was really only the mood of Prabhupāda's circumference at a given point in time. Even what they saw as "Prabhupāda's Teachings" was only the teaching *they* had managed to *evoke* from him, and what they propagated was only what they had managed to comprehend of the teachings they had evoked.

This Song is for all the Ladies Here Tonight...

When we got back from the old world, I tried to book a string of shows and make 108 actually happen. It was something I had never done before and have never done again.

The first show would be on Saturday, October 10th at the Unisound in Reading, Pennsylvania with Another Wall and one or maybe two other bands. The next Friday we would do a "108 Spoken Word" at the Baltimore ISKCON temple. It would be a regular Hare Krishna event with kīrtan, "class" and a "feast," but the subject of the class would be our lyrics. That Sunday we booked a show at the Apocalypse in Norwalk, Connecticut, this time with Supertouch, Another Wall and one or two others. We planned to hold another spoken word somewhere in Norwalk the next day... but that never worked out.

I had three similar shows and spoken words booked for the following two weekends, too.

Norm Arenas had recently moved into the temple, so we got him to play second guitar, but before we could even practice as a five-piece, Rob quit. That left us without a singer... a week before we were finally supposed to play our first shows.

I wouldn't admit defeat and decided to sing *and* play guitar.

The first show, at Unisound, went surprisingly well. I wore my bleach-splattered black pants and a cool shirt with Lakṣmī and Viṣṇu seated together on the sea-dragon, Ananta Śeṣa. With a thick black marker I had drawn the Hare Krishna *mahā*-mantra around my left wrist, and wore a bracelet of red, shiny beads that the Rādhārāṇī deity in DC had worn. On the inside of my right forearm I drew a heart with the word "Vraj" in it. We played practically every song from the Holyname record, plus a few I had written since then: thorn, hostage:i, and woman. I drew up and handed out a flier with 108 lyrics on it, and explained the songs from the stage with semi-psychotic Krishna-banter.

I had been working lately with two women from the Baltimore temple, who came to the show and stood at the side of the room on a raised bench of some sort. I dedicated Woman to them; "This song goes out to those two ladies over there, Kārtika and Tracy. They are Hare Krishna women. They're *real* women because they know what a *real* man is. They can tell a *real* man from an imposter. They know that the *real* man... is Krishna, and every other man... is an imposter."

I Give Up (Take One)

Rob came to see the show the next weekend in Connecticut. We couldn't manage to find a place to have a spoken word the next night, so after the show we suddenly decided to take Rob and visit one of the craziest, most controversial Hare Krishna places of all time: the farm in West Virginia called New Vṛndāvana. We figured we could stay there for the week and then go straight from there to our next leg of shows in the Ohio area.

"Guys, I can't take off for a week," Zac explained. "I've got a girlfriend, and I've got a job."

Instead of realizing that we couldn't prance along on our fun filled adventure, we decided that Zac would have to transport himself home and catch up with us in Ohio the next weekend.

He had to beg to be let onto an oversold bus, where he sat in the stairwell. Arriving at Port Authority in New York City, he was physically threatened by one of the many madmen there while waiting for a connecting bus. Finally arriving in DC just before dawn, he called a friend who drove him to the temple where his car was parked. Having hardly slept a wink, he drove home as the sun was rising. Merging onto the highway, a gasoline truck came speeding up behind him, veered off, and slammed head on into the pillars of an overpass - bursting into flame.

Zac stopped his car and the driver ran towards him, screaming and in flames, to collapse and die on Zac's windshield.

Traumatized and infuriated that our childish selfishness had caused all this misfortune and subjected him to so much madness, he quit the band. We cancelled the rest of the shows and returned to the temple in DC. First Rob, now Zac... forget it. This was too difficult, and I wasn't even into doing it, anyway - I would rather follow my dream of being a Vṛndāvana bābājī.

108 broke up before Holyname even came out.

Śrīla Jesus

As for New Vṛndāvana, that was a right good freak out in its own right.

The place had been developed and lead by one of ISKCON's former infallible gurus, His Divine Grace Śrīla Bhaktipāda Swāmī — who turned out to be one of "the bad apples," to use a forgiving phrase. A misogynist conspirator to murder accused pretty soundly of pedophilic homosexual nefarities, Bhaktipāda was not just a menace, he was a good old-fashioned Jesus lover. While not proving himself a threat to women, children, and rival gurus, he focused on transforming Krishna consciousness into something that Jesus fans and followers of all other faiths and denominations could appreciate.

Like every ISKCON temple, New Vṛndāvana had a statue of Prabhupāda on a fancy guru-seat. Unlike ISKCON temples, however, a similar statue of Jesus sat on his own guru-seat just to the left and a little below Prabhupāda (because Christians would really appreciate *that*, right?). Also unlike other ISKCON temples for the past few years, there was an empty guru-seat on Prabhupāda's right. That one was for Bhaktipāda himself.

Instead of wearing Krishna clothing, almost all of the residents of New Vṛndāvana wore the brown robes, hoods, and rope-belts of Christian monks. There was a pipe-organ in the temple room, which played along with acoustic guitars during the morning temple program, in which all the songs were sung in English instead of Sanskrit, with decidedly hymn-like translations replete with "thy" and "thou."

Yeah.

Umm...

Now I knew *just how weird* things could get in the name of "following your guru." It scared the shit out of all of us, except Rob who found the whole thing pretty hilarious. We cut our trip short and left ASAP.

Bats in the Belfry

After calling off 108, I relocated to the Krishna Temple in Dallas, Texas. At first I lived in a bare, square servant's room next to a suite of lavishly furnished rooms set aside for the former zonal-guru of this temple Tamāl Krishna Goswāmī. After a few weeks, the Goswāmī came to the temple and his servant needed the room, so I went looking for somewhere else to set up camp.

I found a spot in the adjoining building that had formerly been a boarding school, I think. A large theatre had a backstage that was like a hallway above and behind the stage. It was literally full of a heap of costumes and other bric-a-brac left behind since God knows when. I pushed it all more tightly to one end, clearing enough space to lay out a sleeping bag and set up a small desk for my computer.

I preferred my own space, even if it was in an attic-closet.

I sat there for hours every day, answering letters, putting together a doomed 7th issue of Enquirer, and writing a very small book called Mādhurya-Kādambinī-Bindu, my explanation of a book of almost the same name by the 17th Century guru Viśvanātha Cakravartī.

I sent a copy to Dhanurdhara Swami, with a letter:

> I've enclosed a booklet which I hope you will be happy with. There are so many kids in the hardcore scene who are already becoming devotees, but there is little attention paid to them compared to the attention paid to get them in the door. I think this is one of the reasons why devotees come in from our preaching, but then leave.
>
> Whenever a devotee comes to me with a problem, they are always so satisfied to hear something from the Madhurya-Kadambini relevant to their situation. I've found this to be true again and again. So I wanted to present the book for the new devotees - in a

> language that they could understand, and with emphasis on relevant stages.

I also gave a copy to Tamāl Krishna Goswāmī here in Dallas. Less than a week later I sent another letter to Dhanurdhara Swami:

> *Because of the wonderful association of Tamala Krishna Goswami, I can see that the book I recently sent was a complete waste of time, as far as preaching is concerned (although he said it was great for study notes and stuff along those lines). I'm sorry it takes me so long to get the right idea and mood and to learn the right lessons. But with the help of the Vaishnavas, who are manifesting your mercy, I am gradually coming around - and I pray to soon become qualified as your follower.*

It's hard to imagine myself accepting someone's rather questionable criticism as "wonderful" and then apologizing for being such a lame follower. But maybe this was just me being showy and trying to look humble and sincere. After all, it's evident that I never really gave up on that book. A year or two later I would get sections of it published in my Back to Godhead column, and decades later I would develop it fully and publish it as To Dance in the Downpour of Devotion.

Up here in the belfry I also wrote another booklet, called "The Hare Krishna Movement." This was the kind of thing I was *supposed* to be doing, apparently. Its articles were for brand new people who didn't know anything about Prabhupāda or Krishna or vegetarianism or any of that stuff. Guṇagrahi Goswāmī printed a few *thousand* of them and devotees started handing them out by the dozens.

A Kali-Jolly Christmas

I had booked another trip to Vṛndāvana and sent a letter to Dhanurdhara Swami trying to convince him to let me transfer there permanently. In the meantime, I had to survive December. That wasn't easy because December is Christmas time, and that means the "Christmas Marathon" a.k.a. "Śrīla Prabhupāda's Transcendental Book Distribution Marathon."

I found myself in that famous bus with a bunch of other Hare Krishna boys and men, including a pretty significant number of straightedgers-in-dhotis, headed off to Somewhere-or-Other in Georgia.

Stereotypically, Indian people in America are either scientist-doctors, or owners of convenience stores and motels. The motels they owned were dubbed by the bus devotees as, "Patel Motels." It was relatively easy to convince their owners that their moral obligation to spreading Vedic wisdom would be fulfilled by granting us free use of their facilities.

I didn't like the sound of "Patel Motel." Many ISKCON members had a less-than-respectful attitude towards Indians. Initially, that confused me, but later I realized that Indians tend to naturally know a lot more about Indian culture than other people do, which was a challenge and often an embarrassment to ISKCON's western converts, who preferred to pride themselves on being the most ideal representatives of Vedic culture. Defaming their rivals, they referred to Indians as "hodge podge Hindus."

As for me, I loved almost everything about Indians - their languages, their cultural idiosyncrasies and mannerisms, their so-called hodge-podge (which was in many cases really a sophisticated and mature conception of plurality), and, especially, I loved their food - which was always light-years more delicious than the approximations of Indian food cooked up by western devotees. So, for me, the best part of the whole "marathon" was the one or two times the "Patels" invited us into their apartment to eat.

Besides that, December was not fun. A troupe of big-league, full-time book distributors joined us at the motel, and I tried my best to avoid them. Partly this was out of fear of arguing to the death about the efficacy of this whole thing, but partly it was out of fear of being crushed to dust by my absolutely inadequate salesmanship compared to them. Actually, it would bring hell on your head if you referred to book distribution talent as "salesmanship." Supposedly it was your purity that caused people to buy books from you.

The cool thing is that the big-league book distributer in our motel room was Kaustubha dās, a mysteriously silent and serious devotee who, I was told, used to hang out with the Cro-Mags.

We small-fries commiserated and tried to cheer one another up, as a car would drop us off in the parking lot of some shopping mall where we would spend the entire day trying to stop shoppers as they loaded their cars, attempting to convince them that they needed to buy a book from us about something they had never heard of or thought of before.

It all just felt so awkward and weird, and every day seemed to last a month.

To take a break we would glide around the lot on the shopping carts. I probably would have wound up doing that all day long, but then I would have to face the disappointment and disapproval the next morning, when everyone's "saṅkīrtan scores" were read aloud and mine were zero.

Even when I tried hard all day long, my scores were only a little above zero anyway.

Before reading those scores each morning, we would do kīrtan in the motel rooms, trying to maintain some semblance of temple life and spiritual practice. Once, while some of us were hitting drums and cymbals and others were getting dressed and brushing teeth, a loud and persistent knock fell upon our door, accompanied by a semi-delirious shout from a clearly big man with a southern drawl, "Hey man! Open up! Let me in man! I know Kālī! I know Kālī! I been to Vietnam. I know Kālī!"

We ignored him.

He showed no signs of fatigue, banging on the door at 5am, probably high on cocaine, shouting, "I know Kālī! Let me in, man, I know Kālī!"

Kālī is a ferocious, fearsome goddess of ghastly destruction - so saying "I know Kālī, let me in!" didn't exactly put anyone's mind at ease.

We looked at each other like frightened little chicks. For some reason, someone got up and timidly opened the door.

A huge, bearded trucker smiled from ear to ear as he stumbled into the room, exclaiming, "My maaan! I been to the temples in Vietnam! *I know Kālī!*"

Kaustubha suddenly strode out from the bathroom, silent and dressed in nothing but his *gamcha*.

"My man! My man!" the trucker told Kaustubha, "I know Kālī! Let me play those little cymbal thingies."

Kaustubha wasn't interested in making friends with a Vietnam vet who drove trucks in Alabama while snorting cocaine. He *plowed* full force into the mountainous man, forced him out the door, and promptly slammed and locked it before returning, still without saying a word, to finish his hygiene in the bathroom.

The trucker spent another ten minutes pleading for us to let him in, and then finally gave up.

I decided that Kaustubha was likely hardest guy I had met so far, and daydreamed about what the whole Cro-Mags scene must have been like with people like him involved.

CHAPTER TWENTY-EIGHT:

YOUR NAME IS... VRAJA KISHOR

Editing the Guru

Back in Vṛndāvana, Dhanurdhara Swāmī again took me as his guest and let me stay in his office, adjoining his own room. I was fascinated to see what books he had on his bookshelf. One of them in particular grabbed my attention, "Notable Horoscopes" by B.V. Raman. Horoscopes? I thought horoscopes were something shallow women read in Cosmo magazine. I never expected to find a book about them on a guru's bookshelf in Vṛndāvana. Thumbing through the book, however, I was amazed. It contained complex astrological charts and elaborately detailed interpretations for dozens of famous people — including Jesus, Buddha, and Krishna. Mahārāja explained that astrology was one of the ancient Vedic sciences and is still taken very seriously in India.

"You would probably be very good at it," he said.

I attended his VIHE classes again. He was considering compiling his notes into a book to serve as a study guide for Nectar of Devotion. Since I was a writer, I immediately offered to edit them. An hour or two later I showed him my edit of a few pages, and he agreed that I should edit the whole thing, and not be shy about suggesting changes.

I really dug into that task.

First I would have to understanding everything in a section clearly, then I would alter, restructure, rewrite, or add to the section, sometimes making diagrams, until everything was as clear and complete as possible.

The task was huge and would take more than a year to complete. Working on a computer in Vṛndāvana wasn't easy, either, because the power would go out often and stay out for who knows how long. It was then that I developed the enduring habitual instinct of hitting "control-s" (to save the file) every time I wrote even two or three words.

Your Name is...

In February, on the anniversary of Nityānanda's appearance in the world, we went down into the temple room for an initiation ceremony, Dhanurdhara Mahārāja would officially accept me as his disciple, and I would officially promise to follow his guidance, beginning with the instruction to chant a certain amount every day, and to follow certain rules of moral behavior.

A few days earlier I had gone into town to buy chanting beads. Yesterday I had given these to him, and this morning he used them to count his own chanting. Soon, in the ceremony, he would give them to me to use as my own.

Jagadīśh Mahārāja was also initiating several disciples at the same ceremony. Raghunath was there, getting his "second initiation" along with our godsister Jāhnava.

Jagadīśh Mahārāja spoke for a while about the significance of initiation. Dhanurdhara Swāmī said a few words too. Then he called my name, "Bhakta Vic."

I came closer and bowed, stretching out fully across the floor.

"What are the four regulative principles?" He asked.

"No intoxication, no meat eating, no illicit sex, and no gambling," I answered.

"Do you promise to chant at least 16 rounds every day?"

"I promise to chant at least 16 rounds a day."

"And try to do more on *Ekādaśī*?" he added.

I nodded in agreement, saying I would try to do 25 on *Ekādaśī* days. Then he held out the large chanting beads and I came forward to accept them.

"Your name is…" he said, placing the beads in my hands as the beating of my heart provided a drum roll that only I could hear. "…Vraja Kishor dāsa."

Whoa!!!

Vraja Kishor dāsa!?!? I Couldn't possibly have dreamed of a more perfect name! *Vraja* is a name of the realm of Vṛndāvana. *Kishor* literally means "teenager." Dāsa means "servant." I was now The Servant of The Teenager of Vṛndāvana! What "teenager"? Krishna, of course! And what was the significance of his being a *teenager*? That is the age where romantic love blooms with the most excitement! So, I had been named as a servant of Krishna as the teenage lover of the gopīs.

Perfect!

Nārāyaṇa Mahārāja

Working very carefully on Dhanurdhara Swāmī's Nectar of Devotion notes, I became deeply involved in understanding everything in that book, including the fascinating topics of *rasa, prema, bhāva,* and *rāgānuga.*

Rasa was the experience of transcendental joy, an exhilarating state resulting from having strong affection for a subject which becomes stimulated and expressed in just the right ways. *Bhakti-rasa* was the supreme experience of joy, in which affection for Krishna was the fundamental subject. *Prema* was the perfection of divine love, which forcibly attracts Śrī Krishna himself to come directly before you and form a face-to-face, person-to-person relationship. *Bhāva* was the preliminary stage of that perfection, the goal of practicing Krishna consciousness, a state where one was still in this world, but hardly, and where the immanent attainment of Krishna himself made one delirious in so many ways. *Rāgānuga* was a special way of practicing Krishna consciousness, which was not inspired by the desire to be righteous and follow rules, but was inspired directly by a passion to achieve a specific type of relationship with Krishna in Vṛndāvana.

All these topics were so much more inspiring than anything else I was learning as a Hare Krishna — how to wear monk's underwear, how not to use toilet paper, how to distribute books, how to shower, how to tell people about vegetarianism, etc. — and here in Vṛndāvana I had the opportunity to really dive deeply into exploring them. It was a great feeling, like I was exactly where I wanted to be.

In the course of editing, some of the questions I would ask wouldn't be easy to answer immediately. Half a dozen or so of these piled up, and then Dhanurdhara Swami decided that he would take me with him and a few of his godbrothers to see Nārāyaṇa Mahārāja for the answers.

We got on a Rickshaw together, sitting side by side, and went from the quiet of Vṛndāvana's outskirts into the bustle of the small nearby city, Mathurā - where Nārāyaṇa Mahārāja had his headquarters in the "Keśavjī" temple. I thought it was a nice temple: small, loud, busy, painted in pastels. I liked the altar, it was the first time I saw Rādhā Krishna and Śrī Caitanya together on one altar. We waited around for a while, and then went upstairs to a small room where Nārāyaṇa Mahārāja sat on a simple bed with one or two other devotees at the bedside. I was beside myself with excitement, almost as if I was meeting Prabhupāda himself.

Everyone bowed to the respected sādhu. He seemed unmoved by any of it, in a good way. They exchanged greetings pleasantly, for what seemed to take a very long time. Finally, my Guru Mahārāja introduced me. "This is my disciple. His name is Vraja Kishor dās."

Nārāyaṇa Mahārāja raised his eyebrows a little, nodding his head, expressing in that typical Indian way that he found this to be a very agreeable name. I moved myself forward from where I sat on the floor, and touched my head to his feet. He put his hand on my head for a moment.

"He is a musician in an important band," my Mahārāja continued, "preaching Krishna consciousness to young people in the west."

He didn't seem particularly interested in that or impressed by it.

"He is intelligent and is a good writer, so he is helping me edit my notes on Nectar of Devotion - which we make into a study guide in the form of a book."

He nodded his head, looked at me and said, "Be a good boy."

"Wait outside," my Mahārāja said, "in the temple."

I waited there for a very long time, maybe an hour or more, while the Prabhupāda disciples I had tagged along with put their questions to Nārāyaṇa Mahārāja and heard their answers. I was a little sad that I wasn't allowed to be there, but at least I had time to think about the fascinating thing Nārāyaṇa Mahārāja told me, "Be a good boy."

It seemed so ridiculously simple and random, but at the same time, something in my heart recognized that it was neither. It was exactly pertinent to me. I was busy doing all sorts of "big" things - being a big musician in a big band, a big preacher, a big paṇḍit in training helping my own guru write his book... Nārāyaṇa Mahārāja had told me not to let these things replace the simple essence of bhakti - just being "good" in a humble, quiet, normal way.

108 + Shelter: Must Work Together

I was lobbying pretty hard to have Dhanurdhara Swāmī transfer me here to Vṛndāvana permanently.

"What would you do here?" He asked.

"I could serve you and help you write books," I said enthusiastically, "and study at the VIHE and do the 24 hour kīrtan in my spare time... just like I am doing now!"

"It sounds good, *maybe*," he said. "But I have to discuss it with your authority, Guṇagrahī Goswāmī, and with Raghunath."

A week or so later we discussed it again. "Raghunath and Guṇagrahī Mahārāja both think that what you are doing in the West is too valuable to be stopped so soon. I told them about the practical difficulties you faced in maintaining your party and they decided that 108 and Shelter should work together. That will make it easier for you. Some of the members from Shelter can play in 108 if you need them, and you can share equipment if you need, and you should go on tour together this summer."

My heart sunk.

"In a few years, you can come to Vṛndāvana," he concluded, "but for now you have to serve the preaching mission and continue your service in the West."

CHAPTER TWENTY-NINE:

THE KRISHNA CARNIVAL ROADSHOW

Rob Fish is no Temple Thief!

And that's how 108 wound up doing a US tour with Shelter in the summer of 1993. Shelter would be the main band. We would be the tag-alongs.

Touring with them would mean touring big. The tour would be long, five-months. The venues and audiences would be bigger. *Everything* would be exaggerated, larger-than-life, and almost circus-like. There would be a school bus full of devotees, for example, with big kīrtans and *prasādam* at every show... Shelter had cultivated a *modus operandi* that seemed to want to test just how much of the Hare Krishna temple they could teleport directly into the middle of the mosh pit, before the scene would say, "yo, enough already."

Before the tour could begin there were a few problems to iron out, the biggest of which was: who would be in 108? We only had Tony and I, and you definitely need more than two people in a band.

The first thing I did was get in touch with Rob to see if he was interested in rejoining the band.

He was, but there was a problem: he was unwilling to tour with Shelter.

He had learned that Raghunath had declared him a thief, and felt extremely betrayed and maligned by that. Now, Rob has stolen more than his share of bubblegum and Kit-Kats in his day, and shenanigan'd far more than the average Joe - but Raghunath didn't just accuse him of thievery, he claimed that Rob was a devotee-robber and temple-thief, and this cut Rob to the core.

The controversy had started from Shelter's first night in Philly, when our van was robbed. Over the next few months, the temple itself regularly had break-ins - people going behind the altar to steal a few silver valuables and other things that looked like jewelry.

Raghunath decided the robber had to be the fucked-up kid, Rob.

Nobody, not even me I guess, really challenged him with any logic like, "How does Rob sneak out in the middle of the night, heist our van, rob the temple, offload it all at some pawn shop or something, and manage to be back in his bunk by 2:30 in the morning when some of us start waking up to chant?"

At one point someone actually saw the robbers and realized it wasn't Rob. But by that time Rob had moved out.

Rob told me "I will only tour with Shelter if Raghunath sits down with me and clears the air."

I set up the meeting, asking Tony to join us as a "neutral party."

We waited for Rob in the backyard of the temple. When he arrived, Raghunath immediately bowed on hands and knees with his head all the way down on the grass.

Rob stood there and spent the next 30 minutes cursing and yelling at him. "How could you be such a fucking two-faced, lying, heartless coward?"

At one point, Tony couldn't tolerate it anymore and said, "Yo man, chill the fuck out. Who do you think you are? You can't talk to Raghunath like that."

"I know who the fuck I am," Rob retorted. "But I don't really have any idea who the fuck you are, or why you are here, or why any of this is any of your business."

All of us were just in awe of how *pissed* Rob was and how openly he was letting it pour out of him.

Raghunath just sat there, patiently, the entire time, continuously apologizing. Each apology took just a little bit of steam out of Rob's anger, and after a half hour of it, Rob couldn't do anything but accept the apologies and forgive. In fact, he became deeply impressed by how fully Raghunath was willing to own up to the emotional grief he caused. From that day on, even though he would often strongly disagree with Raghunath, he always respected and felt a genuine love for him.

Jealous Against the Machine

My dad had sent me a copy of the *hugely* popular Rage Against the Machine record, as if to say, "Look how bad you screwed up by joining those Krishna's, son."

The cover was the burning Buddhist monk protesting the Vietnam war, which was supposed to be Inside Out's album cover for our LP named Rage Against the Machine. Some of the lyrics and maybe even a riff or two were ideas we were just beginning to throw around right before I quit. Even the band's logo looked to me a lot like the lettering style I had developed for Inside Out.

108's first record had also come out. Reviews of it in hardcore zines mostly said, "It's good, but I liked Inside Out better."

The 108 record was jacked.

When I saw the cover I was like, "...how did this happen?" But people thought it was cool and intentional. It was just a big blank white thing with a 108 logo in a small corner instead of covering the entire front as it was supposed to.

It was pressed as a CD too, which was cool except the mastering was totally messed up: The entire record wound up as a single track, making it impossible to jump forward or backward from track to track. Everyone assumed we did this on purpose as some sort of statement. Some said, "This way we can't skip all the Krishna stuff in the middle and at the end, right?"

Listening to Rage Against the Machine gave me a reason to want to do 108. Bullet in your Head and the rest would play over my Walkman as I ran around the block in Dallas, trying to build up some muscle and get into shape for a hardcore tour. As my Vans went from sidewalk to asphalt I told myself, "108 will become just as big, even if I have to pull it together with my teeth."

Or, in my less insane moments, "So Zack's huge, so what? I would rather have 20 people sincerely interested in Krishna than an arena of people who just want to headbang."

Ironically, as I worked up a sweat on the streets of Dallas, Zack was trying to call me at the temple in Philly. Whoever answered the phone there didn't seem to know "Vic DiCara" or where I lived. So, Inside Out did a reunion show that summer without me.

Multi-tracking with a Boombox and Walkman

Before the tour got started I had written a few new songs in that big empty Dallas temple theatre. I would use my boombox and Walkman to multi-track: recording a guitar on the Walkman, then playing that recording over the boombox while the Walkman sat right next to the speaker and recorded the playback along with me playing a bass line, and finally, doing the same thing with me tapping out a drum beat on my legs.

Hi-tech.

I didn't bother trying to record vocals. Screaming and shouting in the empty temple theatre just seemed too freaky. I would show Rob the vocals in person.

That's how I wrote and demoed Deathbed and Solitary Confinement, adding them to the set list we would play, along with Thorn, Hostage:I, and Pale, and Noonenomore, mixed in with all the material recorded on Holyname.

They Have a Girl in the Band

I thought Ekendra from Shelter could play drums for 108, pulling double-shifts every night, but Rob had a better idea. He brought in Chris Daly — the drummer from his other band, Ressurection. Daly's work commitments wouldn't allow him to do the whole five-month tour, so Ekendra would wind up playing drums for 108 for a bit. But it turned out to be a short bit, because Daly would soon quit his job and return to finish the tour.

I had a bright idea, too, though. Steve Reddy had moved away from the temple for some time, and came back just recently with a partner, a lady named Kate who was a musician and guitar player with a legitimate background in our scene. I asked her to play guitar along with me in the band, because I thought it would make a very powerful statement:

The hardcore scene complained that Hare Krishna's treated women as second-class citizens, but here comes 108 with a woman up on stage rocking a guitar in front of a completely male-dominated scene. "So who really treats women as useless," it seemed to challenge, "us or you?"

Not only would it be a statement to the hardcore scene, it would be a statement to ISKCON, too. "You treat women like background noise, but that doesn't mean we, the new generation of Hare Krishna's, will follow in your footsteps."

To my delight, Kate accepted the offer.

But a protest arose from Romapāda Swāmī, the main swāmī of the Brooklyn temple, "How can a single woman be allowed to travel on the road with single men, and even share the same sleeping arrangements? It's unacceptable." He called Kate to a meeting and delivered an ultimatum, "Either marry Steve immediately or I will transfer you to another temple and allow no contact between the two of you, and I definitely won't allow you to be in 108 and go on the road with them."

Terrified of losing everything, especially the man she loved, Kate told Steve what had happened. Steve replied by proposing to her on the spot. They married the very next day, without the presence or even the knowledge of their families. Kate didn't let her parents know until it was done, because she was sure they would have gotten her out of the temple before it could happen.

Now duly sanctified and blessed, Kate could come on tour with us without violating any Hare Krishna fanaticism about "intermingling of the sexes," for she would be with her husband the entire time; Steve would be the tour manager, being the new owner of Equal Vision Records (Raghunath had recently decided to transfer ownership).

We also added a whole other van to the tour, to be filled with Hare Krishna women so Kate wouldn't be the only one. Only two of them were from the hardcore scene: Nancy, and Sarah. Sarah, also known as HLS ("Hard Line Sarah"), was a Vegan devotee from Arkansas. Nancy was a Boston hardcore kid, the girlfriend of Jay from Eye for an Eye, who also came along to roadie for Shelter. Apparently Nancy and Jay were exempt from sanctifying their "association" with marriage because they didn't live in a temple.

Another woman in the van was Robin, the sister of one of the hardcore guys who had moved into the Philly temple and gotten initiated. Another was a simple, nice woman from England. I'm not quite sure why she was there, unless I remember correctly that she was thinking of trying to do something similar as a musician in Europe, completely outside any connection to the hardcore scene. Finally, there was Śrī Keśava a potential bride for Raghunath — which, to me, made the tour feel like it had an aspect of being a pre-honeymoon-trial-tour. I didn't dig that at all. Nor did I find it easy to like the candidate, an Australian blonde who wanted to be in a band too; thin and self-consciously pretty with a matching personality and ambition.

The "girls van" - or, more properly, the *mātājī*-van[3] - would breakdown more than any other car. Nancy impressed me a lot, because she knew how to use wrenches, fix cars, and get dirt and oil under her short fingernails.

Thus the "tour caravan" would wind up being a school bus full of male devotees, a van full of female devotees, and two vans full of musicians and equipment.

Something like a carnival.

Tar and Feather Ego

I poured an incredible amount of passion into every show, each song, every single note — as if the entire universe was at stake. In a sense it was, at least the only universe I knew: the one centered around the massive, swirling black hole of my ego.

Since getting back from Vṛndāvana at the beginning of the year, my consciousness had really gone nowhere special. It was fixated in the typical materialistic rut of jealousy over the success of others.

In June, just before the tour, my guru came to Dallas. I wasn't there. I was already up in Philly, practicing with the new lineup. Philly was like a party-house compared to the way I had been used to living. We were staying up late, eating ice cream, talking about hardcore for hours... Normally I would have made a big, pompous protest and tried to shame everyone into being more "strict," but this time I just went with it.

---

[3] *Mātājī* means "respected mother." The convention in ISKCON is to address all women as *mātājī*, and all men as *prabhu*, "powerful."

Mahārāja came up to Philly a few days later and, honestly, I felt inconvenienced, not thrilled. I was busy building up my ego for a battle against the world, and was in no mood to suddenly recall that this was the antithesis of the true essence of what I was supposedly battling for. Other people were eager to ask him questions and hear his classes, but I would sleep late and miss them, arguably because I had to stay up late practicing.

He came along to several of the first shows on the tour. That proved even more difficult. I was supposed to be the big enigmatic focus of attention up there on the stage, but here was my guru walking around the show — whom I was supposed to make the focus of my attention and respect. I wanted to upstage and outdo everyone, but here was a person who I was supposed to bow down to on sight. I would avoid seeing him at the shows because I didn't want to bow down to him in front of everyone.

Our tour took a break at the Krishna farm in Pennsylvania, Gītā Nāgarī, where we attended the Vaiṣṇava Institute for Higher Education (one of the first transplants of what Vṛndāvana Institute for Higher Education was doing). It dawned on me that even here all I really wanted to do was upstage people. I sat in the classes feeling special, like I knew everything so much better than all the other students, because I had been editing Mahārāja's notes and learning everything directly from him.

Ego is such a tar-and-feathers thing.

No Visions to Impress Zack

I saw Zack and a few other Inside Out era friends when our amazing Krishna Carnival Roadshow rolled into Salt Lake City for a show at what I remember to be a wooden skatepark. He got on stage with 108 and sang No Spiritual Surrender with us.

After the show I went to hang out with them all.

"I've been reading a lot of Carlos Castaneda," Zack told me as we sat under the clear Utah stars. "Have you read his stuff?"

247

I felt illiterate. In the past few years I hadn't read much that was not written by Śrīla Prabhupāda.

"He's into shamanism and stuff," he told me, "the spirituality of the Toltecs. He talks about all these mystical visions and stuff, it's really interesting."

Spirituality of the Toltecs... Mystical visions... I didn't know what to say.

"Have you had any mystic visions from the chanting and the meditation and everything that you do?" He asked me.

Not only was Zack's band 96 million times more powerful than mine, but now my spirituality was about to seem equally impotent next to his newest literary expeditions with this Don Juan Carlos Castaneda guy. "It's not like that," I said. "Krishna consciousness is not like, 'here take peyote and see all these colors swirling around and realize God in the desert.' Krishna consciousness is a scientific philosophy that you learn, and by practicing it you come to see it in practical ways. In *practical* ways, you come to see how God is in everyone and everything - but it's not like a big trippy vision or a hocus pocus."

I couldn't even speak in the first person.

Vegans in our Midst

Hard Line Sarah, as her name implies, was vegan. In fact, I think she may have been the very first vegan ISKCON devotee. She explained herself to us, and seeing that she managed to pull it off without too much trouble, Rob and I decided to go vegan too.

Holy John Henry, that was a controversy and a half.

It was not just a change in diet, it was a *statement*: "VEGANISM... IS... BETTER." Raghunath and the rest of the devotees on the tour just weren't in the mood to have that statement thrown in their faces every time we sat down to eat.

A swāmī who joined our tour for a bit, along with a van full of Hare Krishna kids, had to mediate a formal debate at one point. We all sat on the floor in a temple room somewhere in Florida, arguing the merits and demerits of our choice. I don't remember the swāmī's exact verdict, or if he even gave one, but we kept on being vegan, much to the chagrin of Shelter - which, honestly, was probably part of the reason we kept on being Vegan.

But it was a pain in the ass. My life was already hard enough. After a month or two I gave up on my own, probably in deference to a huge plate of ghee-soaked walnut halava.

Still, I never ceased to acknowledge that veganism really was more non-violent than vanilla vegetarianism. I just realized I couldn't handle it on top of everything else I was doing, and I actually managed to cope with the fact that I might in some ways be less than the world's most perfect ideal of absolutely everything.

Chapter Thirty:

SOS on the LES

Peanuts in Pockets

Finally, summer drew to a close, as did the grueling *Māyā* Mosh-Down Tour. It had become unbearable, and I was miserable and confused.

Rob, Tony, and I found ourselves in New York without a penny in our pockets, despite all the shows played and all the shirts and records sold for the past five months. We had plans for the future of the band — immediately record for Equal Vision, and then do another tour, on our own — but we had no idea what the future would hold for any of us as individuals.

I didn't want to go back to Dallas; I needed to be in the Northeast with the rest of the band members. I didn't want to move into the Brooklyn temple — that place was just too big, empty, cold and frightening. I didn't want to go down to Shelter-land in Philly — over the past few months I'd had enough conflicts with Raghunath to last a few years.

We heard that ISKCON had recently re-acquired a lease for 26 2nd Avenue on the Lower East Side of Manhattan, and were using it as a "preaching center." Although nothing more than a storefront next to a gas station near the Bowery, it was special. It was the very first ISKCON temple, the very first Krishna temple in the Western world. Prabhupāda literally started ISKCON from this place, living in the apartment in the rear building, and holding kīrtans, lectures and *prasādam* feasts for the '60s hippies and bohemians in the storefront itself, which, above the front window continued to bear the sign from its previous tenant: "Matchless Gifts."

As soon as we walked in the door, I felt it — as if a clean and refreshing river started to trickle into my tour-beaten, ego-abused and dimmed heart. It was like I could almost hear and feel the Prabhupāda of those early days, who was almost an entirely different person from the way he seemed in the huge ISKCON of later days. At 26 2nd Ave, Prabhupāda was "Swāmījī." ISKCON had a few dozen members, and Swāmījī could personally interact with each and every one of them. The mood was much less formal, much more open, and not yet totally dominated by young western males like Kīrtanānanda, with their odd intensities and decidedly western minds and viewpoints. The ISKCON of 26 2nd Avenue was so much more spiritually raw, uncensored, and exciting — just like Vṛndāvana.

The storefront was only a few blocks away from the studio we would be recording at: Don Fury, so we got permission to stay there.

Spiritual? Yes. Practically located? Yes. Comfortable? No.

ISKCON hadn't been able to get the apartment. They only had the storefront itself — a single, open room with a toilet and sink in a closet-like area; no tub, kitchen, refrigerator, closet or anything remotely private. We showered by pouring water from the sink over our heads while standing on a plastic basin that we would then dump into the toilet. We cooked on a small green Coleman camping stove, pooling our quarters and dollar bills to buy peanuts, broccoli, and, sometimes, cream cheese. Once a week or so, devotees would hold a feast here, and we could really eat.

At one point I ran out of quarters and dollars to rub together, and didn't even have enough money to buy a razor to shave my head.

On a more positive note, I started holding Nectar of Devotion classes every week. It really felt like an honor to be able to explain Nectar of Devotion at this sacred place.

I also realized that wearing the "magic robes" really did make a difference for me. For the past five months I was dressing like a hardcore kid - and started feeling a lot like a hardcore kid. Now that I was dressing in the robes again, I started feeling more like a devotee. I decided I would always wear the robes, even at shows, even on stage, even when walking outside in the winter.

Songs of Separation @ Don Fury's

Most of what we did at 26 2nd Ave was to get ready for recording. As typical for me, I used a notebook to map out the guitar tracks and other details I wanted to record. As was also typical for me, my plans didn't include other people any more than absolutely necessary. Kate and Tony wouldn't be on the record, I decided. I would do all the guitars and bass.

Somehow, they didn't seem to mind.

Some of the songs were older than the Holyname record: Woman, Thorn, Hostage:i, and Nononenomore. Two others I had written with my Walkman in Dallas just before the tour: Deathbed, and Solitary. Still others I had written on the road, taking advantage of Porcell's four-track and drum machine: Opposition, Son of Nanda, Weapon, Pale, and a loopy/trippy thing called Govinda-Virahena that we didn't even try to play live. Over the last few days at 26 2nd Ave I had written a few more — Shun the Mask, I am Not, and Request Denied — to get a tally worthy of being called an LP.

Don Fury's studio was a basement in Little Italy, below the namesake's apartment. It felt authentically "New York" to open the sidewalk trapdoor and climb down there in the late-summer sun while pedestrians walked around and trucks unloaded their cargo. It has an impressive setup: a control room and a room for playing, which had a semi-partitioned area to isolate the drums behind Plexiglas and foam-covered wood.

The Alesis ADAT was the newest thing at the time. Fury had 3 of them, granting a total of 24 digital tracks, recorded to VHS tapes you could buy at any convenience store.

This was my fourth experience recording in a studio, but I was still just starting to grasp how it all really works. According to Don, in the digital age it was absolutely imperative to record using a click track. I had my doubts but I gave in when he said, "Alan Cage used it for the BURN EP." Alan was the most incredible drummer I'd played with, and his drum sound on the BURN EP was monolithic. Daly took a while to get used to the heartless imposition of having a metronome playing in your ears while you are trying to wail, but he got the hang of it soon enough, and laid down his rhythms with his trademark tasteful precision.

Then I recorded my two guitar tracks. Fury would allow more only for leads, in fact he was one of the Genii who all but deleted the third rhythm guitar on the Inside Out EP. I had a few leads here and there, and a few feedbacks and other sound effects. My favorite was the overdub for Opposition: detuning and retuning a string while playing it.

When I recorded the bass, Fury tried to stop me from bending the strings. "That's for guitar," he said, "don't do that on the bass."

I told him it was what I wanted, but still his comment affected how I played.

Mosquitos would come down from the open trapdoor into the cool basement. Don Fury would kill them. One of us said, "Maybe you shouldn't kill them, they are living beings just like us."

"Yeah, but they suck our blood and spread disease." He countered.

"Ok, but at least say 'Krishna' right before you kill them," we said.

And he would. Bzzzzzt. "Krishna." Clap!

Kate and Tony would come down to be a part of the whole thing and to give moral support. Other devotes would sometimes come with food from the temple. Rob was nailing his vocals. I had set aside a few parts for myself, mainly the verses of Deathbed, and asked Kate to lend her vocals to a Sanskrit part in Son of Nanda.

Govinda Virahena was a loose rendition of one of the more heart-wrenching Sanskrit verses of Śikṣāṣṭaka, with the actual Sanskrit being screamed in the background. Don Fury's way to remember the pronunciation of Śikṣāṣṭaka was to combine two brand names he knew, "A razor and a soda... Shick Shasta." All the vocals on that song were mine, and when it came time to do them, all the stress of the tour and my intense life in general came to a head. It was just too much stress and I broke down in tears for a while.

The whole recording took only a few days, and we wound up finishing on Rādhāṣṭamī, the anniversary of Śrīmatī Rādhārānī's appearance in the world.

I wish the sound of the drums and guitars was even a little bit more like the BURN EP, but at least the songs came out basically the way I had envisioned them.

Where's Towaco?

With the recording finished, it was time to figure out what to do with my life. Staying at the storefront forever just wasn't a reasonable option. Tony got something set up and headed out. Rob made ready to return to his home base in New Jersey. I was still clueless.

Then one evening a whole lot of devotees came to 26 2nd Avenue for some event. Subāl, a Latin musician and Venezuelan devotee with a soft heart and huge smile, asked, "How are you doing Vraj Prabhu? What are your plans?"

"I'm in a bit of distress, Prabhu," I said. "I have no idea where to go."

"Why don't you come to the Towaco temple?" he asked. "It is almost empty and we are looking for new people. Lakṣmī Prabhu is the temple president, I think he would be happy to have you."

"Towaco?" I asked. "Where is that?"

"It's in New Jersey. It's not far."

I arrived by public transportation at a beautiful, spacious property on a hill with an impressive old house at the summit. Inside were beautiful, kind-eyed deities of Nitai and Gaura. The building was run down but still felt nice, like a home in need of repair.

I met Lakṣmī in his spacious office on the second floor, with a great view overlooking the hill. He seemed like a very nice and reasonable man. He said had recently worked as an A&R for a major record and was familiar with John and Harley from the Cro-Mags.

"Once I met Harley in a health food store, and he was trying to tell me that he was a kṣatrīya warrior. 'Harley,' I told him, 'If a real kṣatrīya like Arjuna walked in here right now you would pee your pants.'"

I thought that was great.

He asked me what service I would do if I lived there.

"That's the thing," I said. "I do a lot of preaching and am very busy with the band. Sometimes I might not even be here for months at a time. And I go to Vṛndāvana for a few months, too. So I'm not sure what I can do, because even when I am here I have a lot of writing to do, answering letters and stuff like that. So I don't really do any normal service like selling books or washing pots. So…"

"That's fine," he said, to my total surprise. "There is *one* service I want you to do, and do it really well: start a program on Saturday nights for young western kids. We have a huge Indian congregation and our Sunday feast is completely Indian. I want you to create a Saturday program for westerners. Can you do that?"

"Sure!" I said.

"OK, there are a few rooms available..."

Green Marble and Candlelight

The modest room I picked was in the corner at the end of the second floor hall in a section of three rooms with a shared bathroom. My parents stopped in for a visit soon after I transferred here and seemed happy that I was no longer in the hot-dog shack in the middle of the dilapidated old summer camp in DC.

The floor, though, was unpleasant. It was beat up linoleum tile, completely worn out in some areas, and very yellowed in others. I had been trying to scrape off the yellowed parts, but it was very slow work.

Mom and dad offered to buy and help install a new floor.

We went to a Home Depot and I selected self-sticking linoleum tiles that looked like gorgeous, rich green marble. We first laid down a base, because the old tiles were uneven. Then we glued the tiles into place one by one, cutting some to fit the edges and corners.

It was like old times, as a kid I enjoyed helping my dad build patios and decks.

When we were done, the place looked awesome!

We also bought two brass, wall mounted candleholders. I started using candles instead of electric light for a while. With my deity pictures on the wall, and the candles at either side, my room looked like a temple itself; exactly as I wanted it!

Franklin, Slayer of Monists

The first writing project I undertook in my new room was a zine. I had given up on Enquirer, but wanted to release Songs of Separation along with "wordsong" — a zine explaining all the 108 lyrics and music and interviewing the band members.

Tony had left 108 by the time I got to interviewing the band members, so I interviewed his replacement, Franklin Rhi.

I ran into Franklin often at the Brooklyn temple and I liked him a lot. He was a hardcore guy, not a "straightedge kid." Long, straight, black Asian hair reached far down his back, but to my dismay he cut it off just before joining us. He seemed perfect for 108 because, like me, he was serious, silent, moody, and really into obscure ideas. He hated *māyāvāda* philosophy — an extreme form of absolute monism that many Westerners wrongly assumed represented all Indian philosophy. He would say, as annoyed as most people get when they talk about someone snaking their parking space, "'We are all one, we are all God,' that's just downright bogus *māyāvāda*."

Śrīla Thanks List *ki Jaya*

Being on the road with peers every day for the past five months had revived a little bit of the sense of humor I once had, and I tried (maybe a little too hard) to let it show in the zine and on the liner notes to Songs of Separation. Rob, "E-luv Swamee" in the zine, was credited in the liner notes for "vocals, spiritual sarcasm." "Kate-O-Eight" got credit for "guitars, vocals, and bangles." I credited myself for "metal leads, and vocals."

Speaking of the liner notes, the thanks list was always a big deal. In hardcore it's almost like an honor role. Usually these lists start off with "Thanks to:" Ours dispensed with that and instead ended with "*ki jaya!*" which is sort of funny if you've hung around a Krishna temple a bit and seen how people use the phrase.

I started the *ki jaya* list with "Tony, Norm, Zac & Ekendra 109" crediting the former members of 108 (apparently I forgot again that

Jay Holtzman was our singer once). Then followed the people who practically helped the recording in significant ways, "Steve & EVR; Furious Don; Raghu & the Shelt-ettes; Josh." (Joshua Wildman had taken photos of me in Krishna garb, in the 26 2nd Avenue basement, holding my smashed guitar and looking simultaneously pensive, miserable, and crazy. One of those photos was used on the record's back cover.) Then followed people and things relevant to the recent tour: "H.L.S. & Kṛṣṇa Grrrl Fanzine; Mates from the "Maya Moshdown Tour" '93." (Kṛṣṇa Grrrl was a fanzine Kate did with Sarah) Then, thanks for the people who arranged for and permitted our lodging while recording, "Romapada Swami, Prema Bhakti, Kathleen, & 26 2nd ave." Finally, we expressed sincere gratitude to mom and dad, "z Mommaz and z Poppaz."

When the record was released a few months later, on the anniversary of Nitai's appearance in the world about 500 years ago, I gave a copy to my guru, Dhanurdhara Swami, with great hopes of hearing him say something positive about it.

A few days later he said, "Romapāda Swāmī showed me how you mentioned him on the 108 record."

"Oh?" I said hopefully.

"He didn't seem to mind, but I think its a little insulting."

Why would anyone be insulted to be mentioned on a *thanks* list?

"You really don't understand culture. He is a *sannyāsī* and a guru, but you just mixed his name in there with everyone else, and didn't even refer to him with an honorific."

I was speechless.

"You put Śrīla Prabhupāda, and Śrīla Dhanurdhara Swāmī and Śrīla Satsvarūpa Goswāmī, and you put us at the top in bold. Then you just threw Romapāda Swāmī's name in there next to Bhaktin Kathleen and Hard Line Sarah."

I couldn't believe the pickiness. "You are my guru," I said, "and Satsvarūpa Mahārāja is Rob's guru... that's why we put 'Śrīla' in front of your names and put you at the top..."

"Romapāda Swāmī is a guru too. You should have put him at the top of the list or at least used an honorific like Śrīla or Śrīpad."

Supposedly *women* had this trait, being difficult to satisfy, even when you try.

I looked down and mumbled, "I thought he would have been happy to be thanked. I didn't have to mention him at all, he didn't really do anything, he just said 'OK' to Prema and Kathleen's request that we could stay at 26 2nd Ave."

"Vraja," he concluded, "just try to be more sensitive to Vaiṣṇava culture."

I was quite confused as to what "Vaiṣṇava culture" really was. Bhaktivinode had described a Vaiṣṇava as an "essentialist" (*sāragrahi*), not a "formalist" (*bahirgrahi*). The Swāmīs in this case sure seemed like they missed the essence of gratitude in being thanked and instead got hung up on the formalities of how and when I thanked them.

But I was just a punk rebel at heart. No wonder I couldn't grasp the finer sensibilities of culture and good manners.

Saturday Night Life

I was supposed to be in Vṛndāvan when Songs of Separation came out, during the first few months of 1994, but I was still broke. Dhanurdhara Swāmī suggested that I come in October, during the very special Vṛndāvana Kārtika festival and VIHE seminars.

Meanwhile I turned my attention to fulfilling my one responsibility to the Towaco temple: developing a good Saturday night program. I made a flier with a few 108 graphic elements announcing "Saturday Night-Life", and handed it out at a show in New Jersey. A hardcore girl named Billie-jo showed up the first weekend with her younger brother. I cooked the feast, gave the class, and led the kīrtan. She and her brother were the only participants.

It was great.

The next week she brought a friend from Rutgers, Matthew Dasti. The third week Matthew brought a few more friends. Within a month or two we had some really happening "Saturday Nightlife."

Soon Billie-jo, Matthew and some of his friends had moved in and Towaco started to hum again.

The Saturday program was nice, but I really loved the Sunday program. The guests were almost 100% Gujarati Indians, and to be honest I definitely preferred the company of Indians. Week after week I happily merged myself among them and soon began to develop some significant friendships.

Irritating Whippersnapper

One person at the temple was not at all happy with me, the oldest and most long-term temple resident: Maitreya *Brahmacārī*, a British Bachelor approaching his 50s. Maybe it was just bad chemistry, but mostly he was infinitely irritated by the fact that a whippersnapper like me was getting away without selling books, pandering stickers, or even washing pots — and was instead being treated like a respected sannyāsī preacher.

Within a few months he left.

He moved to New Vṛndāvana, which had recently evicted Bhaktipāda and began to undo all the Christian weirdness. (They finally gave up imagining that Bhaktipāda was God's pure-devotee-emissary when they found him having sex in the back of a Winnebago with a young male disciple.)

CHAPTER THIRTY-ONE:
M.A.D. LIKE INSANE

Grandma Mindi

That summer, my Great Grandmother, "Grandma Mindi" died.

I always had a tremendous amount of love and respect for her. An established Italian-American man brought her to America to marry him, but upon arrival she discovered she didn't like the man at all, and refused the marriage. This kind of defiance from a woman was practically unheard of, but she didn't care. She wasn't going to marry someone she didn't love, even if he had arranged all the paperwork and paid to bring her to America.

A palm reader in New York City told her, "Clementine, when you walk out of this room you will run into a man wearing a sweater, riding a bike. He is your husband."

Sure enough, she walked onto the sidewalk and a man riding a bike, wearing a sweater, almost crashed into her. That was my Great Grandfather, "Papa Joe."

Grandma Mindi was an archetypical Italian woman; she loved to feed people and would cook incredibly and in incredible quantity. When we visited I would make Olympic medals out of masking tape and award them to the people who had eaten the most. My dad usually won.

For the past few years I would visit her whenever I visited my parents, because she was living in a nursing home quite near them, and my mom was going there often to keep her company. She barely spoke any English, but that didn't really get in the way of our relationship.

She didn't seem to mind my shaved head and robes, I explained that it was religious and she seemed to respect that.

I went to her funeral dressed in my normal Krishna getup. It was one of the first times the whole family saw me like that. Everyone seemed a little confused, but managed to digest it. I also made a little effort to be slightly normal. My Uncle Joe had recently had two kids, and I had a little fun playing with them.

Makeshift Lineups

108 kept the ball rolling after Songs of Separation came out with a short one-week tour of the East Coast in the spring, followed by a six-week tour of the US in the summer, followed by another month or so on tour in Europe.

Unfortunately, the US tour wasn't with our full line-up. Equal Vision Records was running on a higher level now, and Steve couldn't be away from the office for six weeks. Since Steve couldn't come, Kate felt that she couldn't come either. Romapāda Swāmī's ultimatum on this topic, and its reinforcement from every direction in ISKCON, had traumatized her with the fear that she would be excommunicated from Krishna consciousness and lose everything if she broke the laws of "chastity" by traveling with men without her husband.

Steve and Kate did join us for the European tour (with Refused as our support) but we still couldn't manage to bring the full line-up. This time it was Chris Daly who couldn't come. Commitments to his job prevented it.

The booking company, M.A.D., provided a drummer.

Unfortunately this drummer could play the songs *his* way, but couldn't quite play them the way they were recorded. I kept trying to show him the specific details, but he just couldn't seem to get it right. It drove me crazy. I eventually became so frustrated that I realized it would have been better to have cancelled the tour instead of playing without being at our best.

Red Light Japa Walk

Just prior to the tour's start, Rasaraja (the artist formerly known as Rob Fish) had gone to Belfast, Ireland to be among the final group of people initiated by the increasingly reclusive and introspective guru, Satsvarūpa Dās Goswāmī. From there, he journeyed with his new name by bus and ferry to the Amsterdam temple, where he was greeted in the street by a fistfight between two of the temple devotees.

Those two brawlers turned out to be his roommates for the night.

At around 2am, he decided to get up and do some chanting. Walking towards the temple room, he bumped into a swāmī named Suhotra.

"Oh," the swāmī said with obvious sarcasm, "you're one of the rock and roll devotees? Straightedge? *Hardcore?*"

"Yeah," Rasaraja answered. "Is there a peaceful place around here for a *japa* walk?"

"Why not chant in the temple?" The swāmī asked.

"I'm just tired of being cooped up in a bus for so long."

The swāmī gave Ras directions to a peaceful place to walk and chant.

By following those directions, Ras found himself in the middle of Amsterdam's Red Light district in the wee hours of the morning, with naked women waiting for customers in storefront windows and people selling drugs openly on the street. Returning confused to the temple, he found the swāmī sitting with a few young men. When they saw the mixture of confusion, anger and shock on his face, they broke down laughing.

Incidentally, this swāmī was soon exposed for walking this same route quite often.

Worn Out

Ras joined us the next day in Germany, and the tour began.

Lately, he had been dealing with extremely serious headaches. During the tour, he would need to spend long periods of time alone in the van, seeking whatever meager quiet and comfort he could find there. Often he would have to get up on stage and scream while under the grip of intense migraines.

A really dark, desperate, and depressed mood began to overtake him.

The tour was wearing on *everyone*. Franklin started to get annoyed easily. When Kate made a comment about his EMS sleeping bag, "It should say DMS," he felt insulted and a serious rift developed between them.

Things were looking grim.

Blue Busses

It was nice to meet Śacīnandana Swāmī — a 30 or 40-year-old German man with a kind heart and deeply spiritual motivations who came to several of our shows and was extremely supportive and encouraging.

A group of his disciples had a blue bus, painted beautifully with Viṣṇu lying in the ocean of causes, generating bubble-like universes. They called it "The Spiritual Skyliner." The young men on the bus came to a lot of our shows, cooking for us and the kids who attended, and doing kīrtan with us.

Deathbed Music Video

In Berlin, a camera crew from our European distributor, Lost and Found, filmed us for a music video for our song, deathbed. We recorded ourselves awkwardly lip-syncing in an empty room, in front of a blank wall. I told them that I wanted the video to mostly be live footage, like the video for I Against I, by the Bad Brains.

They didn't listen. The video came out looking like a bad psychedelic trip with us poorly lip-syncing over strange paisley patterns.

I hated it.

It didn't go anywhere anyway. I think MTV Europe played the video a few times at best.

Ras, Under Arrest

Towards the end of the tour we went to Sweden, Refused's hometown and an all-around great country. In Karlstad we arrived at the venue and followed a wonderful scent through the hallways behind the club. The scent led us into a mini mall, to a door that opened on a kitchen where devotees greeted us, "Haribol! Haribol!"

They had a restaurant in the same building as the club we were playing, and had cooked for us and for the show!

They also had a television show, and they interviewed us for that. Following that, a local newscast came to interview us, and stuck around to film at the show.

During the show a group of young Hare Krishna ladies did wonderful kīrtan next to our merchandize table. They would come to all our shows in Sweden, doing kīrtan and handing out *prasādam*.

The show was packed wall to wall, and when we played the entire place went absolutely nuts. Kids were flying everywhere in absolute insanity.

During a break between songs, two rent-a-cop types came on stage, took one of our microphones and lectured the crowd in Swedish. We couldn't understand a word.

When we played the next song, the place went even more berserk. One of the security guard / rent-a-cops got back on stage in the middle of the song and started motioning for everyone to stop.

Rasaraja made a gesture of disgust, and the bassist of Refused ran out from behind the drums and threw the guy into the crowd, while the crowd went beyond mad.

After the set we were busy at our merch table, talking to people and signing shirts and records for almost an hour, when the promoter suddenly came over and told Rob, "You have to come out front to talk to the police."

The rent-a-cops were not rented.

They arrested Rasaraja, charging him with inciting a riot, and put him in a holding cell.

It was clean, and had a private bathroom and a very cozy looking cot. Compared to the squats we had been sleeping in, it seemed like heaven.

Just as Ras began to happily doze into what would surely have been his best sleep in weeks, his cell door opened. The drummer of Refused, the promoter, and the newscaster who had interviewed used their footage to prove that Rasaraja had done nothing to "incite a riot," and he was released.

If only they could have taken at least a few hours more!

CHAPTER THIRTY-TWO:
KĀRTIKA IN VRAJA

Once Italian, Now a Brahmin

Superman can change from mild-mannered to super-powered, and I pretty much learned to do the same. One day I was a hardcore punk rocker living from one German squat to the next, thrashing and screaming violently on a stage. The next day I was a modest, quiet *sādhu*-in-training, chanting and studying scripture in the sacred dusts of India.

Here in Vṛndāvana I was about to pull off yet another incredible transformation. An Italian-American from New York, an outcaste with no position whatsoever in Vedic culture, was about to be transformed into a member of the highest caste.

I received "Brahmin-initiation."

Now I not only had the Brahmin's shaved-head and pony tail, I also had the Brahmin's "sacred thread," a strand of several strings draped over my left shoulder, signifying that I was permitted to chant Vedic mantra and do formal ceremonies and temple worship.

I received seven new mantras, including one from Ṛg Veda which only "Brahmins" were supposed to chant[4], and was told to chant them ten times each, three times a day, at sunrise, noon, and sunset. I was also shown a special way to wrap the sacred thread around my right thumb and to use that thumb to count the ten repetitions on my right hand.

No one ever attempted to explain what the mantras meant.

Essentialists, or formalists?

Anyway, to be honest, more significant than the mantra was the social status granted by my new thread. It was like getting a promotion at work.

When I first joined ISKCON I was just Bhakta Vic, without any special symbol or nomenclature to mark me as being any different from any other Joe who came around the temple now and again. Then I was allowed to shave my head and wear the robes. That was my first promotion. The next came when I "got my first initiation" and changed my name to Vraja Kishor das, proving that I was more committed, more "surrendered" than the plebes with normal names. Now I had my third promotion, a special thread for an even higher echelon, extending my superiority over the rank and file Krishna *dāsas* and *dāsīs*.

---

[4] In truth, in Vedic culture, "Brahmin" is not a birthright, it's a way of life. And the Vedic mantra are chanted by all "dvija" — a term that is not entirely synonymous with "brahmin", but refers to anyone from any caste who receives formal education. I didn't know any of this at the time, and am just using the ISKCON lingo here. In fact, I didn't even know that the mantra was from Ṛg Veda at the time!

Ironically, then, these initiations didn't change all that much in my heart. I had *always* believed and behaved as if I was superior to everyone else. Now I just had some evidence for it in a strange and very niche context.

The only people above me now, I thought, were the ones with *three* initiations: the sannyāsīs. I fully intended to change that, too.

You Should Study Sanskrit with Him One Day

Over the past year and a half I had done a lot of work editing Dhanurdhara Swami's notes on Nectar of Devotion, helping to get them into a format fit to publish. One thing I liked so much about doing this was that I was *good* at it: organizing, clarifying, and expressing information succinctly is my thing. I also liked that it gave some meaning to my becoming a Hare Krishna disciple: I was actually learning authentic Vedic philosophy in detail, with significant reference to the primary source material.

The source material was Bhakti-Rasāmṛta Sindhu, a Sanskrit text written by Śrī Rūpa Goswāmī in the early 1500s. We only had a partial translation of it in those days, from Bon Mahārāja. Prabhupāda had translated a scattering of the more important verses when they appeared in the text of Śrī Krishna Caitanya's biography, Caitanya Caritāmṛta. For everything else, or to resolve any questions about these translations, we relied on Nārāyaṇa Mahārāja and a few Sanskrit scholars.

The nearest and certainly the best of these scholars was only a few doors down from Dhanurdhara Swami's office: Satyanārāyaṇa Prabhu, a small, quiet, bright-eyed Indian man, the Gurukula Sanskrit Teacher. He studied philosophy at unparalleled depth from the most learned man in Vṛndāvana, a mystical, quiet, elder sādhu named Haridās Śāstrī, whom Dhanurdhara Swami described as a man "with nine PhDs." As a result, Satyanārāyana Prabhu was translating Jīva Goswāmī's extremely philosophical Sandarbhas into English. These six extensive essays are outstandingly important because they form the founding philosophical "constitution" of Śrī Caitanya's school of thought.

I was delighted and honored when Mahārāja brought me to his room and introduced me. "This is my disciple, Vraja Kishor. He is the one editing my Nectar of Devotion book."

Prabhujī's mannerism was uncommonly calm and quiet, so much so that it almost seemed loud. There was so *much in there*, I could tell, and he was holding almost all of it back, patiently, humbly. But it would leak out loudly through his smallest expressions and gestures. All the expression we usually put into words and gestures seemed to shine through his eyes alone. He looked at me very happily, respectfully, and hopefully.

I noticed a curious plaque on his green desk that said, "Prabhupāda said, 'I never said...'"

"One day, Vraja," said Dhanurdhara Swāmī, "you should study Sanskrit with him."

I thought that was a *fantastic* idea! Prabhujī seemed to agree, and gave me an abbreviated copy of Jīva Goswāmī's textbook on Sanskrit grammar.

Love Krishna, but Not *too* Much

Since the very beginning, two things had really fascinated me about, and attracted me to, Krishna Consciousness. The first was its incredibly detailed, systematic and logical philosophy, revealing the ultimate root of reality as a conscious entity named "Krishna." The second was Krishna himself, the most incredibly relatable, attractive, pleasurable, and lawless expression of divine consciousness.

Ironically, both facets of Krishna consciousness proved very difficult to pursue in ISKCON.

When I first read Prabhupāda's books, I assumed ISKCON would be full of thoughtful philosophers. When I got involved, however, I realized that ISKCON's atmosphere was thoroughly anti-intellectual. Free thought was considered undesirable "speculation." One must note speculate. One must listen to authorities and accept their opinion. Vṛndāvana, especially the VIHE, was the only place where freethinking had enough elbowroom to actually grasp the details of philosophy.

Vṛndāvana was also the only place in ISKCON where I could sense the real Krishna — the relatable, attractive, and lawless supreme enjoyer enjoying his own supreme joy. Outside of Vṛndāvana, ISKCON made Krishna seem distant and otherworldly, his most attractive aspects were made abstract and taboo, his lawless intimacy made to seem inconceivable and irrelevant.

No wonder I wanted more than anything to spend most of my time in Vṛndāvana!

Then, it seemed someone gave the ISKCON governors a memo, "Hey, you missed a spot. There is still one place where Vraja Kishor might actually thrive in Krishna consciousness."

They turned their eyes to Vṛndāvana, to stomp out the last strongholds of everything I loved.

Through my studies of Nectar of Devotion and its source, Bhakti-Rasāmṛta Sindhu I learned quite assuredly that the intimate and unrestrainable Krishna could be realized only by an equally intimate and unrestrained practice: *rāgānuga-sādhana*. ISKCON, however, abounded with misconceptions about *rāgānuga-sādhana*. They thought of it as an extremely advanced perfection dramatically unlike what they were already doing on a daily basis. The truth, however, is that *rāgānuga* is a practice (*sādhana*). Sure, it is the most powerful, rare, and special form of practice aiming for the most exalted perfection, but it is a practice nonetheless, not something that only perfect souls should dare to even think about. It also became clear to me that what ISKCON devotees already did every morning — chanting, dancing and discussing Śrīmad Bhāgavatam — could easily be approached as *rāgānuga sādhana*. ISKCON however, seemed to think *rāgānuga* was practiced as a wild free-for-all, perhaps even with an abundance of cross dressing and midnight *rāsa* dancing.

Despite having no clear idea what it was, they decided with firm conviction that it must be curbed, stamped out entirely if possible.

There was a showdown between those who had studied *rāgānuga* carefully and those who wanted to enforce ISKCON's long-held beliefs about it.

It didn't go well for us.

Maybe we should have tried to avoid the showdown by explaining *rāgānuga* to them more clearly?

It probably wouldn't have worked. Deep, broad and thorough understanding of sacred texts held much less importance in ISKCON than the opinions of its leading managers and figureheads.

On the threat of excommunication and punishment the GBC laid down strict resolutions and declarations. "You are forbidden to discuss these things, this is not Prabhupāda's mood." A lot of their anger was directed towards the main person who had been guiding us towards a better, clearer understanding of *rāgānuga*: Śrīpad Nārāyaṇa Mahārāja. "You are forbidden to learn from him, and he is forbidden in ISKCON."

All this "forbidding" felt like living in Orwell's 1984.

The only thing I really *liked* about ISKCON was that it was somehow connected with Krishna, and thus somehow connected with Krishna's passionate relationship to the gopīs and the supreme gopī, Śrī Rādhā. But now ISKCON was taking pains to make it clear that it considered all of that illegal, "unbonafide."

Love Krishna... but not too much.

Actually, I doubt they would give a cold chickpea whether I "loved Krishna" or not. They were more interested in "ISKCON," and to them "ISKCON" meant "Prabhupāda," and "Prabhupāda" meant "Prabhupāda's teachings," and "Prabhupāda's teachings" meant "Prabhupāda's orders." And nobody could comprehend Prabhuāda's orders better than the organization Prabhupāda set up for establishing those orders, the Governing Body Commission.

Nothing could be allowed to threaten the authority of the GBC. If anyone openly questioned their decrees, they would most certainly find themselves accused of being anti-Prabhupāda and anti-ISKCON.

If they persisted, they would soon find themselves exiled. And if anyone started to gain more prominence than they, threatening to be a better guide for the society, that person would be banned, prohibited, defamed, denounced and eliminated.

And that's exactly what happened. *Rāgānuga* was not the real issue. Power was the real issue. ISKCON managers saw Nārāyaṇa Mahārāja becoming alarmingly important in ISKCON. That put them on edge, and when some people began to express their opinion that his guidance should be accepted more thoroughly throughout ISKCON, the GBC could tolerate no more.

They stamped out the Vṛndāvana mood because they didn't want a rival who would clearly outshine them. The long-standing phobias and misconceptions of *rāgānuga* and *vraja-prema* were a very convenient and effective tool.

Like most casualties of modern warfare, I was just caught in the crossfire.

Hollow Are the Bones of Lonely

Until now I had fantasized that I could help improve ISKCON. I gave up on that. Or, more accurately, I gave up trying to do it on their terms. My attitude changed. Now I was ready to apply the PRA (punk rock attitude) to the ISK.

No one was going to tell me to curb my interest in Vṛndāvana Krishna and also expect me to accept them as an authority on Krishna consciousness.

Challenges to real Krishna consciousness came from everywhere. Not just from the world, but from within my own ego. Not just from the *karmī* non-devotees but also even from the spiritual organization that claimed it would nurture me. There was very little support anywhere, yet somehow I had to keep trying.

I wrote the lyrics to Arctic:

i'll try for you.
I'll cry for you.
trial.
trial by ice.

i can simply extend my finger in a pose of exquisite pain.
my pain.
i can only stretch my arms.
stretch, reach, for you.

i need a blanket to warm me from the chill of my emptiness.
i need a blanket to exsulate me because it's cold inside.

try not to freeze
try not to die

a jolting phone: cataclysmic in the bone-marrow night.
i need a blanket to warm me from the chill of my emptiness.
where is sleep to hide me,
from the fact that you're so absent in my heart?
where is sleep to hide me,
from the fact that i'm too dead to care?

hollow are the bones of lonely.

i stand: hollow.
i die: hollow.
but I'll try.

I had cut myself off from a loving family, and people of the world looked at me as a weirdo. Now I also felt cut off from ISKCON, who also seemed to look at me as a deviant. All I had left was a few kindred souls in Vṛndāvana.

Trivikrama Dasa & Baby Gopal

Perhaps out of compassion the Goddess of Vṛndāvana sent me a new companion: Trivikrama Dāsa.

I met him outside Dhanurdhara Swami's rooms, a guitarist with a long blond ponytail *śikha* and an expansive, creative spirit. We quickly developed a friendship and I offered to take him and his wife, Līlā Vṛndāvana, on *parikrama* to some of my favorite Vṛndāvana spots.

Trivikrama had experienced some friction and rejection from Shelter (which by now seemed to me a necessary prerequisite for playing in 108). He said, "When I set up my equipment, they gawked at me like I was from another planet... which, I am, but I mean, you know? Then their bassist told me, 'Why do you use such heavy strings? Change them, you sound like Tony Iommi!'"

We looked at each other sympathetically, and he asked rhetorically, "What's wrong with sounding like Tony Iommi?"

Triv had wound up on tour with Shelter because Līlā Vṛndāvana had become the first bass player in a new band called Baby Gopal, Shelter's opening act.

Like almost everyone, I hated Baby Gopal, which is odd because I really wanted to like a predominantly female Hare Krishna band. Their first problem was that they came across less like a band and more like a plan; a plan to bunny hop the hardcore scene and land in some midsize indie label, soon to bounce again onto Epic or Sony. Another problem was that their music was 100% Alt-Rock, but they always played hardcore shows. The biggest problem, however, was the singer: the irritating thin blonde Australian who had her trial run with Raghunath on the Shelter 108 Tour.

But Triv wasn't interested in talking much about any of this. He had heavier things on his mind, carrying the ashes of his sister to the Ganges river.

I loved him.

"108 also just finished a really awful tour," I told him. "I think just about everyone is frustrated and will probably quit soon, especially our bass player, Franklin. If he quits, would you be willing to play bass for us?"

CHAPTER THIRTY-THREE:

THREEFOLD MISERIES

This Demo Sucks

The tour was hard on everyone, but at least we weren't penniless anymore. I had enough money to buy some musical equipment, including a Tascam 488 8-track cassette recorder and a Boss Doctor Rhythm 550 drum machine. A few weeks later I had already cranked out about 8 songs, put them together on a demo called "108 III," and gave copies to Ras, Franklin, and Chris.

Ras *hated* it.

He played it for Norm, who agreed to accompany him and explain to me that the songs did, in fact, suck.

There was a trippy Into Another -esque acoustic/electric song about Buddha, the cat who lived in the Towaco temple basement. Another song was about devotees who weren't particularly serious, and chanted "16 rounds of Gorilla Biscuits gossip." Another made reference to, "Standing on the shore and dancing in the Holyname."

It was out there in left field, and the music backing it, though good in some parts, was like a quilt torn apart and put back together in the wrong sequence.

Everyone agreed that at least one song, "Panic," was a keeper. It was a fast one, with rhythmically "backward" beats, and lyrics about people I knew through the mail who had to go through deprogramming and other heavy-duty intimidations from family who hated Krishna consciousness.

Killer of Triangles

A day or two later, I felt inspired while looking out the window of EVR's office in Manhattan. I tuned an acoustic guitar to drop-d and then looked at the fretboard. An interesting shape appeared: triangles merging at an apex to form an "x" in a box.

It was the main riff for Killer of the Soul.

The title came from the 3rd Mantra of Iśopaniṣad:

> *asuryā nāma te lokā andhena tamasāvṛtāḥ*
> *tāṁs te pretyābhigacchanti ye ke cātma-hano janāḥ*

The "sunless realms" obscured by blinding darkness soul-killers, one and all, enter that afterlife.

"Soul-killer" has two meanings, (1) to destroy other creatures,[5] (2) to destroy yourself. The first verse elaborated on the first meaning, set in the context of meat-eating, and borrowing a reference from Śrī Caitanya who declared that those who kill a cow will enter these

---

[5] Sanskrit sometimes refers to the soul as a "creature," an "animal."

dark regions for as many thousands of years or births as there are hairs on that cow. The second verse elaborated on the second meaning, set in the context of drowning oneself in intoxication.

All the lyrics had a dark, intense, and satanic mood to them, as did the riff.

Scandalous Triangles

I looked for other shapes in different places on the frets. The next one I found was a triangle-chord way up past the 12th fret, hovering up there like the ships in Space Invaders. It became the main riff to Scandal.

The lyrics were a protest against slanderous anti-Krishna propaganda circulating in the hardcore scene:

> *Slanderous how scandalous*
> *ludicrous how fallacious*
> *is the preponderance of ignorance*
> *that you cast upon my people.*
>
> *Publication of fabrications*
> *dislocated misquotations*
> *that try to cast my culture*
> *as a creature, of scorn.*

The initial wave of Anti-Krishna protest from the hardcore scene had been pretty much crushed by the Shelter / Inside Out / Quicksand tour in 1990, but a second wave gradually built up over the next few years and developed into a few branches. Born Against represented the main branch, survivors of the first wave. Of all the anti-Krishna's, they were our favorite. Ras, especially, just *liked* the band, and refused to have an "us vs. them" attitude about it.

Other branches of the anti-Krishna camp, however, didn't have any redeeming qualities. Chokehold, for example, were whinny little brats connected somehow to a straightedge kid named Josh, who did a fanzine called Trustkill. An entire issue of Trustkill was set aside just to make fun of Krishna. Some of it was funny. There was a page with pictures of people given names like Bhakta Basics and Bhakta School-sale. Most of it, however, was just obnoxious and asinine. I decided to make Josh Trustkill my enemy, and wrote the lyrics to Scandal in reference to his cheap slander.

Spin Magazine

Nirvana was now the biggest band around. Rage Against the Machine was practically as big as Metallica. Quicksand and Into Another were signed to major labels and seemed ready to be the next big things. Krishnacore... Well our music wasn't as groundbreaking or great as most of the above, but even if it was, the very *concept* just seemed doomed for commercial failure.

So, we were shocked when Spin Magazine published a huge article titled, "KrishnaCore."

> *From Robert Johnson to Sinead O'Connor, rock and religion have shared a storied, oft-contentious relationship. The latest odd couple? Hardcore musicians turned Hare Krishna. Text by Erik Davis. Photographs by Ray Lego.*

The full-page photo beneath this text? Me rocking out on my dad's purple starburst Gibson Les Paul, with my tongue sticking out.

My parents were psyched!

Me too. Maybe there was hope after all that I might not have made the wrong career choice by quitting Inside Out? Maybe my aspiration to catch up to Zack might have some hope of getting a measure of success?

Who's Triv? Where's Kate?

Franklin had quit during the discussion of how much the 108 III demo sucked. (He actually liked most of the songs on it.) We immediately replaced him with the fascinating guy I had met in Vṛndāvana, Trivikrama.

Triv was a mad scientist of music, a lead guitarist with incredible skill, deep creativity, and impeccable taste not only for the subtleties of melody and rhythm, but also for tone itself. He collected all sorts of equipment and experimented with endless combinations of amps and pedals in search of the most appropriate bass and guitar tones for our band.

He and I sat down together one day without any amplification and I showed him the bass lines to all the 108 songs. He easily grasped everything, so I began to show him the finer details. To my amazement, he considered them all carefully — most people just get frustrated and give up when it gets this specific. He wound up being the only person who not only could comprehended all the fine details but could improve them. Playing music with him became an enjoyable experience in and of itself. It was the first time I had really felt a perfect artistic match since I quit Inside Out.

After a single practice at a rehearsal studio, Trivikrama played his first show with us: a huge, a completely sold out event at the Wetlands in NYC.

It was also our first show without Kate, and someone shouted from the crowd, "Where's Kate?"

It's hard to remember exactly why we kicked her out, probably because there wasn't really an exact, clear reason. The trauma of the swāmī's ultimatum made her not want to tour with us unless her husband came along, but her husband needed to give his attention to Equal Vision Records, not to tagging along on an endless string of tours.

I sat with her on the green futon couch at Equal Vision and said, "We are going to do a lot of touring now, and I know you don't want to do that without Steve. So, it's probably better to make a clean break."

She seemed OK about it, but when I left she collapsed in tears.

We had broken her heart.

"Yeah, Where's Kate-oh-Eight?" someone else echoed, closer to the stage.

My stage persona had somehow developed into something of a bizarre, dry comedian with his head in another dimension. I had been making such comments into the microphone all night, so I reflexively stepped up to do the same in reply.

By the time I started talking, I realized I had no idea what to say. That's when you're supposed to shut up.

I didn't.

"Kate's not with us anymore," I said.

"Where is she?"

"She... merged... into the *brahmajyoti*.[6]"

Not only was it an insult to pass up an ideal opportunity to express our gratitude and respect to Kate, I made it seem like not having Kate in the band wasn't that important. It was just another joke, a bad joke, too, with insulting overtones for devotees.

And to make it still worse, she was *right there* listening to it all. At the last minute she came down to the show, arriving just after we began to play.

---

[6] This was almost like saying, "she become nothing." *Brahmajyoti* is the "great white light" of undifferentiated consciousness. Merging into it constitutes absolute freedom, liberation and enlightenment, but it is only the foundational beginning of spiritual liberation.

Can't Catch the Roadrunner

Shelter had signed a deal with Roadrunner Records. If not exactly a "major label," at least it was definitely a big step up from self-run hardcore labels. The A&R who signed them also had an interest in us.

After one or two meetings we signed a contract to record a demo for their further consideration. They set us up in a NYC studio run by a hardcore legend from the Icemen, Noah. It was in a basement, with a pump down the hall making strange industrial noises that we recorded and used as the intro to Panic.

We also recorded our two other newest songs, Killer of the Soul and Scandal.

Roadrunner heard the demo and declined to develop it further. Those were three great songs, but I think the label just knew the truth: both the music and the band were just too far from mainstream to be commercially viable. Plus, they already had one Krishnacore gamble in their portfolio, did they really need two?

Fuck Korn, and Fuck You if you Support That Shit

We all wanted to get bigger and have more influence on a wider audience. Steve wanted the same thing for Equal Vision Records, and was already finding some initial success. He had developed a friendly working relationship with Sick of it All, and they agreed to take us along on their huge tour with Orange 9mm.

But then, at the very last minute, major-labels screwed it up. Epic / Immortal had a brand new act named Korn, who paid Sick of it All a fat sum to kick 108 off the tour so they could take our spot.

At least we played the tour's first show.

"What the fuck is Korn?" I shouted from the stage during our set. "Kiddie porn? What the fuck is *that*? Child abuse is not a fucking gimmick. You know what I say about Korn? I say, '*Fuck you* Korn.' And 'fuck you' to anyone who buys that shit and supports them."

They were probably smoking a joint in their tour buses parked outside and couldn't care less. My outraged boycott certainly didn't stand in the way of their becoming absolutely huge. Maybe their child-abuse theme wasn't a gimmick; maybe it was about real issues they had to face growing up. I don't really know. I didn't really care. I was just pissed.

Daly is the Reason

It seemed like everyone except 108 was on the road to the big leagues, even 108's band members and ex-members. Norm and Chris were doing a band called Texas is the Reason, who were exploding. Chris realized that both bands needed his full attention, and he chose Texas over us.

I don't blame him, but I wasn't happy to be thrown back into "no-drummer limbo."

Lenny was a Canadian Shelter had recently tried out and passed up. His style of drumming was fast, light and sloppy — the kind that would work well for chaotic and noisy punk. 108 rhythms, however, needed metallic precision packed into unhurried grooves. Ras felt strongly that Lenny was not the right drummer for us. I wouldn't listen. You would have thought I might have remembered all my frustration with the quick-replacement drummer on our last European tour.

I just wanted to move forward somehow, and convinced Ras to give it a try.

One of my typical dumb moves.

Chapter Thirty-Four:

Misery on Wheels

I Slashed the Fucker's Tires

We had hoped to spend the Summer of 1995 touring with Sick of it All, with Chris Daly playing drums. Instead we had Lenny and a self-booked tour with two good but relatively unknown hardcore bands: Bloodlet, and Coalesce (who *later* became big).

Rasaraja's headaches were worse than ever and his moods reflected that: he was seriously depressed. We had to go to emergency rooms several times to get him shots and painkillers so that he could manage to keep going.

One such occasion happened in Mesa, Arizona. That's why we arrived at the venue much later than the other bands. Ras, dazed from the medication, stayed in the van to try and get some sleep, while the rest of us discovered that the venue was just a small rental hall somewhere out in the middle of nowhere.

And barely a dozen kids had shown up.

The other bands informed us that this was all intentional. The promoter hated Hare Krishna and had a vendetta against Coalesce's singer, who had given up on his hardline Veganism.

"Let's go talk to this guy," I said.

A huge mob of us surrounded the promoter in the "backstage" room.

"Look," I said, "we know what you're doing. OK, Ha ha... very funny. 'Let's mess with the Hare Krishna's.' Great, but our singer is a fucking lunatic and he wants to *kill* you. I'm trying to calm him down and solve this *peacefully*, OK? So, work with me. Fine, you had your joke and fucked up a show for us. Yay. Thank you very much. Now the fun's over. Now you have to think about the money you guaranteed us: three hundred and fifty for 108, two hundred for Bloodlet, and a hundred for Coalesce. You are going to pay us that — I don't know how and I don't care how — or you're going to find yourself in a *whole lot* of trouble."

As if on cue, Rasaraja walked in to the room, dazed and drowsy, looking more like a confused and crumpled bunny-rabbit than an angry bear.

"What?" he said, *completely* unaware of what was going on.

We just couldn't help but burst out laughing.

Ras assumed that everyone was laughing at him for no reason. "What the *fuck*?" He shouted, suddenly becoming exactly the violent lunatic we had described, throwing things around the room.

The promoter left, got the money, returned, and paid us. We then played to the dozen or so people who managed to find out about the show, sold a few shirts, and proceeded to pack our van to leave.

It was then that Shree, a girl touring with Bloodlet, walked up to the van holding her bleeding hand.

"Do you guys have any bandages?"

Just then, in the distance, "Holy shit! They slashed his tires! 108 slashed his tires!"

We looked at her like disappointed parents, "What did you do?"

"I slashed the fucker's tires!" she proudly declared.

Our roadie Maha Jay — an ex-marine with a heart of pure gold — walked over and informed us, "I just ripped the sink out of the men's room wall, and the toilet out of the floor."

We stopped laughing and decided to leave immediately.

Vanessa (the other girl traveling with Bloodlet) lived nearby, so we went there for the night, expecting to see police cars when we arrived. But everything was quiet, and we took our stuff inside.

"Where's the merch box?" Ras asked Maha.

Maha Jay stopped in his tracks, and his face went pale. "I left it at the club... on the merch table"

All of our money was in that box. We *had* to go back and get it.

Jeremy, the Kung Fu master from Bloodlet, Maha Jay, the big ex-marine, and Ras, the lunatic, got out of the van and approached the building. Jay and Jeremy flanked the door imposingly, which Ras nonchalantly walked to the merch table, where the box still sat, unnoticed.

The promoter and some friends were standing in a circle, like people who had just gone through an earthquake, discussing what an amazing bunch of assholes we all were. They all fell silent when they realized we had returned.

Ras smiled as he picked up the box and walked out calmly, saying "Goodbye fellas."

Promoter sent faxes to every other promoter for all the rest of our tour, telling them what we had done. It was not the first time Ras and Jeremy had to convince adolescent promoters to pay their guarantees — banging on their front doors in the middle of the night, waking up their entire house, and accompanying them to ATMs. As news and rumors spread, promoters were getting worried and called Steve at Equal Vision to complain.

The next time we talked to Steve, he was furious. "Slashing tires and ripping out toilets? Have you lost your minds!?"

Yes, we had.

We were sick, depressed, uncomfortable, sexually repressed, dirty, hungry, sleep-deprived and insomniacal, frustrated, and backed by a drummer who couldn't play the songs quite right.

Yes we had lost our minds, and had *no idea* where to find them.

Frustration x Caffination

I had been doing the Krishna thing for about five years now. That's five years of the strictest celibacy and utmost commitment, pushing everything else aside for the sake of Krishna consciousness. What did I actually have to show for it? Had I developed any significant relationship with Krishna, or any significant realization of reality and my true self?

In a sense, yes... but almost none of my moments of significant realization and progress seemed at all connected to this frustrating dung-ball of sweat and anger on wheels known as "hardcore." My few truly spiritual experiences and realizations had come from Vṛndāvana - either chanting with Aindra in the temple room, or visiting sacred places with Dhanurdhara Swāmī, of studying the primary texts of bhakti-yoga at the VIHE. So what the hell was I doing *here*, in a van with people from Bloodlet, losing my mind?

Was I, "Serving Śrīla Prabhupāda's preaching mission"?

Seemed I could serve it a lot better if I wasn't falling to pieces like the rubber from the tires being worn down into the road.

I sat behind the steering wheel, driving down who-remembers-what freeway in the middle of who-remembers-what black night, with chocolate and soda caffeine wiring me into a jittery waking-dream of quasi-reality. Eyes open, mind neither asleep nor awake. I don't remember where we were headed, but I was already at the final destination: wits end.

I couldn't keep going like this, I needed a big change: either get myself to Vṛndāvana permanently, or else get on with it already and see if one or both of those girls in the back was up for something much more interesting than all this driving.

You Are Yamaraja Das

The guys in Bloodlet said they were jealous of our cool names. I humorously offered to make them my disciples.

They loved the idea.

We did the "initiation ceremony" at a park somewhere along the road. I can't remember all the names I gave, but I remember that the singer became "Yamaraja das" — servant of the lord of death — and was stoked about it.

I wrote the names out for them in Sanskrit, because they said they wanted to get tattoos.

The Daughter of my Godsister is my...

At some point our tour hobbled into Connecticut to play at some veteran's hall without a stage or sound-system. It was *ekādaśī*, the "no grains" day. Jay and Nancy came out to the show early and brought a friend, a beautiful young lady, exactly "my type" — curvy, mysterious, dangerous, understated and wearing her extremely long black hair in two braids over her shoulders. They introduced her to us as Shyama Sakhi.

I thought it was the best name I had heard since Vraja Kishor.

Shyama Sakhi was the daughter of Bhanu-nandini, a Japanese lady who was my "godsister" (student of the same guru). I knew Bhanu-nandinī had unusually good character, and it seemed her daughter did, too.

She had brought some soup in a thermos, along with other delicious *ekādaśī*-safe things she had cooked, and the whole band went with Jay, Nancy, and Shyama Sakhi into our van for a picnic. I talked to her a bit, not like a leech, more like an uncle (I still much preferred the Vṛndāvana option over the other extreme). She had an intriguing personality.

I didn't know it at the time, but we had already met once in Germany, on the Shelter tour. As I was walking upstairs in the Koln temple she had asked if she could buy a Shelter shirt and I had told her, "no," giving the excuse that all the shirts were in boxes, locked in the van.

We met again a few weeks later and a show we were supposed to play with the Cro-Mags (they cancelled). We ran into each other backstage and I gave her a glass of orange juice.

One, Two, THREE, Four...

After the tour we wanted to do something positive, for a change. We had plenty of new songs, so we wanted to record, and went to Brian McTernan's Salad Day's studio in Maryland.

In the studio it was even more obvious than on stage: Lenny wasn't going to cut it.

The straw breaking the camel's back fell just before the heavy part in Blood, the part that goes, "'Pessimist,' but ain't it so factual?"

Lenny just could not count it off the right way. Triv and I could adjust to his count, but Ras couldn't come in correctly if the count wasn't the way it was supposed to be. It should have been really simple, honestly. The previous riff ended on a "3" so Lenny just had to rest on the "4", and then start a four-count from the "1." Simple. Ras would come in on three ("Pes-"), again on four ("sa-"), and then the full band would come in at the start of the next measure ("mist"). It might sound complicated on paper, but it's not, and nobody could figure out why Lenny couldn't grasp it.

I tried to explain it to him. Then Ras tried. Then Brian tried. Then Triv.

It was maddening, and Lenny was yelling for us to stop telling him how to play drums.

I finally saw things Rob's way: it's better to wait and do things right, instead of rushing and doing everything wrong.

We decided to cancel the recording.

CHAPTER THIRTY-FIVE:

MISERY ON OTHER CONTINENTS

108 minus 1

I had been in San Diego visiting my parents for a few days, and then flew with them from to Chicago to visit my grandparents and my Aunt, who I had not seen for six years. 108's second tour of Europe would begin tomorrow, so I made a quick call back home to check that all the preparations were going smoothly.

They weren't.

Several months ago Ras had married Prema Bhakti Mārga, who had joined ISKCON quite a while before us, and was part of the Hardcore Scene from the mid '80s, when the Bad Brains were very active in New York. She had just recently become pregnant and had just today gone into a serious medical emergency.

Ras certainly could not leave for a six-week tour with her in that condition.

At the Chicago airport waiting for my flight to JFK in the "Admiral's Club" (my parents roll that way) I ate a few complimentary peanuts and made a complimentary phone to call to Trivikrama. We decided it was too late to cancel everything; we should try to do the tour without Rasaraja.

Without a singer?

A booming voice would announce "Gentlemen and gentlemen... all the way from the streets of New York... we give you the Slayer of Krishnacore... 1... 0... 8!" Then, as only three of us walked on stage, a fast, low-pitched, monotone would read off the side-effects, "The band regrets to inform you that their singer, Rasaraja dasa, could not be present tonight due to medical complications. Please mosh responsibly."

I mean, what band would tour without their singer?

Hold the Plane for our Guru

Maha Jay and Lenny picked me up at JFK Airport and took me to Towaco where I rushed to pack all my things and head back to board our flight to Germany. On the way to JFK we stopped in Manhattan to pick up some merchandise from Equal Vision Records. Leaving their office, Kate humorously gave us an intentionally mom-ish farewell, "You boys all have your tickets and passports, right?"

That's when I realized I *didn't*.

My passport was still somewhere in my room in Towaco.

It was already 9:30pm. The plane was scheduled to leave in two hours. It would take 45 minutes to get back to Towaco, and from there about an hour and fifteen to get to JFK. That's two hours in travel time alone, foretelling that we would be walking into the international departure lobby while our plane was leaving the ground, even if nothing slowed us down and we spent no time at all getting into the temple and finding my passport.

I called Towaco, but everyone was asleep.

I kept calling.

Finally someone answered and I hurriedly explained the situation and begged, "If someone could bring my passport to Equal Vision, it would save a precious 45 minutes and we could still make the flight!"

They said it would be impossible. I forget the reason.

Mahāmuni, the one devotee I would have expected to do it, was already with us, waiting to drive the van back to the temple once we got out at the airport.

Impossible?

Yes, but Śrīla Prabhupāda has a saying that is extremely popular with his followers, "Impossible is a word in a fool's dictionary."

Steve took Trivikrama and Lenny directly to the airport. I jumped behind the wheel of the van with Jason and Muni, literally put the pedal to the metal... and kept it there. The van groaned, rattled and complained as I kept it pushed way past its maximum speed, sounding and feeling like it might suddenly shake itself unbolted and just fall apart on the road like a Warner Brothers cartoon. I would sometimes back off the accelerator, but only when the steering wheel started shaking too violently to control. Gripping that wheel with white knuckles I barreled down the road like an immortal, weaving in and out of traffic.

It's a miracle was that we didn't die and take a few others with us.

It's another miracle that the police didn't stop us.

After about 30 minutes cheating death of his golden opportunity, we shot up the Towaco driveway and came to an abrupt halt behind the temple. I knew the doors would be locked at this time of night, so I bolted up the fire escape. The second story window was open in the warm September night, and I ran into my room to begin rummaging through my things. After five or ten minutes of desperation, I finally found my passport, raced back down the fire escape, and took the van back through the same harrowing death-race.

It was 11:15 when we jolted to a halt at the departure curb, Jason and I leapt out for the check-in counter.

To our surprise and relief, Pakistan Air personnel were rushing toward us, shouting in that Indian-English accent I loved so dearly, "Hurry! Hurry, please! Plane is now leaving, you must hurry! We are holding the door open for you only, please hurry!"

Amazing.

Somehow Trivikrama managed to keep the flight from closing its doors a half hour before takeoff. Somehow these people were *checking us in* for an international flight *fifteen minutes* before departure.

As we ran towards the gate, we found Trivikrama still busy convincing the airplane crew not to close the door and pull away from the gate. "Please, you have to hold the plane for our guru. We are touring Europe with him to do kīrtan and bhajan for the benefit of the world. Swamiji will be here any moment now, I promise. Please wait for him."

Sure enough, I leapt on board in my saffron robes, greeted as guruji and swamiji by Trivikrama's bow to the floor, namaskara from some passengers, and even one or two elated exclamations of "Jaya Mahārāj!" from the cabin crew.

We flopped into our seats, exhausted, and broke out laughing in awe of the amazing miracle.

A Taste of the Big Leagues

On arriving in Frankfurt the *karma* of making all those people wait for us seemed to immediately bear fruit. We stood around outside for *seven hours*, waiting for our tour bus to pick us up.

But it was a tour bus!

M.A.D. had managed to get guarantees big enough to afford sharing a bus with our supporting band, Abhinanda. It had a back room with a couch and a tv-vcr built into the walls; we used it as our "temple room" for doing kīrtan, hanging out, and telling stories from Krishna-līlā. The middle of the bus had a toilet and shower, and twelve beds arranged in bunks, each with its own curtain. The front had a table and a few places to sit. The shower didn't work, but everything else did. It felt to me like we were Led Zeppelin, traveling in a mobile Hyatt Regency.

These Next Songs... are Covers

I knew I could sing and play guitar at the same time, because I had done it before — that's how we did the very first couple of 108 shows back in 1992. But it was difficult to do it with our more complex songs, and on such short notice. To give myself a break, and give the crowd a chance to have a singer to look at, Maha Jay would come out and take over the mic on one or two songs. We also covered a few Cro-Mags songs, letting the crowd basically handle the vocals and keep themselves entertained.

A devotee named Amara Prabhu came on most of the tour too, helping with the merch table and translating for us whenever there was a language barrier in Germany. He basically played the role of a tour manager.

Two or three shows into the tour, Rasaraja called and said that Prema was feeling better, so he could fly out and join us. That was a relief, but to be honest, a part of me had gotten a little comfortable with the opportunity to have the entire "spotlight" on me.

After about a week, however, Prema's condition had become very bad again, and Rasaraja returned to New York. 108 was again a three-piece, with our roadie as an occasional guest star.

Swedish Friends, German Dungeons, Italian Nuns, and James Bond's Briefcase

Sweden was an immense success, the devotees really went out of their way to take care of us, catering our shows and arranging programs for us in their restaurants and temples. At the Govinda's restaurant in Umeå, about a hundred straightedge kids paid for a kīrtan, class, and *prasādam* program where I tried to rally them to adopt the spreading of Krishna consciousness as the essence of all "movements" for bettering society.

At the show that evening, the opening act was a punk-reggae Ska band. From the stage, their singer held up a Bhagavad-Gita and said, "We hate 108 for turning kids into a bunch of chanting fools." Then, they started tearing up the book.

Trivikrama leapt onto the stage, spat in the singers face, and pulled the book from his hands. Maha Jay followed and slapped the singer across the face.

Almost every show had one or two interviews scheduled from a local TV, radio, newspaper, or at least a local hardcore fanzine. I loved that.

Rasaraja rejoined the tour after being away for two weeks and losing his child to a miscarriage.

In Freiburg, Germany we played in the dungeon of a castle that had been used by Nazi SS, where they had executed thousands of Swedish soldiers. The whole city seemed possessed by ghosts. I wandered into a gothic church with horrifyingly gruesome depictions of the crucifixion, and dozens upon dozens of tombs and coffins. When I tried to leave, all the doors were locked.

I fretted about the place for a few long minutes, till I saw a priest crossing the altar. He let me out.

In Italy I took the opportunity to visit the Adriatic shore, where I washed myself and my clothes and then sat to chant my newest mantras.

I noticed a young nun in black robes standing at a bit of a distance, facing the water, praying. It felt good to feel like I had something common with someone. At the club that night, though, I felt jealous of her. She was probably back in the sanctity of her monastery, while here I was in a nightclub surrounded by loud music, alcohol, and cigarette smoke.

In Geneva, a famously political city, we found a briefcase stuffed into the crack of a large tree in a park across from the club. Inside were identification papers of a Polish astronaut and a dozen other indecipherable political documents. We closed the thing and returned it to its crack, hoping James Bond was not about to assassinate us for the secrets we might now know.

We were supposed to play France for the first time, but the promoter suddenly cancelled the show on the grounds that, "108 and Hare Krishna are sexist fascists." France was very hostile. Earlier we simply traveled through the country en-route, and at the border they boarded our bus with dogs and machine guns. They kept us for hours, interviewing us in separate rooms, trying to get us to admit to smuggling drugs and so on. When we finally left, we had not traveled more than five minutes down the road when another patrol pulled us over and also insisted on searching everything in the bus and trailer.

Leaving Lenny

The toilet on the bus worked, technically, but it was a much better idea to use the restrooms at rest stops, or else the bus would quickly begin to smell like a cesspool. So, we would stop every few hours for the bathrooms, drinks and snacks, and a chance to just get out and walk around while the hired driver replenished his nicotine levels.

When stopping, the driver would note everyone who got off the bus, and before leaving would make sure all of them had gotten back on.

Nothing was out of order when we arrived at a club one evening and began unloading equipment from the trailer hitched behind the bus. Lenny wasn't helping, which wasn't unusual. After a while I told Jay, "Go wake up Lenny and tell him he has to get out here and set up his drums for sound check."

A few minutes later, Maha Jay returned saying, "Braj... Lenny's not in the bus."

Lenny had a trademark: he would stay in his bunk *all day* with the curtain drawn, doing a combination of sleeping and listening to a Walkman (probably while sleeping, too). We went into the bus looking for him.

"Lenny? Lenny?"

I pulled his bunk-curtain all the way open: the only thing there was his Walkman.

We drove back towards our last rest stop, which was more than an hour and a half away. A few kilometers before we got there, just as the last light of dusk was fading, we just barely spotted Lenny walking down the side of the freeway, towards the city our show was in that night.

"You guys are assholes!" He said, on the bus as we drove back.

"I didn't see you get off the bus." The driver explained.

"That's because no one told me you were making a rest stop! I woke up and there was no one on the bus and I had to pee, so I got out. Then you left without me. That's really not cool."

"We didn't 'leave without you,'" I explained. "No one knew you weren't on the bus."

"Don't you check to see if everyone is in the bus before you just drive away?"

"Yeah, we did," I said, "and everyone who got off *was* back on the bus."

"You didn't even notice I wasn't there?"

"How would we notice?" I shouted, "Your curtain was closed, just like it *always* is. All you ever do all day is sleep with your curtain closed! We thought you were still there, like always, sleeping like a vampire in your coffin!"

Lenny, however, was convinced that we intentionally left him, as a practical joke.

By the time we made it back to the club, people had already seen the two opening bands, waited around for an hour, and then gave up on us and went home.

The promoter didn't want to pay.

I picked up a crate of his records, which looked rare, and carried them onto the bus. Ras talked him into paying something, and Jason and I returned the records.

Past Life Regression

England was hit or miss. In any case it was nice to spend a little time at the beautiful and active temple George Harrison had given to ISKCON - the Bhaktivedānta Manor.

While we were there, a devotee who was famous and very successful with past-life regression through mass-hypnosis invited us to stay at his home. There, he introduced his daughter, who had maybe just entered her teens, and explained matter-of-factly that she was Wolfgang Amadeus Mozart in her previous life. He had determined this through hypnosis, but confirmed it with some other evidence. I don't remember all the evidence, but I remember him saying something about asking her to sign Mozart's name, and having her watch the movie about Mozart's life, and correct several details with historical accuracy.

Of course, we were completely fascinated by this, and he offered to do a group regression on all of us.

So the four members of 108 and our roadie sat in comfortable chairs in his living room and he set out to put us under hypnosis. It didn't work on me. I guess my critical mind refused to stop analyzing the situation and allow someone else to tell it what to do. I thought everyone else would experience the same disappointment, but when I looked around they were all obviously in a very different mental state.

Trivikrama was the first one to describe what he was seeing, shocked by the vividness of it. He saw through different eyes: he was a woman and could see blonde curls of hair and refined hands. This woman sat at a table, dining with her beloved, a brown-eyed, brown-haired person, in a room that seemed to be in a tower near a body of water.

Then the hypnotist turned his attention to Rasaraja. A memory was emerging there as well, more slowly, dimly and reluctantly. Bricks surrounded him. He was just a child, thin and hungry and alone. He felt the strong urge to escape, but it was impossible. Eventually it became clear that he had been a child prisoner of the Nazi Holocaust.

Maha Jay also had a very interesting tale to tell. "I see fire everywhere, but it doesn't burn. The whole battlefield is fire. I am a warrior, in armor... and Braja. It's Braja! He's dying in my arms. He has the legs... Braja has goat legs!"

Each person had come back to normal consciousness while explaining their memory. The only one still in hypnosis was Lenny.

"What do you see, Lenny?" The hypnotist asked.

"A lot of water."

"What does the water look like?"

"It's the ocean."

"Are you in the ocean?"

"No, I am walking in the sand next to it... I can see my feet in the sand... I have nails... long nails... like claws... wait, what the hell? I'm a *bear*!?"

Lenny, the guy who hibernated all day long, was a bear in his last life! It was the perfect, comedic ending to a session that otherwise left everyone in a mixture of awe and shock.

A small, beautiful, Indian painting hung on the wall of that room — depicting Rādhā and Krishna walking through the Vṛndāvana trees. It was painted on cloth, and framed in what looked like bamboo. I complimented it and our host took it off the wall, handed it to me, and said, "It is a gift for you."

My appreciation for that painting never waned. Krishna's face, especially, was painted with a lot of feeling. Years later I would use it for the cover of one of my books.

A Stupid *Karmī*'s CD Walkman

After the final show, the bus dropped us off at the Frankfurt Temple and we said our goodbyes to Abhinanda and Amara. Then, only a few minutes later, Amara appeared again in the temple and explained that the bus driver was missing his portable CD player and a few other small items.

We immediately suspected Lenny, who was not only a loose cannon but also hated the driver for "intentionally" leaving him at the rest stop. We knew Lenny would deny it, so we went through the motions of being fair and excluding all other possibilities. We brought everyone into a room and searched everyone's bags, one by one - in an overly dramatic, comedic manner, making it obvious that we knew exactly in which bags would find the stolen items.

Eventually there were no more bags to check except the prime suspect, Lenny.

"You're the only one left, Len." Ras said sarcastically. "I wonder what we'll find in your bags...."

"Alright, alright," Lenny finally shouted, "you don't have to be such jerks about it. I did it. I stole his stupid cd player. So what? Why do you have to make such a big huge deal out of it? It's just a fucking cd player, man, and he's just a stupid *karmī*."

We gave everything back to the driver and then said goodbye for real.

Chapter Thirty-Six:
Cursed Instincts

The Incredible Missing Drummer

Our immediate plan on returning from all that touring was to record. The first thing we told Lenny is that we would look for another drummer to do the recording.

A few days later, the president of the Brooklyn temple, where Lenny stayed, called Rasaraja in an angry mood. "Your Bhakta Lenny disappeared and took a case of our books with him. You're going to have to pay for those books, you know."

We wouldn't hear a single word from or about Lenny for more than ten years.

Screams of Death

I had been trying to break up 108 since late 1992. I was sick of touring and playing shows and just wanted to stay in Vṛndāvana studying the philosophy of Krishna consciousness and trying to practice it and realize it.

At the end of 1995 my guru finally agreed, partially.

I could stop doing 108, but I couldn't move to Vṛndāvana.

Instead, I could bring Vṛndāvana to New Jersey, by opening the first branch of the Vṛndāvana Institute of Higher Education. I would be the headmaster and main teacher for ISKCON's *bhakti-śāstrī* degree - which teaches the Bhagavad Gita, Nectar of Devotion, Nectar of Instruction, and Śrī Īśopaniṣad in detail.

I was thrilled!

The newest 108 songs were among our very best, and we had almost enough for an LP - so we decided to do one more record and one more world tour before pulling the plug.

We had five songs already. I took out my 8-track and drum machine to write another four: the slow, heavy Being or Body? With its Hare Krishna *mahāmantra* ending; the strange, fast When Death Closes Your Eyes, a paraphrase of centuries-old poetry by Prabhodānanda Sarasvatī; Mantra Six, with a name referencing an Upaniṣad's Mantra and a riff inspired by a mix of Guns 'n' Roses' Sweet Child and Quicksand's Baphomet; and Serve and Defy, an attempt to do post-I Against I Bad Brains a bit better than they did.

Recording the vocals on these demos in the quiet temple made me self-conscious, so I got a huge extension cord that reached all the way down the hill where I parked the 108 Van. I set up the 8 track inside, and screamed my head off down there. To a passerby it would have probably sounded like a murder-in-progress at the Krishna temple.

Lost and... Well, Just Lost

Ras was friends with Matt Cross, the drummer of Orange 9mm, who agreed to do the recording with us. I gave him the demos of the songs and we rehearsed once. Then we returned to Maryland and Brian McTernan's Salad Days studio.

We wouldn't be recording this one for Equal Vision Records. Instead this was for EVR's European distributor, Lost and Found.

That was weird.

The first reason had to do with scheduling. The first semester of the school I would open was set to begin in the summer of 1996. That means our farewell tour would have to be *over* by the summer, when tours usually *begin*. We wanted the record out *before* the final tour, and Steve said Equal Vision couldn't do it. Lost and Found said they could.

The second reason was financial. Rasaraja had no job and no health insurance, and his wife's medical emergency had resulted in huge hospital bills. Lost and Found offered us $20k. They would give us eight thousand immediately, to record and split however we liked. They would give us another six after we gave them the masters for the record, and the final six once we had recorded a live show for them in Berlin. This would solve a lot of problems for us, especially for Ras.

For the record, Lost & Found never gave us the final payment.

Baked Potatoes and Portable Ovens

Armed with a lot of potatoes, a portable oven, and a *really* good drummer we set up shop at Salad Days studio. Within a few short hours Matt had laid down impeccable drums for every song. With time to spare we wrote and recorded two new songs on the spot: Curse of Instinct and Pyro Stoke.

How strange that the last songs 108 wrote were the first songs we wrote collaboratively, organically. Ras wrote all the lyrics to Curse, and used a poem given to him by Bhurijan Prabhu (a close friend of our gurus) as the lyrics to Pyro Stoke.

We also recorded three cover songs, Coptic Times (Bad Brains), The Bars (Black Flag), and Death Comes Ripping (Misfits). The Misfits song was for a Misfits tribute compilation that Norm was doing through his Anti-Matter zine. We figured we could use the other two along with the two new songs we just wrote, to put out an EP in addition to the LP.

Three days later we indeed emerged with masters for both an LP and EP.

To me, these are recordings of 108 at its peak.

Chapter Thirty-Seven:

The Train Wreck

Ashes, Ashes, The Soul Falls Down

I went to Vṛndāvan again for three months immediately after recording Threefold and Curse. It was January of 1996. From India I planned to join 108 in Europe for our final tour, return with them to America to play our final shows, and then immediately start the first semester of the new VIHE in New Jersey.

But Vṛndāvana had a different plan, beginning with the final pulverization of my hope that there might be some viable intellectual space in ISKCON.

Satyanārāyaṇa Prabhu, the Sanskrit Scholar I had met last year, had completed his translation of Jīva Goswāmī's Tattva Sandarbha. The Bhaktivedānta Book Trust, who had funded the work, refused to publish it.

They claimed it did not match Prabhupāda's teachings.

Prabhupāda, they said, had taught that we all once existed with Krishna but fell from that condition due to envying his superiority, an idea that sounded an awful lot like the Adam and Eve / Paradise Lost mashup. Jīva Goswāmī, on the other hand, clearly established in Tattva Sandarbha that our current ignorance of Bhagavān is beginningless. According to the BBT, Śrī Jīva and Prabhupāda were at odds, and since it was Prabhupāda's book publishing company, they would not publish Jīva Goswāmī's book unless Satyanārāyaṇa Prabhu found some way to make it sound like Śrī Jīva agreed with the Paradise Lost theory.

Well, hey, Jīva Goswāmī's teachings are the foundation of the Gauḍīya Vaiṣṇava tradition that ISKCON was supposed to represent. If they "didn't match" Prabhupāda's teachings, that wouldn't speak highly at all of Prabhupāda's teachings, since Prabhupāda himself always stressed that a guru is only as good as his loyalty and fidelity to the tradition he represents.

Satyanārāyaṇa Jī and his team had a much saner conclusion: Yes, someone was at odds with Śrī Jīva, but it was not Prabhupāda. The people who were really at odds with Śrī Jīva were the GBC and BBT.

They attempted to demonstrate this thoroughly by producing a whole book explaining in rigorous detail how Prabhupāda's teachings were not out of harmony with Śrī Jīva's.

ISKCON banned it.

I immediately bought and read it.

The book, In Vaikuṇṭha Not Even the Leaves Fall, elaborately evaluated all of Prabhupāda's sometimes contradictory statements on the issue and showed how Prabhupāda often directly stated the same conclusion as Śrī Jīva, and his other statements could very easily be resolved to be in harmony with Śrī Jīva. It also showed how Prabhupāda's immediate predecessors were in harmony with Śrī Jīva, and how Śrī Jīva was in harmony with the conclusions of other Vaiṣṇava groups.

In other words, the only ones out of harmony were the ones holding the official ISKCON opinion.

No wonder ISKCON banned it.

I saw the whole issue as a farce. Not only did it reveal the ISKCON leadership to be the people who conduct inquisitions, censor journalism, and burn books, it also revealed their intellectual capacity as subpar.

It perfection developed a flaw, was it "perfect"?

If we lost our attraction to Krishna, was he "all-attractive"?

These are very simple, basic points that should not require genius philosophical intelligence to comprehend.

The ISKCON official opinion claimed that the soul's "choice" to "leave Krishna" was required for freewill. "If there was no choice not to love Krishna, then there was no freewill involved in that love. If there was no freewill, love couldn't be real, because love can't be forced."

Indeed, there is nothing wrong with the logic about freewill, but there is no need for the soul to have to previously be with Krishna before effecting its freewill. Consciousness exhibits it inherent freewill by orienting itself towards or away from the root-consciousness, Krishna. It does not need to switch its orientation to show that it can choose an orientation.

The biggest problem with the Paradise Lost theory, though, was simply that Prabhupāda always said that a bonafide guru has to be loyal to his gurus and present the same philosophical conclusions they presented. So if ISKCON insisted that Prabhupāda's teachings contradicted Jīva Goswāmī's they were inadvertently saying that Prabhupāda was not a bonafide Gauḍīya guru.

What a joke.

This debacle destroyed the final shreds of any willingness I still retailed to follow ISKCON's official leadership, the GBC.

Child Abuse

There was an even bigger disaster that had been brewing, simmering and fermenting for several months or more, and was now waiting at my doorstep like a package with a bomb inside. It was less compelling or intriguing than the *rāgānuga* crackdown or the Paradise Lost debate, but far more repulsive and demoralizing than either.

It was child abuse.

And it involved my guru.

I found myself faced with so much disgusting material to sift through. Trying to find the truth in it was like searching a vat of vomit for an important piece of paper.

What did I discover in there?

From very early on, ISKCON had been entwined with negativity towards women and family. It would seem that several of the key early leaders of ISKCON had mental disorders of misogyny, misopedia, and pedophilia, which they could legitimize by extracting and/or focusing on negative statements about women and sexuality from Prabhupāda. And the whole thing became labeled as "traditional," "Vedic," and "Krishna conscious."

The ideal ISKCON member was a sannyāsī — a man without a wife or family, and absolutely no contract with women. A married man was a "second class devotee" at best, following a "lower standard of devotion." Women (even a wife) were *māyā*'s temptations, and the further a man could stay away from them (even his wife) the "higher his standards." Children were nothing to be proud of, they were only public announcements of at least how many times you must have succumbed to your animal instincts and done ISKCON's absolutely anti-spiritual cardinal no-no: sex.

Of course there were many members of ISKCON who didn't embrace these divisive and hateful attitudes, but most of the leaders did, wholeheartedly, and this affected all the rest of us, even if we didn't always know it.

The atmosphere of misogyny and misopedia imposed on Krishna consciousness by some of the movement's earliest western leaders attracted more people with similar disdains and perversions; and it pushed even those with relatively normal mental equilibrium to emulate or at least accept everything.

Those who protested were demonized and ostracized.

Like many societies, ISKCON utilized a school system to free mothers from the burden of raising children so they could continue working for the society. A lot of the ISKCON schools, called gurukula, were boarding schools. A lot of these boarding schools were really far away, like in Vṛndāvana, India, where my guru was the headmaster. The leaders encouraged the mothers and fathers to send their children off to these wonderfully spiritual schools in wonderfully spiritual places, where they would learn how to be just like the wonderful child-saint, Prahlād Mahāraja.

"Give your child a spiritual education," they said, "and he will thank you for a lifetime."

As in most boarding schools and summer camps, ISKCON's children in these schools became easy targets for the mentally disturbed, and helpless outlets for all the anger and frustration pent up in the supposed "devotees" who were supposedly taking care of them and teaching them. At the very least, they were excessively disciplined, and often became the victims of physical and emotional abuse and manipulation, and even perverse sexual abuse from fellow students and from their supposed caretakers.

What did the ISKCON leaders do about it?

Nothing.

"Preaching" was more important. And, by "Preaching" we mostly meant going out and peddling junk on the streets all day long to pay the never ending bills incurred by the grandiose ambitions of ISKCON's divinely-appointed leaders.

ISKCON tried to hide it all, censoring the student's communications with their parents and pretending that nothing was wrong. People, of course, found out anyway, but preferred to pretend it didn't exist. Everyone wanted ISKCON to be blissful. Everyone wanted ISKCON to be perfect. No one wanted to be a "fault-finder."

This dynamic was so pervasively oppressive that even the parents remained silent.

But by the mid '90s all those little kids had grown into young adults trying to make sense of the extreme emotional challenges they faced as a result of the hellish conditions they suffered growing up.

They started speaking out.

And they got lawyers.

It's a good idea to get a lawyer really, because in the end very, very few people give a damn about being right or wrong, moral or immoral, spiritual or material - people care about *money*, and lawyers threaten their money. Sure enough, as soon as lawyers got involved, ISKCON stopped ignoring the issue.

Faced with the great likelihood of losing almost all of their North American assets in a huge and very ugly public lawsuit, ISKCON formed a "child-protection committee" to hear the complaints of their alumni and figure out what to do about it.

My guru was practically the only leader of a gurukula from that earlier era who still remained active in ISKCON. He came to symbolize all the terrible injustices suffered by those children, not only the injustice that he might have done, not only the injustice that might have occurred in his school and under his watch, but all the injustice done in all the schools by all the stressed-out and mentally deranged teachers and students.

Everyone's outrage and anger was focused on him, the face of the scandal.

This confused the bonkers out of me, because I had known Dhanurdhara Swāmī since 1990, not just as an acquaintance but as a roommate and coworker. I had literally *lived with him* for months at a time, year after year. He seemed cool to me, not a violent or angry type. In fact, I had *lived with him in the Vṛndāvana gurukula* and as far as I could see he seldom dealt with the kids directly and they seemed to *like* him, at least as much as any student likes their school principal.

Most of the claims of abuse, however, were from pre-1990, so maybe he had been a very different person before I met him? I didn't know, and no one, including him, offered me any clear, decisive, complete information.

I very gradually learned that he used to be too disciplinarian, pulling kids by the ears, slapping them in the face, publicly humiliating them, and so on. And, the bottom line is that he *did* fail to keep the students in his school safe from the physical, emotional, and sexual abuse of the teachers and other students.

Surely he had significant guilt in all this and should make reparations and accept punishment, but there was a much deeper root, and people seemed to be completely ignoring it in the rush of finally being able to vent their anger upon a single, human face. The real root of the problem wasn't limited to an individual, or even a group, it was spread through the culture and attitude shared by almost the entire society of ISKCON.

The blame was ISKCON's for allowing the views of misogynists and misopedists to be accepted as Vedic tradition. The blame was ISKCONs for being more concerned with maintaining their in-bred pure and perfect image than with actually striving to become something close to pure and perfect.

The blame was ISKCON's for caring more about preaching than about children.

Dhanurdhara Swāmī was a part of that ISKCON, and so surely deserved part of the blame. But to let *all* the blame focus on him, all the anger, all the punishment? Signal the press releases for our latest statement (the only statement we ever released): "ISKCON is perfect, pure and blissful. There are but for a few bad apples we are vigilant to purge from our midst."

But it was not just the apples that were rotten; the tree itself had a disease. Burning the rotten apples would not cure it. Sure enough, even 20 years after Dhanurdhara Swāmī was removed as the headmaster, very similar abuses of children continue in the Vṛndāvana school.

Realizing that my guru was involved in very serious mistreatment of children was hard on me.

No, I didn't conclude that he was a "bogus guru." He was teaching me Bhagavad Gītā and Nectar of Devotion and trying to help me apply myself to *sādhana-bhakti*. That's what a guru is supposed to do, and he was doing it pretty well, in my estimation.

Of course, it proved that a guru was an authority in *one* area, not all. And might not always be a flawless authority, either. But this had been my opinion for a long time now, anyway.

Then what was so serious about how this affected me? It was something very negative about a person I wanted to have only positive feelings about. But, most of all, the whole experience pulverized the last bit of hope I had that ISKCON might be the place for me.

Child abuse...?

Yeah... uh... no thanks.

It crushed my enthusiasm to be a *sannyāsī* — which up till now had been a major motivation. Not only did I start to see the idolization of *sannyāsa* as the epitome of the very things that ruined ISKCON, I also felt that ISKCON itself, riddled as it was with disgusting imperfections, wasn't worth my absolute dedication.

Seven Days Without Oxygen

In February Dhanurdhara Swāmī and I went to Māyāpura, where all the managers would be meeting and discussing the child abuse case with him. Bring in *Māyāpura* at this time of year always made me tense, but this year was just off the charts.

In a few days, I started to get asthma symptoms. Soon it was so intense that I could barely move. I didn't have enough breath even to chew and swallow food. I could just sit in one spot the whole day, sweating from the effort to get enough oxygen into my clogged lungs.

Dhanurdhara Swāmī would come back to the room at the end of the day, in a very somber and silent mood. Apparently, the powers that be were deciding his fate, and it wasn't looking pretty for him.

I stayed in that spot for seven days, unable to move or eat, until Dhanurdhara Swāmī said, "Rādhānātha Swāmī also has asthma, and he gave me this to give to you."

Thank god! An albuterol inhaler.

Now that I could breathe well enough to walk, I went to a homeopathic nurse nearby. She had me inhaling steam from a pot of boiling herbs, and did reiki, which I had never heard of before. She told me that the pollen at this time of year from all the flowers planted around the gardens were probably what was triggering the asthma.

I went to a dial-up internet booth and sent my dad and mom an email about my health, asking them to send more inhalers just in case. A little after doing that, my computer, an AST Ascentia 810N, died for the second time. I borrowed someone else's computer and sent another email to my dad, asking him to help me get it repaired once I sent it back to New York with someone.

Dhanurdhara Swāmī suggested that I go back to Vṛndāvana, giving me the key to his rooms, his briefcase and laptop, and Girirāja, a sacred stone from Govardhan Hill that he usually worshipped each morning, along with all the paraphernalia for it. He arranged for Bhagavān Dās, a friend of mine who had traveled a tiny bit with me when I was in Shelter, to accompany me on the journey back and asked him to help me take care of Girirāja.

The Train Wreck

The taxi from rural Māyāpur to filthy Calcutta was bumpy, sooty and smoggy, but even with all the exhaust in my face, I could breathe more easily than I did amidst the manicured gardens of ISKCON Māyāpura. At the Calcutta station we purchased tickets for the best, fastest train to Delhi: the Rāj Dhānī Express. It wasn't a typical sardine-can of chaos; it had air-conditioning and reserved seating that was actually enforced.

As the train started rolling, my spirits went up. I was returning to Vṛndāvana!

Porters walked up and down the aisle shouting, *"Garam chai, garam chai, garam chai. Chai, chai, garam chai, garam chai"* ("hot tea, hot tea!"). Sometimes they would switch to English, with that thick accent I absolutely loved, *"ve-ge-table cut-let... ve-ge-table cut-let..."*

Eventually the Sun went down. We pulled out the bunks and went to sleep.

I was sleeping comfortably in the middle of the night when a heavy, iron thud shook me out of my dream, and made me sit upright in the bunk, with wide open eyes.

I was airborne.

The whole train bounced and clanged.

Was I really awake? It was like peering through a heavy fog into a low-visibility reality. I started chanting loudly, "Hare Krishna. Hare Krishna. Hare Krishna ... Hare Krishna!" Louder and louder each time.

We were slowing rapidly, and seemed to be sinking into some kind of slime or mud. An awful scraping sound came from outside. Sparks flew everywhere as the source of the sound passed my window.

Then, abruptly, the train came to a stop: sudden yet viscous and murky.

There was a moment to breathe a sigh of relief, thinking it was over. Then the train started slowly tilting to the left. I imagined us atop a bridge, about to tip over the side.

Then the lights went out, making it pitch black.

The fans in the ventilation system spun down and shut off. Panic threatened to grip me as I contemplated the fact that all the windows of this air-conditioned car were *sealed*.

No ventilation.

65 breathing Indians... and me.

I took the Asthma inhaler from where I had tucked it into the upper roll of my *dhoti*, and shot some into my lungs.

The train had tilted to about forty-five degrees and then stopped. That was a welcome surprise, but even if we didn't fall off a bridge, I figured we would probably explode. India Railways had a cartoon of an exploding train above every ashtray.

I needed to get out of this death-box!

Then I noticed that all the passengers were calm, talking to one another in Hindi. Bhagavān shouted through the darkness, "Where is Girirāja?"

Girirāja was in a box secured by a chain with our briefcases and computer cases, to a rail of our bunk. Fumbling with that lock in the blackness might take forever, and the train could explode at any moment. "We need to get out," I replied.

Getting out, or getting *anywhere*, was not easy with the train at a forty-five degree angle. We had to *climb* from one berth to the next, which was made no easier by the fact that we could barely even see our own hands in the darkness. Nor was I feeling very capable to mountain climb after seven days of being unable to eat or even breathe.

Luckily, our berth was close to the doors. Once, we got to them, however, we discovered that all the doors were locked, by big iron padlocks.

Had someone intentionally done this? Were terrorists about to storm in with machine guns?

It was really hard not to panic now.

"Should we break the window?" Bhagavan asked me.

"Break it," I said.

He grabbed a fire extinguisher and started ramming the window. Shards flew everywhere, but the damn thing wouldn't break. "This has got to be the only thing in India that *won't* break!" I cursed.

Some passengers spoke to us in English, convincing us that the doors were open at the other end of the car. Somehow I made it all the way there. These doors were wide open.

Someone helped me jump down, and then patiently explained, while looking deeply into my eyes, "God has saved us. By *karma* we were meant to die, but God has saved us."

Hundreds of passengers were at a short distance from the tracks, at the edge of a thicket. Most were spreading blankets on the ground, where they opened up tiffins to share *chapattis* and pickles.

The underbelly of the train was exposed, like a felled dragon collapsed on its side. Gasoline leaked out of the cracked tanks, onto the stone track-bed, which I guessed was what had slowed us down like slime and mud. The car leaned with all its weight upon a single electric pole - that's why the car hadn't tipped *all* the way over.

At the front of the train, the engine car had jack-knifed at 90 degrees across the track. The first passenger car was off the tracks entirely, in a ditch, on its side. Our car was next, leaning up against the electric pole. The tracks were mangled. The changing point on the track must not have gotten all the way into place, maybe a rock or something got in its way. The wheels of our train hit the protruding track, sending the car airborne and causing the track itself to buckle, snap, and twist, slicing into the side of the derailing train, sending sparks everywhere until, just two cars behind ours, the rail went through a window into the passenger compartment, where it had forced the train to come to its abrupt stop.

Now, it stuck garishly out the gnashed window, stabbing the black night with all the theatrics of Indian flashlights, like a rusted and splintered bone hanging from the mouth of an ogre. Two bodies were carried on stretchers out of that car. One seemed very dead.

A man walked up to me and said, "Because we must have done good things for others, therefore we did not die here."

Another told me, "We have survived the crash, but we won't survive the dacoits."

Dacoit is a word Indian's use for criminals. They were talking about the Indian mafia, who would most likely be monitoring this most wealthy of all Indian trains, and would show up any minute now to loot us.

Somehow, no one seemed worried. They just kept each other company, and fell asleep on their blankets beside the tracks. I decided to do the same, using our valuable bags as an uncomfortable pillow. (Bhagavān had gotten Giriraj and the important bags off the train.)

I awoke with a flashlight in my eyes, and could make out a shotgun.

Was it the police or the dacoits?

It was the police.

As the Sun began to rise, they packed us all into the undamaged cars and carted us backwards at half-speed to the previous station in Gaya. With everyone packed into half as much space as normal, it felt like a normal Indian train. People were everywhere.

Sitting next to me was the wife of a supreme court judge. We had an extensive and very respectful conversation. A man came to introduce himself, saying, "I used to visit Gauḍīya Maṭh when your

Śrīla Prabhupāda was still a married man." He became enthusiastic and started glorifying Krishna to all the passengers.

At Gaya we headed forward again, but on an alternate rail, around the toppled cars and damaged tracks. This took us into Patna station as the sun set. There, new cars were added to replace the damaged ones and we were no longer packed together like sardines. Four hours later, around 10pm, we arrived in Delhi, which had never looked so beautiful.

CHAPTER THIRTY-EIGHT:

THE TRANSCENDENCE

It was Beautiful, for a Moment

What a relief and joy it was to be back in Vṛndāvana. Dad had gone to Tijuana to buy the inhalers and ship them, but the asthma had reduced to a mere occasional cough on its own. I was eating papaya and lemon, which was so delicious. There wasn't an ISKCON World War Three of stress happening all around me. Life seemed happy.

For a day or two.

Looking in the mirror one morning while brushing my teeth, I noticed that my tongue was black. The Ayurvedic doctor in the gurukula, Dr. Partap Chauhan, brother of the Sanskrit scholar Satynārāyaṇa Prabhu, gave me some powders and the blackness went away.

Then dysentery started.

Dhanurdhara Swāmī returned from Māyāpura and headed off to Delhi, giving me a few errands to run. The first one took me to an old King's house at Govardhana Hill, which had recently become an ISKCON property. I delivered a message or something, and then headed back to Vṛndāvana by motor rickshaw.

When the ride started it was warm. By the time we arrived, I was shivering from the cold.

Seven Days to Live

I shivered under a blanket all through the night, and went to see the school nurse when I woke up late the next morning. "I think I have a fever," I said, shuffling into her office where she was taking care of a half a dozen kids.

She looked at me carefully and said, "I think you have more than a fever. Come with me to get your blood checked, I am taking some of the students anyway."

I didn't want to, but she convinced me.

The rickshaw bumped us downtown to Loi Bazaar, stopping in front of an open wooden box that was a medical lab. A plank made it easy to cross the open sewer at the roadside and enter. The man who worked here reached up on top of a shelf and pulled down a microscope, blowing on it to remove the dust.

It was the same microscope I had seen in my grandfather's house, 20 years ago.

The nurse turned to me and quietly said, "Don't worry, I always bring my own needles."

He drew blood from the half-dozen school kids in their yellow dhotis, and took mine too. I waited around for ten or fifteen minutes, feeling lousy and upset that I was wasting my time when I could be busy writing all the materials our new school would need.

Finally we were called to hear the results.

These kids all had horrific diseases with terrifying names that I thought had been stamped out centuries ago. One had malaria. Another had typhoid. They all had *something* horrible. Then I heard my own name, followed by the words "falciparum malaria."

What!? Brain malaria?

"When did the fever start?" The nurse asked me.

"Yesterday, around sunset."

"Good," she said, obviously very relieved, "then you have seven days to live… unless you take the medication."

I felt numb. It didn't seem real.

She took me straight away to get the medicine. The dispensary had more people in the waiting room than usually fit into an Indian train. We gave up waiting when they announced that it was a government holiday or something, and they were closing early.

We went across town to another dispensary.

It was also closed.

I started to panic. I had seven days to live, and the stores were closed!

"Don't worry," she said, "I think I still have one or two pills left over in my office."

I was deeply relieved when she found those two crimson red, oval globes at the bottom of her file cabinet.

"Take these," she said. "Tomorrow I'll go back downtown and get the rest of what you'll need. Don't try to do anything strenuous, the medicine is very, very powerful."

I took the red pills and called Dhanurdhara Swāmī. "The medicine is poison," he said. "The only way to get rid of the disease is to poison yourself. The poison kills everything, and almost kills you, too. Eat a lot of mosambi and drink a lot of water."

I walked out to the fruit vendor and bought a huge bag of mosambi — which is like a cross between an orange and a lime — and several bottles of water. Then I returned to Dhanurdhara Swāmī's rooms where I lied down in a corner with a sleeping bag and blanket.

An Evil Presence

Everything became a blur; a shivering, sweating, aching, hallucinogenic blur punctuated by stumbling into the bathroom to vomit or diarrhea. Luckily Dhanurdhara Swāmī's rooms had an attached, private toilet.

The nurse noted that my fever was getting up to 106, but she said that was normal. Amara, our tour manager from Germany, came over to do reiki on me. I could actually feel small serpents crawling beneath my skin, following his hands.

Once a day or so, I would slither out of the room and down the steps into the street, where I would deliriously buy more mosambi and bottled water. Between the sweating, vomiting and diarrhea I was losing water faster than I could get it in.

As I drifted further and further from a normal state of perception I began to become acutely aware of an evil presence focusing its attention on me from above. It seemed to me to be a powerful, vengeful ghost. I used a bottle of Yamuna water to make a magic circle around where I lay on the floor, to keep the evil presence from getting any closer. But I had to throw up or diarrhea so often that I decided to break the magic circle and make a magic lane leading to the toilet.

One day, as I prepared to slither out, I discovered that the door would not open! It had been bolted shut from the outside!

I panicked, feeling trapped and imagining myself dehydrating fast. I shouted out the window. "Haribol? Hare Krishna? Haribol?" until a group of older students headed by Jīva (the son of my Japanese god-sister) showed up and opened the door.

I wasn't coherent enough to realize that the powerful, vengeful evil spirit with its attention on me from above was actually one of the older Gurukula students who hated Dhanurdhara Swāmī and wanted to mess with his disciple.

A Skull at the Edge of Forever

After four or five days of intense fever, vomiting, and poison I couldn't even move any more. I just lay in the corner alternating between violent shivers and violent sweats. I started to see things similar to dreams, but since I wasn't asleep, the visions were much more detailed than an ordinary dream.

The walls of the room dissolved and I saw a dark world outside, with meteors of fire raining from the sky, smashing everything and setting it ablaze. I saw the wall of a beautiful home. Zooming out I saw that only the corner, window and curtain remained; the rest had been destroyed by the constant barrage. Behind that wall, in the last shred of a tranquil house, my mother and father cowered in fear.

Feeling the urge to take cover, I suddenly realized that *there was no cover*. There was no safety. In a world of constant destruction all we can do is huddle in the safest corner we can find. There we build whatever life we can, for as long as we can, before time and hunger and violence smash everything we have built, like meteors smashing through umbrellas.

A new scene appeared, a crowded sidewalk. Everyone looked like me: young but riddled with pain and disease. I understood that I was not the only one suffering. *Everyone* suffers, almost all the time.

Then a most amazing scene unfolded.

A pillar of energy emerged from my naval as I lie on the floor, like the stem of a lotus. I left my body behind, watching it recede as I ascended through that stem towards outer space. People came out to see my ascent. The higher I went, the more amazing the beings who came to see me, each of them inviting me to stop my upward course and follow them to see what wonders they had in store for me. Above the clouds, beautiful, bejeweled but otherwise naked men and women flew towards me playing fabulous music and moving gracefully.

I was dying.

I was leaving my body and ascending on the path through higher and higher planets! If I just kept going to the highest apex, I would wind up with Krishna in Vṛndāvana! So, I took my attention away from the angelic nymphs and rose still higher into the depths of space, passing fantastic sight after fantastic sight. At the end, a line of great sages full of incredible knowledge and wisdom came towards me with hands folded.

I continued upward.

Finally I arrived at the blossom atop the stem. There, in the distance above me, I could see Viṣṇu. He was standing with his back towards me, with infinite legs, arms, and heads expanding into, merging with, giving shelter to space itself.

He slowly turned around.

Oh my God, I was *really* about to see Viṣṇu!

The face that looked upon me was not what I expected. It was not a beautiful face reminiscent of Krishna; instead it was a horrifying skull, reeking of death.

Without words, it said, "You may go to Krishna, *through me.*"

I was literally on the threshold of death, pausing, hesitating. There seemed to be ropes tied around my waist, invisible ropes with faint hints of personality. Some of them I seemed to already know, others were familiar, but unknown.

Some of the ropes seemed to be children.

I could not go any further forward. Destiny was calling me downward, back to the manifest and tangible world where there were still so many things waiting for me to accomplish.

I declined the opportunity to go "Back to Godhead."

Get Me Out of This Filthy Place

The Malaria had been beaten, almost taking me with it.

Someone knocked on my door and said my father was on the phone. I went down to the office and spoke with him. He wanted to get me out of India immediately, and that sounded great to me. Within a day he had arranged a ticket from Delhi, laying over in Frankfurt, ending up in San Diego. All I had to do was get to the airport.

A friend named Madhusudan arranged a taxi for me. I packed my few things and was ready to go. I hadn't been to the temple room in over a week, so I slowly walked down to say goodbye to the most captivatingly gorgeous deities in the world, Śrī Śrī Rādhā Śyāmasundar.

About 15 minutes later I slowly returned to the room, finding the door slightly ajar. Inside, none of my things had been moved, but one of the zippers on my duffle bag was open. It was the zipper to the pocket where I kept my wallet and passport. Both of them were still inside, but when I opened up my wallet the only money left in it were a few US dollars. All the Indian rupees were gone.

Just then Madhusudan arrived, "The taxi is here, Prabhu."

"I've been robbed," I said. "I don't know if I can go. I don't have any money."

My Japanese god-sister arrived, carrying a bag lunch that she had kindly made for me. She came with Billie-jo, the young woman who had been the first guest at my Saturday Night-Life program in Towaco a few years ago. The two of them gave me the money I needed to pay for the taxi.

My emotions were frazzled down to the barest nerve endings and the thought of enduring the death race of an Indian taxi into Delhi petrified me. Madhusudan agreed to come with me and, literally, hold my hand the entire way.

The flight from Delhi landed in Germany, where I had more than a 24-hour layover before my journey would continue. Śacīnandana Swāmī kindly sent devotees to pick me up from the Frankfurt airport. After calling my dad from the temple to let him know I had made it this far, I slept until the devotees woke me and brought me back to the airport.

Chapter Thirty-Nine:

The End

Center for Tropical Disease

My parents were in shock when they saw me in the San Diego airport. They took me straight away to UCSD's Infectious Disease Treatment Center, where the doctors were also in shock to see me. In India I was just another face, but here I was a medical miracle.

I weighed just a little over 100 pounds, having lost about thirty-five over the last two or three weeks. I was dehydrated, and had several varieties of parasites inside my bowels. And in a week or two I wanted to fly to Europe to do a hardcore tour.

My parents were against it, but I explained that the tour was already booked, and it was the last tour I might ever do, so I didn't want to miss it. "Then you have two weeks to put on at least 25 pounds," my father said. "Otherwise you're not going."

I started feeling better, and made it my mission to gain weight. In two weeks I weighed 125 pounds.

Descent to Berlin

The flight from San Diego to Berlin had a lot of turbulence. Having just escaped death narrowly in India, I was particularly sensitive and fearful. I wrote in my notebook:

> *Having once seen the face of death, I cannot purge him from my eyes. He lurks in every possibility. He stands on every corner. He dwells in every home.*
>
> *The inescapability of death embraces my mind and drives me to a newer vision: I can see the vanity of every endeavor. It is ludicrous to enjoy objects that disintegrate like gasses in the airs of time.*
>
> *As I approached the doorway of my own death, everything turned grey. All people and things disappeared. One by one, I begged each of them. "You kept me from sorrow and fear. You gave me happiness. Please protect me now, I am on fire with fear and grief."*
>
> *Each one stood blankly staring, slowly turned grey, and disappeared.*

And a poem:

> *Should the chilling black jaws swallow me now,*
> >*would the cars on the freeway stop driving?*
> >*would the children in the park stop laughing?*
>
> *Even if they did, would they not begin again tomorrow?*
>
> *Even if my friends or love ones grieved for the rest of their lives, they too would soon vanish.*
>
> *All is swallowed*
> *All is forgotten*

There is nothing here but shadows shifting shape

The Final Suck

108's final tour sucked.

Ras added Dan Hornecker to the band as a second guitarist, in case I needed to sit some shows out. That was fine with me; Dan was funny and a reliable musician. *Mahā* Jay also came along, which was nice. Ras and Triv had found a good drummer, Mike Paradise (after deciding not to have Harley play in the band, although he tried out and was amazing).

The tour sucked anyway, because our attention was elsewhere.

The only memorable events were arguments and fights.

Sometimes we fought with each other (Ras and Triv ate at restaurants and slept in hotels once or twice, and to us it seemed they must have been spending 108's money. It was hard for me to realize that Triv and Ras actually had jobs, and thus had their own money).

Usually we fought with other people. Some Nazi's came to one of our shows and got violent. Jay, Ras and Dan beat the hell out of them, but the promoter said, "Those guys are national front Nazis! There is a huge meeting blocks away, and as soon as they find out what happened they will come and *kill* you! You have to get out of here!"

We did.

Lost and Found recorded our show in Berlin to release a live record, One Path for Me... It was a half-assed show. We were unglued from our involvement in what was going on. It's a crappy live record compared to what our live shows were really like at their peak.

We got back to America around the end of May and played a string of shows on the East Coast and Midwest. It was the same story: the most memorable parts of the tour were the failures and the fights.

Evan Jacobs came along to film it all and make a documentary, which he titled Curse of Instinct. It's a pathetic documentary. Our van breaks down, our shows get cancelled... and I say ridiculous things, including how I would never get married.

Threefold Misery had come out in Europe, but no one in America had a copy.

Our final show at CBGBs was anti-climactic.

Mr. Headmaster President

VIHE in Towaco, however, was a huge success. I was the "headmaster" and main teacher, and thus got almost all the attention and respect I always wanted. About a dozen students stayed at the temple for about three months earning a *bhakti-śāstrī* degree by studying the Bhagavad Gītā and similar texts in a very systematic manner, which is what I had always thought temple life *should* be like.

After the first VIHE, Towaco's president Lakṣmī Nṛsiṁha decided to leave the post, and I wound up filling his position. Even my parents were proud, and sent me a plaque to put on my desk, "Mr. President."

The best part about being temple president was how close I became with the local Indian families. One elderly couple in particular became so close that I called them *dadu* and *dadima* (Grandpa and Grandma).

The second VIHE semester went even better that the first, and we had repaired and upgraded a lot of the temple to make sure we had enough bathrooms and so on for the dozen or more students who attended.

The temple was really *humming*.

Vṛndāvana? Or Shyama Sakhi?

I should have been happy. I was achieving what I wanted, becoming more influential and thus more able to make a difference in how ISKCON operated. In Towaco, women gave classes and shared the temple room side by side. I even personally escorted the Governing Body Commissioner out of the woman's side of the temple when he came to visit.

I was happy, I guess. But I wasn't satisfied.

Satisfaction is an affair of the heart, and my heart wasn't in ISKCON anymore. The misogyny and other social dysfunctions like hatred of family and demonization of the outside world, the lack of intellectual integrity and knowledge of actual tradition, and the continuing saga of dealing with child abuse, these had piled too much water on the spark of my enthusiasm for "spreading Prabhupāda's movement." The subsequent string of disasters culminating in my near death experience in Vṛndāvana, was like a straw breaking the camel's back, except it wasn't a straw, it was a giant iron anvil.

I didn't want to *deal with* ISKCON anymore. Everything was a struggle; everything was a battle, a disagreement. They wanted to follow exactly what Prabhupāda said, but in the course of all his letters and lectures and conversations and books Prabhupāda had said just about everything on every side of any issue. You couldn't make a statement without having someone prove that Prabhupāda disagreed with you.

I was teaching Bhagavad Gītā, and the clear message throughout the first third of the book was that renunciation of the world should come *after* one has been purified of selfishness by living a responsible and dutiful life, otherwise renunciation is a farce that leads to ruination. This message was what my father had suggested when he read Readings in Vedic Literature. It was what Zack had suggested in his Enquirer interview. It was exactly *not* what ISKCON preached: "Surrender everything to Krishna right now, give everything up and go back to Godhead."

"Complete surrender" (to use the ISKCON terminology) was the ultimate conclusion of Gītā, not the starting point. Yet ISKCON pushed brand new 20-year-olds like me into imitating the ultimate conclusion of yoga before even having the basic foundations.

I weighed my options as I sat on one of the railroad ties that holds some of the hill in place in front of the Towaco temple. I needed a *dramatic* change, and as I saw it, I had two options: to join Aindra in Vṛndāvana and do 24 hour kīrtan there for the rest of my life until I die, or to get married and develop a life independent of ISKCON.

I would have chosen the kīrtan, but after the malaria I could foresee the future. Maybe it would happen in a week, maybe in a month, maybe in a year, maybe in a few years, but eventually I would be looking at the Skull of the Universe again and retreating. I knew I had to figure out what those ropes were and see where they were anchored, *before* I tried to cut them off, throw them away, and try to completely absorb my consciousness in Krishna.

Happily Ever After

I never thought twice about who to marry. If it was anyone it would be Shyama Sakhi, the daughter of my Japanese god-sister, who I had met for the first time at that show in Connecticut when she brought us something to eat on *ekādaśī*. She was exactly my type: strong, independent, artistic, capable, and super beautiful. And, she had been in love with me for a few years despite the odds of it ever going anywhere, and without making a nuisance of herself as people in love often do when they try to attract someone's attention.

Dhanurdhara Swāmī wasn't upset with my decision, as I worried he might be. He was understanding of my need get some distance from ISKCON. But he wasn't sure about my choice of Shyama Sakhi, and suggested I marry her sister instead. "She seems better qualified." I looked at him and wondered if he understood what love felt like. It's not like shopping.

"Well at least call my astrologer and check to see if you are compatible," he said.

335

I did that. The astrologer told me the compatibility was good, *too* good. I probably shouldn't marry her because we would be too attracted to one another and wouldn't be able to "control our senses."

Typical ISKCON stuff. What a joke! That's *why* you marry someone, genius.

I called my mom. It was getting close to my birthday and she asked what I wanted for a present.

"Well it's a little expensive but... Would you be able to buy me a ring?"

She was confused, "A ring? Why?"

"It's an engagement ring."

The silence lasted a long time. It was the happiest she had felt in years.

I had a specific ring in mind, and my parents got it exactly right: a sapphire (Krishna) surrounded by small diamonds (the Gopīs), set in gold (Rādhārāṇī). Once I had it in hand, I called Shyama Sakhi and her mom to a meeting with the temple president. We sat in front of Dhanurdhara Swāmī's Girirāja (who was staying with me for a while) and I asked her mom, "Would you permit me to marry your daughter."

She didn't really understand what I said. Her English wasn't the best. I repeated myself. She looked at her daughter, who was very uncomfortable and blankly said, "I'll have to ask my guru."

I was pretty disappointed.

But when they left and went back upstairs they started shouting in joy and jumping up and down for about ten minutes straight. You could hear them all over the temple.

We got married two months later downstairs in the temple. My mom and dad were there, of course, as was my uncle Joe with his wife and two young children, and my grandfather's brother and sister. My grandfather himself was in the hospital, very sick, and my grandmother stayed with him. Shyama's uncle, aunt, and grandpa came from Japan and attended the wedding dressed in traditional *kimono*. Her grandpa was a very important Buddhist priest. Shyama's sister, Shyama Sundari also came.

Both of our guru's came, and even my guru's mom came. Almost the entire Indian congregation came, including of course Dadu and Dadima.

Immediately, the next morning, Shyama and I flew out to San Diego to begin a new life.

The rest is for another book, if you're interested.

Liner Notes

Thanks List: My **dad**, for coming up with the idea, and funding the writing and initial printing; the many other people helped me write this by sharing their perspectives and memories and giving feedback on earlier drafts:

For the 108 era that was especially **Rob Fish (Rasaraja)** and **Kate-0-Eight (Keli Lalita)**. Other significant help came from **Tim Cohen (Trivikrama)**, **Jason C. Brown (Maha Jay)**, **Jay Holzman (Jai Nitai)**, **Zac Eller**, **Antonio Valladares**, and **Chris Daly**.

For the Shelter era it was especially **Eric Daily (Ekendra)**, who also helped with the early 108 sections. I also got some help from **Ray Cappo (Raghunath)** though he didn't seem very comfortable with most of it.

For the Inside Out era, **Sterling Wilson**, **Alex Baretto**, and **Chris Bratton** helped revive memories, clarify details and get everything in the proper order. **Dave Zuckerman (Deva-sanga)** also helped with some college memories.

For the Beyond and Prehistoric eras, **Kevin Egan** was a huge help, and **Tom Capone**, **Vin Novara**, and **Dom Biocco** also pitched in quite a bit.

✤✤✤✤

We printed a "limited edition test pressing" of 500 copies in connection with the 108 shows we played in America during May of 2016.

If there is enough interest we will also produce a companion volume, with all the photos, fliers, zines, and music that we have.

My father has written his own memoir of the same time period. It's called Krishna's Punk – A Parent's Journey.

✤✤✤✤

I've written several books on *bhakti yoga*. You can find them through **VrajaKishor.com**. Titles include A Simple Gītā and Beautiful Tales of the All-Attractive.

I've also written a few books on astrology. You can find them through **VicDicara.com.** Titles include 27 Stars, 27 Gods and The Beautifully Rational Philosophy of Astrology.

Printed in Dunstable, United Kingdom